MARTYRS' DAY

MARTYRS' DAY

CHRONICLE OF A SMALL WAR

MICHAEL KELLY

RANDOM HOUSE
NEW YORK

Library of Congress Cataloging-in-Publication Data

Kelly, Michael
    Martyrs' Day: chronicle of a small war/Michael Kelly.—1st ed.
        p.   cm.
    ISBN 0-679-41122-4
    1. Persian Gulf War, 1991—Personal narratives.   2. Kelly,
Michael—Journeys—Middle East.   I. Title.
DS79.74.K45 1993
956.704'428–dc20
                                                                        92-50507

Designed by Michael Mendelsohn
Map by Jacques Chazaud
Manufactured in the United States of America on acid-free paper

23456789

First Edition

To my father, Tom Kelly,
for teaching me.

FOREWORD

This book is not intended to be a full history of the conflict known formally as Operation Desert Storm and commonly as the Gulf War. It is meant, rather, as an impressionistic account that might, through detailed reporting, give a feeling for the oddities and terrors of even a modest war.

Where it was necessary for protection's sake, mostly in recounting time spent in Iraq and Iran, I have given false names and changed some of the characteristics of people who spoke to me; this is particularly true in the case of Adnan, who appears in three of the Baghdad chapters. I do not speak Arabic or Hebrew, but, since many people in the Middle East speak English, most of the conversations recounted here were conducted in that language. In cases where I used a translator, I have sometimes mentioned this, and other times not.

This book grew out of four long trips I made to the Middle East between November of 1990 and November of 1991. I was working as a free-lance writer then, and I covered various aspects of the events leading up to the war, the war, and its aftermath for *The New Republic*, *The Boston Globe*, and *Gentlemen's Quarterly*. I could not have done this without a great deal of help from many people, whom I would like to thank here.

I owe a debt beyond what I can say to Madelyn, my wonderful wife (she appears in this book by her nickname, Max), who supported me through a long and difficult two years of travel and writing, and was generous with time, advice, and encouragement. I would not have been able to do this without her constant help; I doubt if I would have tried.

For their support, love, and good humor, I would like to thank my family, and hers: Tom and Marguerite Kelly; my sisters Kate, Meg, and Nell; Irwin and Anita Greenberg; Dan Lloyd and Cheryl Greenberg. I am grateful to my good friends Douglas Lavin, Maureen Dowd, Roger Simon, Peter Jensen, Mark Kane, Jim Helling, Adam Nagourny, and Susan Reed for their sustained encouragement.

At *The New Republic*, I owe a tremendous amount to Martin Peretz, the publisher; to Hendrik Hertzberg, who as editor commissioned and superbly edited most of the articles that appeared in the magazine and took a great chance in assigning a writer he did not know to such an undertaking as covering a war; to Andrew Sullivan, who succeeded Rick and who edited the final two pieces I wrote for the magazine with the same sort of thoughtful care I had come to enjoy; to managing editor Dorothy Wickenden, and to June Haley, Don Harris, and Laura Obolensky.

At *The New York Times*, I would like to thank editor Max Frankel, managing editor Joseph Lelyveld, and then–Washington editor Howell Raines for their patience and generosity in permitting me the time necessary to write this, going well beyond what I had initially requested or had a right to expect.

At *Gentlemen's Quarterly*, my deep thanks to editor Arthur Cooper and managing editor Martin Beiser for their interest in publishing the first three long articles I wrote on the war, for their considerable financial support, and for their generosity in sending assignments my way over several years of free-lancing. I owe an extra thanks to Martin for taking the time and effort to teach me much about the differences between newspaper and magazine writing.

Sharon DeLano, my editor at Random House, greatly improved this book, through many hours of wise and hard pencil editing of the sort I had been told no longer existed in publishing. She is the best editor I have ever worked with and I owe her tremendous thanks. I would like also to thank Harold Evans for taking an initial, supportive, and sustained effort in the idea. Ian Jackman was also most helpful.

Kathy Robbins, my agent, worked hard to get this book published and, as an adviser and friend, offered much-needed support throughout the process of writing it.

I was blessed with excellent researchers in this work: Mervyn Kaiser at *GQ,* Jennifer Pitts at *The New Republic,* and above all, the best researcher I have ever worked with, Arriane de Vogue.

The Boston Globe, for whom I worked as a stringer, paid for a hefty chunk of the $40,000 or so it cost to cover the story, and treated me with the consideration rarely accorded to a stringer, a creature generally occupying a place in the newspaper hierarchy somewhere below classified ad taker. I would like especially to thank H.D.S. Greenway, the senior associate editor; John Yema, the foreign editor; the former foreign editor Thomas Ashbrook; Helen Donovan, the managing editor; Margaret Murray on the foreign desk; and Barbara McDonough on the switchboard.

My friends at CBS News gave me food, telephone access, and much more throughout the war. I would like to generally thank the foreign desk and the staffers in the Baghdad, Amman, Tel Aviv, and Dhahran bureaus, and to single out for special thanks Larry Doyle, the superb bureau chief in Baghdad and Amman, Allen Pizzey, Allen Alter, Nick Follows, Mary Walsh, Doug Tunnell, Tom Anderson, Michael Rosenbaum, Kathy Sciere, Gaby Silon and Eldad Ron in Tel Aviv, Jon Meyersohn, Susan Zirinsky, Mark Knoller, Martha Teichner, and Bruce Dunning. I would also like to acknowledge Nick della Casa, who worked as a cameraman for CBS in Baghdad at the beginning of the war, and who died in Kurdistan at the end.

Traveling in foreign states in a state largely of ignorance, I was helped a great deal by more knowledgeable and competent journalists and friends, including Richard Beeston of *The Times* of London, Geraldine Brooks and Tony Horwitz of *The Wall Street Journal,* Dan Fesperman and Robert Ruby of the *Baltimore Sun,* Bob Drogin of the *Los Angeles Times,* and Patrick McGeough of the *Sidney Morning Herald.* My thanks also to Klames M. Ganji, Chicago's superior travel agent, and to Faik Bisharat, his equal in Amman.

Lastly, let me offer insufficient thanks and admiration to Adnan and all the others I cannot mention by true name, in Iraq and Kuwait and Iran, who were brave enough and good enough to talk to me.

Michael Kelly
January 1993

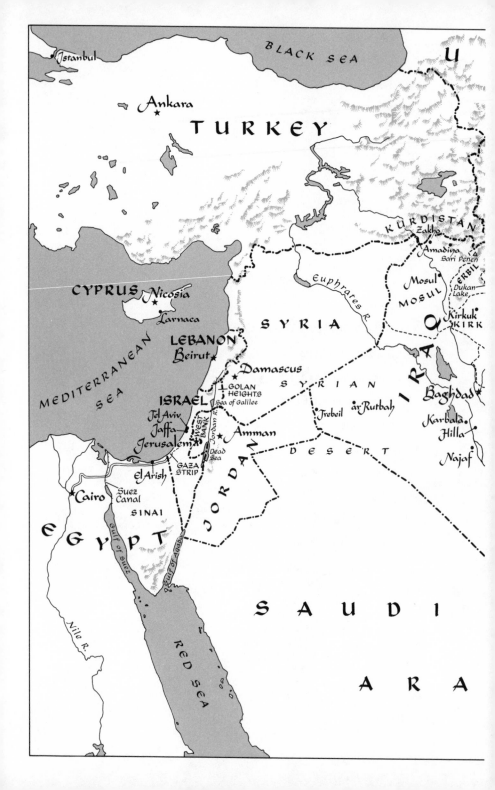

MARTYRS'
DAY

MARTYRS' DAY

B AGHDAD IS RICH IN MONUMENTS to the dead of war. They are, excepting the Leader's many palaces, by far the most impressive pieces of architecture in the city. The most peculiar one is The Tomb of the Unknown Soldier, a pavilion of polished dark-red granite over which hangs a giant upside-down metal clamshell hundreds of feet in diameter. A visitor walks up a long, broad ramp of gray stone that leads, as it were, into the belly of the clam. To one side is a smallish ziggurat, modeled on the ancient Tower of Amara, but in fact as trashily modern as a Burger King, with bright red, green, and black tiles crawling up and down its sides. A square hole in the granite under the center of the clam leads to a staircase, which descends two stories to debouch into a round, windowless room.

The walls of the room, cambered inward to follow the line of the shell, are made of stainless steel and lined with poster-size photographs of the Leader at war: reviewing troops, tasting soup at a field kitchen, firing a rocket-propelled grenade, shaking hands with soldiers, regarding a howitzer. In between and in front of the photographs are glass display cases. Most of the cases contain weapons left over from one or another episode of large-scale killing. Killing has been a more or less continual preoccupation in Iraq since the Great Arab Revolt of 1916–1918. There have been twenty-three coups or attempted coups, five large politico-tribal revolts or massacres, and the country has been involved to one degree or another in eight wars. In a counterclockwise sequence, the displays make up a rough visual history of Iraq's unhappy progression, beginning with the shields, spears, and swords of early Ottoman days, moving on to the elaborate pistols and blunderbusses and hand-tooled Berber long guns of the nineteenth century, then to the sticks, shovels, hatchets, and clubs of the early-twentieth-century anti-British uprising, and so on into the modern era. Each display is labeled with a neat, hand-lettered placard:

"Collection of mechanical rifles used by the Iraqi brave army in some earlier years."

"Thompson machine gun, American-made, gained among the booty in the battle against the Zionist enemy in 1948."

"Machine guns used by a group of Arab Baath Socialist Party Revolutionaries in the operation of blowing [sic] the tyrant Abd al-Karim Qasim on 7th October, 1959." (Twenty-two-year-old Saddam Hussein, the future Leader, was among the participants in the failed attack on air force officer Qasim, who had taken power in a coup against the British-supported Iraqi monarchy the year before. According to his official biography, Saddam received a bullet in the leg, which a friend cut out with a razor blade.)

"Part of Israeli (Mirage) plane shot down by our great forces in 1967 in the H3 area."

On one of the longer glass cases, there is a placard with the word "Martyrs" in a squirm of red Arabic script. Inside are the uniforms worn by various Iraqi soldiers or pilots at the time of their deaths. The uniforms lie flat and are slightly wrinkled. Without bodies to fill them they seem, like medieval suits of armor, too small and somehow false. They have holes in them, and the holes are ringed with rust-colored stains.

A quarter-mile or so down the highway from the Tomb of the Unknown Soldier is the Hands of Victory Pavilion, built in 1984 to celebrate an exceptionally bloody triumph in the most recent Iraqi war save one, the long and awful fight with Iran. The pavilion is a terrible thing. It is approached via a wide asphalt boulevard lined by unusually ugly lampposts, oversized globes set on spindly stalks. The boulevard runs a distance of several city blocks between two matching sets of giant forearms, which rise directly out of the asphalt, one on each side of the road, and loom high into the air, ending in hands clenched in fists. The Leader's own arms and hands were the models for these, the official legend says. The arms are thick with twined ropes of muscle and the fists are the big-knuckled hams of a back-alley brawler; nose-breaker, teeth-smasher fists. Each fist holds a scimitar, and the curved blades cross high above the avenue, so that soldiers may parade, and tourists may stroll, under their protective arches.

At the bases of the arms are huge metal nets, like fishing seines, filled with helmets. The nets are long, pendulous, banana-shaped things, and they have been overstuffed, so the helmets burst obscenely out of their bottom ends onto the ground. What is terrible about the Victory Pavilion lies in this sight and in something all who see it know: the helmets are the real helmets of real dead men, collected on the battlefield from the heads of enemy Iranians. There are thousands of helmets. They are a diverse bunch—American GI models from the Second World War, broad-rimmed doughboy's hats from the First, even a few crested parade-dress hats of a Kaiser Wilhelm style—and battered, full of scars and dents and ragged-edged holes. As they spill out of each net, they make mounds that cascade down onto the avenue, where they are cemented in an artful jumble. Some are set more formally, in rows, upright and mostly buried, but with their tops peeking out like gumdrops in a Candyland road. The rows traverse the road, so that it is impossible to enter the pavilion without driving or walking over the helmets of the dead.

The most traditional, and the most benevolent in spirit, of the major monuments in Baghdad is the Monument of Saddam's Qadisiyyah Martyrs. The war with Iran was called Qadis-iyyah Saddam, after the seventh-century Battle of Qadisiyyah, in which the Arabs drove the Persians from Mesopotamia, and the monument has come to be a sort of all-purpose marker for everyone killed one way or another in service to the Leader. It begins on a horizontal plane, an expanse of gray granite slabs set in a block-long avenue lined with flags and date palms. The avenue leads to the vertical center, a giant blue egg set in a field of white marble and split longitudinally in half. The halves are slightly staggered so that they do not directly oppose each other. They are meant to suggest the dome of a mosque, open to the heavens, to allow the souls of the dead and the prayers of the living to reach God.

On December 1 of every year, the people of Iraq honor their war dead in what is known by decree of the Leader as Martyrs' Day. The focal point is the martyrs' monument, where the principal, official ceremony is held. At a quarter to ten on the morning of December 1, 1991—an unsuitable morning, sunny and blue and unseasonably, sweetly warm—a few hundred people were lined up in patient quietude before the heavy black steel security fence that guards the entrance. The fence is set on wheels in tracks, and opened and shut by electrical impulse. It was a professional crowd of mourners: soldiers, schoolchildren, government workers, and party hacks. Bureaucrats fussed around and through the crowd, herding everyone into just-so order. They were from the Ministry of Information and Culture, and they are known as "minders." As a foreigner, I had a minder assigned just to me, and he hovered at my shoulder like a hummingbird, nervous and eager to please.

In the vast and cruel hierarchy of the Iraqi state, minders are important enough to be disliked by their colleagues and charges, but not important enough to be respected or feared. The spies that matter, the sleek young louts of the Mukhabarat, have the power to torture and kill, and act like it. They wear sunglasses and black vinyl jackets and pleated Italian trousers, and swagger about Baghdad like Toonland gunsels. Minders wear the genteel-shabby suits of the clerking class. Formalized snitches, classroom monitors, they inspire only resentment and sneers behind their backs. They suffer from low self-esteem. In three trips to Iraq, I never learned their proper title. Everyone called them minders, and they even called themselves by this mildly deprecatory term: "Hello, I am your minder today," or "If you are going to go to the market, you must remember to take a minder."

At ten o'clock, the two long center sections of the fence jerked apart with a grinding, clanking rumble, and after a moment's hesitation the crowd moved forward, slowly, silently, up the walk to the big blue eggshells. At the front were the guests of honor, two war widows and an orphan. The widows were suitably dressed in black, but the child wore a bright pink party frock, puffed up with layers of frilly slips underneath.

Behind them came several platoons of boys dressed as soldiers, in crisp fatigues of blue or tan cloth stamped with a camouflage pattern. They wore gold epaulets on their narrow shoulders, and pink and white scarves around their skinny necks. They were no more than ten or eleven years old, and they were members of al-Talaia—the Vanguards—the state organization for citizens between the ages of ten and fifteen. Political indoctrination in Iraq actually begins when children enter school at the age of five or six, but al-Talaia is the first organized politico-military group to which one can belong. The young troops of the Vanguard learn to march and to follow orders, and to serve as junior agents of the state, filing reports on their peers and, on occasion, parents.

The little troopers marched up the walk as a unit, properly, with a childish semblance of military discipline, pumping their arms and swinging their legs in goose-stepping exuberance. Some carried bright paper parasols, which they twirled in ragged coordination. They chanted as they marched: "Long life to the Baath Party! Long life to Saddam Hussein!"

Behind the little Vanguard boys were similar platoons of little Vanguard girls, in blue uniform dresses, carrying flowers, walking along primly and properly, as if they might, by example, teach the boys how to behave. Trailing them was a sort of Toddlers' Auxiliary, children culled from various kindergartens and pre-kindergartens. There was one small boy I liked especially. He was tricked out in a miniature suit of black formal wear, with tails and a bow tie and a red sateen vest. He could not stay still; he danced all over the place.

At the base of the dome, where the gray granite gave way to white marble, the crowd coming in merged with the honor guard already in place. There were half a dozen units, all in parade dress, gaudy and grand and gleaming in the morning sun. The Republican Guards were the most glorious, in uniforms as fine as Victoria's own fusiliers, red tunics with blue sashes, and tall topees, with gold chin straps below and gold tassels stirring in the breeze above. They played drums and horns and clarinets, ushering in the mourners with a tune of a vaguely Sousa-ish nature. "It is a national song, very popular," my minder said. "It is called 'We Welcome the National War.' "

A couple of hundred feet of red carpet had been unrolled up the center of the approach to the pale little flame—almost invisible in the sunlight—in between the eggshells, and the assemblage gathered at the foot of this. Everyone was orderly. The only people making any noise were the musicians of the Republican Guard and the boys of al-Talaia, who had taken up the traditional song on these occasions.

"With our blood, with our souls, we sacrifice for Saddam," they trilled in their pretty, light boy-voices.

The ceremony did not take long. First, six middle-aged men in suits from the Arab Baath Socialist Party walked up and laid down a wreath in front of the small gas flame that burned from a hole set in a granite circle between the two halves of the dome. Then four middle-aged men in suits from the Iraqi National Student Union walked up and laid down a wreath. Then five men in suits and one woman in a suit from the Iraqi National Teachers' Union, etc.

As each delegation approached the end of the carpet, a brigadier general and two soldiers stepped in to escort them. The soldiers flanked the head of the delegation, who carried the wreath, and the three of them walked the last few steps to the flame with a properly slow, funereal gait. When the head of the delegation laid down the wreath, the soldiers did a little dance. Facing the monument, they brought their right legs up waist-high, and then stomped them down, made a half turn so they faced each other, and did it again, then executed a neat half circle to change sides, and a third high step-stomp. Facing front again, they did two rapid stomps, first with the left leg, then with the right; then an about face and a final stomp before the walk back down the carpet.

And on and on it went, all of a bleak, bleached sameness, each party trudging up, laying down its wreath as the honor guard jigged, trudging back: the General Secretariat of Iraqi Economic Advisers, the Iraqi Geologists' Union, the Iraqi Doctors' Union, the Union of Employees of the Ministry of Foreign Affairs, the Iraqi Women's Federation, the Iraqi Friends of the Children Association, the General Federation of Arab Women, the Union of Employees of the Ministry of Information and Culture. As each group approached, the minder read its name off the wreath and whispered it in my ear. Once, he got excited. "Here is a group coming up that has no name on its wreath," he said. The oddity of this caused him to fall prey to a sudden false and wild hope. "Maybe it is just citizens." But then the breeze blew away a palm leaf that had been hiding a tag. "Oh," said the minder. "No. It is the Union of Employees of the Ministry of the Interior."

He seemed a little embarrassed, but the paucity of ordinary citizens was hardly his fault. Over the last quarter century, the Leader had killed off, one way or another, an astonishing number of the ordinary citizens of Iraq, and many of those left living in the winter of 1991 were too crippled or drunk or hungry to gin up much enthusiasm for the celebration of their condition.

A BROWN CITY

A RIVERINE CITY owes itself to its river. The tempo of the river becomes its tempo, the river's coloring its coloring. At its source, in the highlands of southeastern Turkey, the Tigris River is as swift and clear and bright as a baby's eye, but after it has made its way through the great pan of dirt that is the heart of Iraq, after it has picked up the waters of the Kabur, the Great Zab, the Little Zab, and the Uzaym—after all that, by the time it reaches Baghdad, it is a dull, dreary thing, as much soil as water, as thick with sediment as Arabic coffee. It plods along in a thick, straight line, with no shoals or rapids. Its banks are levees made of hard-packed dirt mounded some ten to twenty feet above the mean water line, sparsely adorned with grass that grows in a piebald fashion.

In the fall and winter, the wet months, the moisture rising from the river mixes with dirt and soot and automobile exhaust to form a yellow-tan fog that hangs at the neck and chills to the bone. The fog is so dirty that it has texture, a fine grit that gets in your eyes and hair and, worst of all, teeth. In the spring, the river becomes turbulent and floods, dumping its load of alluvial silt, and the soil for long stretches around its banks becomes a grasping muck that can suck the shoe off a foot. In the hot, dry rest of the year, the mud dries to a brown powder that the overheated wind swirls up and then leaves on everything—the asphalt, the sidewalks, the buildings, the drooping eucalyptus trees—so that with each breath you are an involuntary Hoover.

The city that stretches on both sides of the river is flat and brown like it. It is a sprawl of mostly squat, plain buildings. The poorest buildings are made of rough, dun-hued mud brick (invented in this land of mud six thousand years or so ago), sometimes covered, for variety's sake, with dun-hued mud plaster. The better class of buildings are made of a brick of a lighter, more yellow brown, a sort of mud-and-mustard brick; this is a difference, but not an improvement.

Baghdad was once a much grander place. It was built according to an elegant and intelligent plan by the Abbasid caliph Abu Jafar abd-Allah al-Mansur more than twelve hundred years ago. Roads were laid out in spokes from a great central square where stood the caliph's palace and the main mosque, ringed by the homes of leading bureaucrats, government offices, and army barracks. A double line of walls circled the city. Under the Abbasid caliphate, which lasted from 749 A.D. until 1258, and which reached its apogee in the ninth-century reign of Harun al-Rashid (Aaron the Wise), Baghdad became the greatest city in the world, the capital of the greatest civilization in the world. Here, Abu Nawas wrote his libidinous poems of women and wine; the cartographer Idrisi made the first map of the world; the mathematician al-Kawarizmi defined, in the book *Al-Jabr*, the scope of higher mathematics. The Abbasids built dikes and canals to control the floodwaters of the Tigris and Euphrates and thus encourage the productive farming that was at the heart of the country's wealth. There were bridges, mosques, hospitals, palaces. Visitors marveled.

"The city of Baghdad is three miles in circumference; the country in which it is situated is rich in palm trees, gardens, and orchards, so that nothing equals it in Mesopotamia," wrote Rabbi Benjamin of Toledo, following his visit in the mid-twelfth century. "Merchants of all countries resort thither for purposes of trade, and it contains many wise philosophers, well skilled in science, and magicians proficient in all sorts of enchantment. . . .

"The palace of the caliph . . . contains a large park filled with all sorts of trees, both useful and ornamental, and all kinds of beasts, as well as a pond of water carried thither from the river Tigris; and whenever the caliph desires to enjoy himself and to sport and carouse, birds, beasts, and fishes are prepared for him. . . .

"He has erected buildings. . . . These buildings include many large houses, streets, and hostelries for the sick poor, who resort thither in order to be cured. There are about sixty medical warehouses here, all well provided from the king's stores. . . . The city contains ten colleges."

The glory days ended very soon after the rabbi's visit, when, in 1256, Hulagu Khan, grandson of Genghis, attacked Baghdad. (He was reportedly egged on by his wife, a Nestorian Christian who disliked Muslims.) The Mongol army laid siege for two years, bombarding the city with rocks flung from catapults, and the caliph surrendered in February 1258. Hulagu's men sacked and pillaged with a ferocity notable even for the times. They burned the schools, libraries, palaces, and mosques, destroyed the system of canals and dikes that held back the Tigris and its mud, and stole everything they could carry away. They killed the poets and made a pyramid of their skulls. They wrapped the members of the Abbasid family in carpets and trampled them beneath their horses' hooves.

Hulagu's thoroughness made Baghdad, and Iraq, wretched for a very long time afterward.

"The prime fact of Mesopotamian history is that in the thirteenth century Hulagu destroyed the irrigation system; and from that day to this Mesopotamia has remained a land of mud deprived of mud's only possible advantage, vegetable fertility," wrote the English traveler Robert Byron in his 1937 book *The Road to Oxiana*. "It is a mud plain, so flat that a single heron, reposing on one leg beside some rare trickle of water in a ditch, looks as tall as a wireless aerial. From this plain rise villages of mud and cities of mud. The rivers flow with liquid mud. The air is composed of mud refined into gas. The people are mud-coloured; they wear mud-coloured clothes, and their national hat is nothing more than a formalized mud-pie. Baghdad is the capital one would expect of this divinely favored land. It lurks in a mud fog; when the temperature drops below 110, the residents complain of the chill and get out their furs. For only one thing is it now justly famous: a kind of boil which takes nine months to heal, and leaves a scar."

A cruel description, but not entirely inaccurate, and to a considerable degree still true, although the problems with boils have been largely cleared up. The city the Mongols left behind still has a battered look. There is much, despite the Leader's recent building spree, that is old, and what is old in Baghdad is not old in the buffed and burnished way of, say, Jerusalem, where even the moss in the cracks of the Western Wall seems to have been recently dusted, but old in the true sense: battered and worn and tired. The narrow, potholed, garbage-strewn streets are so thick with honking cars that for blocks sometimes the traffic hardly moves, and when it does, the wheels of the cars throw up clouds of dust. Even a pedestrian stirs up a little dust storm as he walks along, like Charlie Brown's Pigpen, a nebula of brown particulate swirling about him. In scraps of shade in the dirt park by the edge of the river, men sit and drink tea brewed in blackened aluminum pots on tiny fires of eucalyptus twigs, and try to ignore the flies. It is impossible to ignore the flies. They are ubiquitous; fat, loud bullies, so fearless that they will alight on your nose, so sure-winged you will only hit yourself striking at them.

Yet . . . in the soft yellow-rose light of the early morning when the muezzin's call to prayer mixes with the roosters' crows, there is something about the city that is stirring and lovely, something in its shape and smell and look that is at once both fresh and everlasting. There are, every year, fewer places in the world where it is still possible to travel in time, to stand at a spot and see not a monument to the ways of a thousand years ago (as Jerusalem is) but the ways of a thousand years ago still living. You can see that in some spots in Baghdad.

One morning, I went to the suq al-Safafir, the metalsmiths' bazaar, and wandered through the maze of cobblestoned alleys. The smiths sit on stones in front of the cramped brick stalls that are their shops. They are short, strong men who work close to the ground, with their legs around anvils that are iron stakes wedged down hard in slots between the stones. A trickle of clean water runs down the smooth, worn gutter in the center of the alley. Around the coppersmiths are small, gleaming piles of finished and polished pans and pots and trays, and larger piles of dull, rough pieces awaiting their final hammerings and buffings. Some of the bowls and tubs are big enough to bathe in, and stacked waist-high beside them are sheets of milled copper the size of bath towels.

Three smiths sat in a close row, all in furious labor, each hammering a different sort of decoration onto a different sort of container. One held a small, deep pot upside down on his spike so that the rim was resting on the head of the anvil. He turned it a half inch at a time, striking sharp little blows with a medium ball-peen hammer and a square-edged punch like a dull chisel, each blow producing a small crimp, fluting the rim. He wasted no motion; I timed him at twenty-four seconds to the pot. The man next to him was working with a small hammer and a round punch on a large, shallow dish, of the kind used in Arabian feasts to serve a whole lamb on a bed of rice with pine nuts and raisins. He hit the punch with hard taps to make an array of overlapping dents, and when he was done the pan's underside was scaled like the flank of a big fish. The third man, an old fellow with a white skullcap on his bald head, was handling a big wooden mallet, working the rim of a tall pot, rounding the edge with many soft blows to make a gentle incurving lip. The different speeds and tones and pitches of their blows mingled together to make a pleasing sound that was somewhere between cacophony and symphony, like an orchestra warming up.

Suqs are organized by theme. There is, in Baghdad, a *suq* for spices, herbs, and nuts, a *suq* for made-to-measure men's suits (a line of little old men hunched over little old Singers in a dark alleyway), a *suq* for live birds, one for gold, one for electronic goods, one for secondhand tools, and so on. It seems in each as if there is a duplication of effort, each little shop selling something in the same line as its neighbor. But in fact each is selling only one precise part of the line, so that everybody gets a small piece of the overall action.

Thus it was in the metalsmith's bazaar. At the stand next to the three hammering coppersmiths, a small man with forearms like Popeye's was working with a giant pair of tin snips, cutting with one hand a line as straight as a razor's edge through a sheet of galvanized metal, lifting the sheet up and away from the cut with the other hand as he went. He made washtubs and other large utilitarian items out of the metal, and sat in the shadow of a galvanized hill of finished goods. The smith next door worked in secondhand metal, making watering cans and other modest vessels from old boxes and cans. He hammered the boxes flat and shaped the new containers so the old outside was now the inside. Looking down the throat of a watering can, you could see fragments of past-life labels—"vegetable ghee" or "packed with the most modern."

In a twisty side alley hardly wider than a man lying down, I watched a specialist repair a garlic press, brought by a boy on a bicycle who waited while it was fixed. The press was the kind of two-bit tool that in America would be thrown away when it broke, or possibly before. The little sieved box that holds the garlic clove had come away from one of the squeezing handles. The smith had a pot burner set in a metal table, and he heated a brazier in its blue flame until it glowed red-orange, then dipped its tip into a dish of powdered solder, which melted in a wink into a silver puddle. He applied the solder to the join between the handle and the box, touching down a couple of fat drops to make the spot weld, making six separate welds in all; I imagine it was the strongest garlic press in Iraq by the time he was through.

The civilization of man began and flourished in the land between the Tigris and the Euphrates; it was here that man formed the first farming communities, discovered gods, and later God, developed written symbols to convey ideas, made money and a system for its use, built the first planned cities, invented laws, and learned how to brew beer. No land in the world is richer in places that tell the story of early humanity: Al Qurna, where the Tigris and the Euphrates meet and the Garden of Eden perhaps was; Shanidar Cave, site of the earliest evidence of ritual burial; Abu Shanrein, where a six-thousand-year-old temple is the oldest religious structure ever found; Gaugamela, seven thousand years old and some say the place where man turned from hunting and fishing to farming; Ur, primal city and birthplace of Abraham; Nineveh, seat of the Assyrian Empire, and the wicked city Jonah was sent to warn; Al Kifl, where the prophet Ezekiel rests; Kirkuk, where Shadrach, Meshach, and Abednego were delivered from the fiery furnace.

But no spot is of greater importance than Babylon, the seat of the most fully developed early civilization, the site of the Tower of Babel and the hanging gardens that were one of the wonders of the ancient world. The roots of the city go back at least 2,400 years before Christ, to a time when the Akkadians, a Semitic tribe, built on a spot by the Euphrates River a temple to the goddess Ishtar. Seven hundred years later, the Amorite king Hammurabi constructed on that site the capital of a civilization that produced, among other things, a comprehensive code of laws "to make justice prevail in the land, to destroy the evil and the wicked, so that the strong may not oppress the weak."

The Hittites, sweeping down from Asia Minor in the sixteenth century B.C., ended all that, and Babylon languished for a thousand years, until the Chaldean king Nebuchadnezzar II built a new, far greater city on the foundations of the old capital. It is this second Babylon that the prophet Jeremiah called "a golden cup in the Lord's hand, that made all the earth drunken."

The new Babylon covered five hundred acres and had a population of 100,000 people. Its square inner core was bisected by the Euphrates and protected by two outer walls and a canal. "The walls of Babylon were remarkable structures, much admired in antiquity," writes the historian George Roux. "Reinforced by towers and protected by moats, they were made of two thick walls of burnt bricks, joined together by a filling of brick rubble. The top of the outer wall, for instance, was thus more than thirty-six feet wide and could accommodate one or even two chariots of four horses abreast, enabling a rapid movement of troops from one end of town to the other." The horses and chariots belonged to Babylon's guard, and they tooled around the city on the road that ran atop the wall.

The most famous of the eight approaches to Babylon was the great boulevard called Ai-ibur-shabu—"May the Enemy Not Cross It"—popularly known as Procession Street. It brought visitors to Ishtar Gate, a huge three-tiered structure decorated with bas-relief carvings and glazed-brick paintings of bulls and dragons, 570 of them arrayed in prancing rows.

Inside the city were the greatest buildings of the age. Etemen-an-ki, "the Temple Foundation of Heaven and Earth," the structure known now as the Tower of Babel, was seven stories high and three hundred feet wide at its base. The Southern Palace, Nebuchadnezzar's own, covered 52,000 square feet and had five courtyards, a throne room the size of a large modern house, and, on its northeast roof, the hanging gardens of flowers the king built to please his mountain-born wife. The complex of E-sag-ila ("the Temple That Raises Its Head") was Nebuchadnezzar's pet project, and the most lavishly decorated. "Silver, gold, precious stones, bronze, wood from Medea, everything that is expensive, glittering abundance, the produce of the mountains, the treasures of the seas, large quantities, I brought to my city of Babylon," the king wrote, recalling its building. "I made the walls gleam like the sun. With shining gold as if it were gypsum . . . with lapis-lazuli and alabaster. . . ."

It took German archaeologists forty-one years, from 1899 to 1940, to excavate the ruins of this greatness. What they were able to recover ranged from the meager—some walls remained only as stumps—to the magnificent; the bottom part of Ishtar Gate was found, 36 feet high, with 152 glorious bulls and dragons still prancing up and down in rows.

In 1989, the construction crews of the Leader built on top of the ruins of Babylon a new city, the New, New Babylon of Saddam Hussein.

The road to the main entrance runs alongside a shallow, narrow concrete ditch in which sits a foot or so of water that was swimming-pool blue. Bordering the ditch is a swath of lawn mowed to a suburban neatness, and on the lawn are small concrete tables, the tops of which are colored a child's paintbox red or blue.

What is this? I asked.

"It is the Euphrates River," said the minder at my side.

I did not think so, I said.

"No, no. I do not mean it is *really* the Euphrates River. The real river is over there." He pointed to the west. "This is the New Euphrates River of Babylon, Saddam's River."

We drove on to the outer walls of the city, past a sign proclaiming the land to be Saddam Hill, to the new entrance, and walked inside, coming to a broad stone pathway, very clean, surrounded by a strong black iron fence running straight as a shot for several thousand yards.

"It is Ai-ibur-shabu, Procession Street, very famous street of antiquity," the minder said.

Really?

"No, not really. The real Procession Street is there." He pointed to a path running parallel to the fake road, massive old stones as smooth as riverbed rock, partly covered with dirt and weeds.

We walked on to the great old entrance to Nebuchadnezzar's city, Ishtar Gate. The glorious beasts of the bas-relief were strong still, the scales of their armored flesh and the thews and sinews of their great legs taut. The bricks that carried them were big, three times the size of modern bricks, and roughly textured, shot through with small, irregular holes and sturdy, binding pieces of straw and twigs. They were only loosely the same size, and only casually rectangular, in color a soft, warm, pale rose.

But on top of the old gate, and the walls around it, and the foundations of the old buildings—on top of everything that was left of God's golden cup—Saddam's masons had laid down a new city, built precisely on the lines of the old, but of hard, shiny, new yellow bricks fresh from the factory, all exactly the same size and shape, with edges as sharp as the lines of a brand-new split-level rambler. What remained of the old walls rose only four to ten feet above the ground in some cases, and the new additions climbed to fifty, sixty, seventy feet; the effect was less like a prosthetic hand on the end of a man's arm than a prosthetic man on the end of a real hand.

As we walked through the god-awfulness, the minder poked around for bits and pieces of the true Babylon. "Look over here," he would say, trotting off to a corner. "Real bricks!" And I would trot over too and we would look at the few feet of the old brick left visible, sandwiched between the earth and a thousand tons of new wall. A group of schoolchildren walked by, the smaller kids herded along by several Vanguards in blue uniforms.

"We used to come here when I was that age," the minder said. "It was very different. On the ground there was nothing but dirt and old stones, the real ones, and it looked dangerous. It was a little frightening, and that was very exciting. When I was older, in the university, we used to come here and sit on the old walls and have picnics. Now this—they did all this—they say it was to protect the old brick. . . ."

As we were leaving, he pointed out a small scrap of writing in bas-relief on one of the 2,600-year-old bricks. It noted that this city had been built in the reign of Nebuchadnezzar II. Nearby, he showed me a new brick, similarly inscribed. "In the period of Saddam Hussein, President of the Republic of Iraq, this city was reconstructed. The third stage of the reconstruction was finished in 1989."

On the edge of the city, we stopped to look at a man-made hill, terraced and sawed off at the top so it resembled a ziggurat. Planted in sparse rows on the hill were some weak, scrubby, flowerless bushes. On the top, a concrete building, also shaped like a flat-topped pyramid, was half-constructed. "It is the New Hanging Gardens of Babylon," the minder said. "And the New Casino and New Cafeteria of Babylon."

DELUSIONS

THE FIRST BAGHDADI I EVER MET was a minder. He greeted me at Saddam International Airport on January 10, 1991, a week before the beginning of Iraq's most disastrous war, against the United States of America and thirty-nine allies. A small man in a large suit, oddly furtive in manner, he slid up while I was waiting for my bag under a sign that said that visitors who failed to report for AIDS tests would go to jail. All Heepish smiles and flutters of hands, he delivered a strange little welcome speech, the words coming out with hardly any space between them, in a jumbled, jumpy rush.

"Hello, hello. Welcome, welcome. You look worried, my friend, do not worry. Nothing will happen! No, no, oh no. No. There will be no war, you will see, I assure you. Mr. Pérez de Cuéllar will come in and save everything. Oh yes. Or perhaps Mr. Mitterrand. Or, I think this is very likely, Mr. Bush will come to his senses. Yes, I think this will no doubt be the case. You will see. No problem."

It was, I thought later, an ideal introduction to Baghdad the week before the bombs, a city in deep denial, where every man chose his myth: Iraq would pull out of Kuwait; the United Nations, or the French, or the European Community or Yasir Arafat or Mauritania or somebody would come up with a peace plan; the Americans would compromise. Or there would be a war, but, for one reason or another, it wouldn't hurt: the Americans would never attack Baghdad, or the American troops would not fight, or the Iraqi army would inflict losses so great they would drive the Americans to the negotiating table, or Iraq would force Israel into the war and cause a pan-Arab *jihad*, or Saddam's Secret Weapon would save the day (there was a widespread belief in the Secret Weapon, although much disagreement about what it precisely was).

As if the local variety were not enough, the city had become a great importer of foreign delusions, in the form of peace missionaries. Like their ancestors in spirit, the men of God who labored in darkest Africa or among the heathen Chinee, the peace missionaries believed in the power of the Word, and went forth armed with pure spirits and tracts to change the world. For weeks, from all over the West, they had been streaming in a great babbling mass to the land of Babel.

I had encountered them even before I left America, in the airport at New York, waiting for the late-night flight to Amman in a bare box of a room perversely called a lounge. They were a delegation of thirteen under the auspices of the Fellowship of Reconciliation, of Nyack, New York, a group founded in 1915 to stop the war to end all wars, and laboring vainly ever since. Except for an assistant professor of political science and a woman Methodist minister, all of the delegation members were college students. Their eyes were still bright, and their noses still shiny, with the assumptions and oils of adolescence. Their smiling pink faces were soft and downy and open. They wore T-shirts and carried autofocus cameras and bright-colored nylon fanny packs, and if you did not know they were members of a peace delegation, you would think they were en route to Greece or Guatemala to spend the summer hitchhiking and hostel-hopping and playing music in the public squares of small towns.

The assistant professor of political science was J. Stephen Zunes, and he taught at Whitman College in Walla Walla, Washington. He was an earnest man, serious in his purpose. "Media package," he said, as he handed me a yellow folder filled with pamphlets and papers. The centerpiece of the package was a press release with the straightforward title "Why We Are Going to Iraq." It said: "The purpose of the peace delegation is: (1) to call on all nations to refrain from further provocation and acts of war, to de-escalate tensions in the region, and to withdraw all military forces to their home bases. . . ."

It was a big job, Zunes said, but it could be done through the miracle of the Word. "You see, you really can't have war unless you dehumanize the enemy. And dialogue humanizes folks. We will meet with the Iraqis and when we go back we will share with Americans that they are human beings. We will be able to say, 'Look, we talked to these folks and they are human beings and they are going to be killed if we go forward with this war.' "

There was a danger, he allowed, that the Iraqis, who were difficult converts, might try to divert the mission from its true path. "But we are pretty smart people," he said. "If we came up against a situation where it was pretty clear we would be part of a propaganda show, we'd say, 'No way! Forget it!' "

On the flight to Amman, the delegation for the prevention of war and I sat in economy class. In the front section sat another, rather different, group of missionaries: Daniel Ortega, the recently deposed president of Nicaragua; Zhedi Terzi, PLO ambassador to the United Nations; and Louis Farrakhan, leader of the Nation of Islam.

When we landed, the television crews rushed to record the arrival of the Fellowship delegation, and the young people held hands and swayed together and sang Isaiah by the banks of the baggage carousel:

"They shall beat their swords into plowshares and their spears into pruning hooks. Nation shall not lift up sword against nation. Neither shall they learn war anymore."

Their voices were sweet and pure and a little ragged, and the great and lovely words hung in the air. When the moment passed, the singers stood in awkward, unsure silence, like children on a school stage after the recital has ended and before the parents have begun to clap. It was in this brief time of vulnerability that something unfortunate occurred.

As it happened, the media had apparently not noticed the first-class passengers. Fat little Terzi and incognito Ortega took this as their sorry fate, but Farrakhan did not. As the last notes of the psalm drifted off and before the cameras turned away, he swooped down on the soulful singers. His big white teeth gleamed in a brotherly grin as he scooped them up in his arms. "Why, my friends, let us stand together!" he cried and pulled them close to him. He flapped his strong hands. "Come, come, let us all, all of us journeyers for peace, stand together!" he said, and the Fellowship travelers dutifully crowded around and smiled small, slightly nervous smiles. The cameras recorded the scene, and Farrakhan beamed. Afterward, Zunes came up to me, a look of vague unhappiness on his face. "I want you to know, I felt pretty ambivalent about that photo," he said. I believed him, and I felt sorry for him. The path of the righteous is not an easy one.

Professor Zunes and the Reverend Farrakhan and Ex-Presidente Ortega and I arrived in Baghdad five days before the January 15 deadline set by the United Nations for the Iraqis to stop plundering Kuwait. Such is the perverse nature of man, or some men, that the imminent outbreak of war had packed the city. The Al Rashid Hotel, where the minders liked visitors to stay because it was well equipped with listening devices, was booked so solidly with reporters and missionaries of one stripe or another—there was an entire convention of Islamic fundamentalists in town, and the lobby was filled with pamphleteers and men haranguing one another, a scene much like a Democratic convention, except more sober and with less amusing hats—that the front-desk clerks were obliged to double strangers up. I was paired with Tony Horwitz, a reporter for *The Wall Street Journal.* He had been to Baghdad before, and he offered to show me the town. On the way out we ran into Rev. Farrakhan's aide-de-camp, a large man named Leonard Mohammed, who wore a diamond pinky ring and held himself with ponderous dignity. Tony asked him how the Minister's mission was faring. "Not well," said Leonard Mohammed judiciously. "The people here are very resolute on this holy war business, but the Minister does not feel that is the way to go."

The memory of when Baghdad was great is evoked in Abu Nawas Street, named after the greatest poet of the great age. The street runs along the right bank of the Tigris River, and there, in the warm months, couples stroll in the evening, and on New Year's Eve whole families of roisterers fill the big nightclubs. The main attraction, though, is a line of open-air restaurants on the water side of the street that serve a dish called *mazgouf,* which is spiced whole river fish roasted at a tamarisk wood fire.

The fish halls are set in a hard-used little park, a narrow strip of grass and mud and bedraggled eucalyptus trees, with a rusted chain-link fence built along the brown river itself, to keep children from swimming. They are unpromising places: rough, cheap buildings open to the street, with side and rear walls of plastic sheeting or tin tacked to a wood frame, and ropes of colored Christmas-tree lights strung from tin roofs. In the center of the concrete floors are tiled tanks filled with water and small schools of round-bellied, slow-moving fish. It is part of the ritual of eating *mazgouf* that each customer selects his own live fish. Discerning customers make a tour of inspection of the entire strip, studying each tank at some length.

Tony chose the fourth restaurant in the line and selected a

fine, fat fish from the pool. A boy scooped it up, struggling and squirming, in a big long-handled net, and dumped it on the floor; it hit with a flat, loud smack, and before it could flop more than a few times he grabbed it with his left hand, holding it just behind the gills, and with his right brought a rusty monkey wrench down on its head. The first blow probably killed the fish, but the boy gave it a second whack for the sake of a job well done, leaving it lying on the concrete bloody and battered. Grabbing up a wood-handled butcher's knife from the ground, the boy disemboweled the carcass, pulling out the hard-to-get bits of guts with his fingers and raking the cavity clean. He butterflied it from lungs to tail; it was a blood-rich fish, and— gaping open with the thick red dripping from it—looked more like the remains of a hoofed animal than anything piscine.

The butcher boy handed this over to a second boy, who was the cook, working at a fire fifteen feet across with flames three feet in the air over a deep bed of red-and-white coals. Around the edges of the fire, stakes of tamarisk had been driven into the ground to form a circle. After rubbing spices into the meat, the cook staked each fish on three or four of these spikes, anchoring them so they were splayed open toward the flames.

It takes a long time to cook a fish this way, and it was an hour or so before the finished product arrived at our table, along with a dozen big wheels of flat bread hot from the charcoal oven behind us. The bread was very good, chewy and crisp together, but the fish was still flecked with bits of carbon and wood and dirt from its violent end, and tasted of nothing much except smoke.

I washed up afterward at a little sink in the back. Next to the sink, on top of two big sacks of yellow onions, a black-and-white television set was turned on, and as I stood there, the evening news broadcast came on the screen. I expected everything to stop as sudden as a freeze-frame, the butcher boy to pause with monkey wrench in midair, the customers to stop in mid-chew. I thought people in a country five days away from a deadline for war would rush to hear the latest development. But no one but me paid the slightest attention.

I saw why soon enough. The broadcast was a perfect triumph of form over substance. It looked like a news program—a young man in coat and tie sitting at a slab of something that might have been wood and might have been plastic, the magic blue box at his right shoulder matching the pictures to his words—but there was no information in it at all. The carefully smiling announcer read the first item as the box at his shoulder showed pictures of the Leader sitting on a sofa and chatting with a carefully smiling visitor. "His Excellency President Saddam Hussein said today that the belief of the Iraqi people in victory will not be shaken even if the aggressors' force grows several times its number. . . ." This went on for some time, and when it was over there was another piece just like it, and then another, and so on. The only difference from story to story was that sometimes the Leader would be seen talking with solemn advisers, or accepting flowers from children, instead of receiving dignitaries. In twenty minutes, there was not one item that deviated from the pattern; the phrase "His Excellency Saddam Hussein" occurred nineteen times. It was so dull that it was perversely mesmerizing, and I stood there with my mouth open staring dumbly, as if I had never seen moving pictures before.

The following morning, January 11, I went out to the front of the hotel to hire a driver. There was one man, among dozens who had parked their cars there, who seemed different from the others; he carried himself with an obvious, even slightly theatrical, dignity, standing very erect and square-shouldered, with his chin at a slight tilt to the air. I found out later that he had been for many years a high-ranking officer in the army. He spoke enough English that we could talk, and we struck a deal (a hundred dollars a day, I think). His name (for the purposes of this writing) was Adnan, and he agreed to drive me around town so that I could work up some stories to send back to *The New Republic* and *The Boston Globe,* for which I was stringing.

"Well, I will tell you myself what the people think," he said as we started off. "The people of Iraq are not scared. That is what they think."

Not scared at all?

"Well, the women are. But not the men. That is the truth. And the people like Saddam still. That is the truth too. They like Saddam, and they do what he say to do."

Why do they like him?

"Look around." He waved his hand at the scene around us, the broad new highway, the approaching skyline of apartment blocks and office towers. "When I was a child, this city was like a village. A big village, that is all. Your hotel—it did not exist. The roads—they did not exist. Saddam built it all. He built many roads, many schools, many hospitals. Everything, Saddam built. In the past, people did not have shoes. Now they have cars. Saddam gave them all this. So they like him still." He held up a finger. "Aha. I have something to show you that will make you understand."

We drove down the main thoroughfare of Rashid Street. "This is old Baghdad," Adnan said. The unprettified shops slouched against each other, spavined below, crooked above, leaning back on their heels or lurching drunkenly forward, their balconies, held barely up by Corinthian columns of crumbling concrete, sagging like a beldame's bosom over the street. The skins of the buildings were scabrous with flaking, peeling bits of themselves, as if they had been afflicted with a leprosy that attacked mortar and brick and paint instead of flesh.

"Now I will show you the new." We drove, for the next hour or so, through a city of blocks: blocks and blocks of blocks and blocks; apartment blocks, school blocks, hospital blocks, museum blocks, factory blocks, civic center blocks, theater blocks, government blocks—lots of these. The bigger blocks were colored a sort of tan, while the smaller ones were a sort of gray-white. There were, occasionally, doors or window frames painted a primary color, which provided exactly the same sort of false cheer that you would find in exactly the same sort of thing in a public housing tenement in East St. Louis.

In the residential areas, everything was properly ordered, each to his own sort of block. The university professors, for instance, lived in a set of high-rise blocks all in a line, all identical, but with a big numeral painted on the side of each building, so that the professor of Islamic literature did not accidentally wander into the flat of the professor of systems analysis. By the river were the smaller, better apartment blocks of medium-rank party and government men. In the lushly gardened neighborhoods reserved for the most important party members there were very fine blocks; indeed, they were so elegant they were not entirely blocky, but were allowed the grace of curves and bows and angles other than right. There was even a stretch of blocks, on the western outskirts of the city, for war widows. Although there were miles of widows' blocks, there were not enough. There was a waiting list. The poorest of Baghdad, 750,000 of them, lived in a vastness of planned housing called Saddam City, and their blocks, of course, were the worst of all, rough, dirty cement boxes stacked on top of and up against each other; dingy, dismal square upon dingy, dismal square.

We came to a neighborhood, near one of the industrial zones, of medium-size one-story blocks, each with a square yard enclosed by a cinder-block wall.

"This is my house," said Adnan. "Now you can see why we like Saddam. Saddam gave me this house because I was an officer in the army. All these houses, all around, belong to officers. All from Saddam, all this, Saddam built for us. So why should we not like Saddam?"

We went into the living room, cool and dark and bare, in the Arab style; a table with a few chairs and a small sofa. The sofa and the tabletop were covered with clear plastic, to guard against dirt, although there wasn't any. On one wall hung a large studio photograph of a man, perhaps in his forties, dressed in a pressed suit, stiffly unsmiling in the seriousness of the occasion. "My brother," said Adnan. "Missing in action in war with Iran. I was in that war too. Eight years. Plus six years more before that. Half my life, I am fighting."

"Did you like it?"

"No. Except for 1983, I was a volunteer to fight against Israel. That was good, I liked that. The rest—no. In the war against Iran I had to order poison gas against children. Iranians, crazy, coming at our position, thousands. They would not stop. We had no choice. But I did not like it. I am very tired of war. I have many pains because I have had too much cold too often, especially in my knees."

We sat on the sofa covered with slippery plastic, and a young man came in with steaming small glasses of sugared tea. He was Samir, the oldest son, twenty-seven, a chemical engineer by training, but at the moment a junior army officer, at home for a few days' leave. He seemed a gentle, shy young man as he padded about in his socks serving up the tea. When he finished he sat down, and I asked him, as an opening to conversation, what he hoped to do with his life after the war.

"I only say I hope I will live, and get married."

His life's ambition was not unduly modest. Iraq in 1991 was like France in 1919, devastated by a war fought on a scale so large and with such terrible intensity as to destroy a generation. The eight years of war with Iran had killed at least 120,000 people, mostly young men; 300,000 had been wounded, 65,000 had been taken prisoner. The country was full of young widows, aging maidens, legless men, and battle-addled drunks; once financially healthy and growing, it faced a war debt of $80 billion, more than twice the gross national product. Among these ruins, to find love, and the money for a wedding, was to beat very long odds. With the groom's dowry of twenty-two-karat gold and a properly lavish reception, a middle-class wedding cost at least five thousand dollars, more than two years' income for a working man. "This is why I am driving a car," Adnan said. "Because I must get enough money to pay for the dowry. It will take me three more years, I think. When I get enough money, Samir will get married, God willing and if he is not killed in the war."

"I am concerned about the poison gas," Samir said. "They say the Americans will use gas." He went out of the room and came back with his new gas mask and his tool for neutralizing nerve gas, a plastic syringe filled with atropine. "Everybody has them," he said. "They say they work very well, so I am hopeful."

He did not seem hopeful. He stared at the floor and twiddled the gas mask in his hands. "I will die. Fight and die." He gave vent to a deep sigh. "What can I do? It is my country. My house. My blood. I must fight."

"Yes," said his father. "If war comes here, we fight. In the meantime, what can we do? We cannot stay scared in our houses. We work, and eat and sleep and make love. That is life. And if Mr. Saddam says we die, we die."

We all sat there for a minute without saying anything, to linger over the rich sweetness of the melodrama. When Adnan spoke again, he leaned forward and lowered his voice. "Do you know why this all happened?" he said. "No? I will tell you the true story. You know we had a big disagreement with Kuwait about oil prices? So we have a meeting to discuss this. In this meeting, the number two man in Kuwait says bad things to the number two man in Iraq. He says, 'We take Iraqi women to fuck.' Now, Mr. Saddam—and any Iraqi man—will not allow that word to be said about our women. So, when the number two man in Iraq calls back and tells Mr. Saddam what the number two man in Kuwait says, that is that. Mr. Saddam gets very angry, we go to war."

He was talking about (I figured out much later) a meeting in the Saudi city of Jidda on the night of August 1, 1990, between

Izzat Ibrahim, vice-chairman of the Revolutionary Command Council of the Republic of Iraq, and Saad al-Abdullah al-Salem al-Sabah, crown prince of the emirate of Kuwait. The meeting was by way of an old-fashioned shakedown. Saddam Hussein had arrayed eight Iraqi army divisions along the Kuwait border and had sent Ibrahim to demand a great deal of money from Kuwait in exchange for the privilege of remaining uninvaded. The prince declined to pay, and the Iraqi army entered Kuwait a few hours later.

I was to hear a version of Adnan's story all over the Middle East. A reporter in Amman, a fast-food restaurant manager in Dhahran, and a consular officer in Cairo all gave me variations of it. In one account, my favorite, the Kuwaiti prince dismisses the Iraqi messenger with a perfectly calculated insult, delivered in tones of bored hauteur: "But we already give money to Iraq. We give money to your women in Basra every weekend." Basra is an Iraqi port city near the Kuwaiti border that had the usual sexual amenities of liberty towns. I don't know if the story is true in any of its variations, and the people who told it didn't know either. But they liked it, and I like it, because it seems to me to get just so the spirit of the whole misadventure, the mad arrogance of the Kuwaitis, the greedy thuggery of the Iraqis, and the wicked, wanton waste of it all.

When we finished our second glass of tea, Adnan offered a tour of his defensive supplies. In the kitchen, he had filled two big freezers with meat, bread, and vegetables. In the little concrete backyard were five jerry cans of white kerosene, seven of gasoline, and five of propane. In a shed next to these, he had stacked a large Styrofoam cooler full of water, two cartons of potatoes, and three sacks of onions. "Do you have a basement?" I asked. "Where will you go if they bomb Baghdad?"

He pointed to an old army shovel lying in a pile of debris next to a shallow ditch, maybe four feet long and no more than a foot deep. "It is a bomb shelter I dig," he said. "It is all we need. Saddam will protect us." He kept his face straight and

serious when he said this, so that I couldn't possibly know if he
believed what he was saying.

Saddam Hussein and the Arab Baath Socialist Party had held
power in Iraq for twenty-three years, and everyone had learned
to say the right thing with a straight face. It was any number of
hanging offenses to say anything the Leader might object to.
The criminal code listed twenty death-penalty "security"
crimes, including Article 225, which prescribed execution for
anyone who blatantly and publicly insulted Saddam Hussein,
the Baath Party, or the government leadership. The state employed five East German–trained security forces, the principal
one being the huge Mukhabarat, or General Intelligence Bureau. The party permeated and controlled every government
agency, university department, professional organization, and
trade union. Almost everybody was spied upon by someone
close at hand, or at least that is what everybody thought.

The national sense of perspective had become vestigial. The
Ministry of Information and Culture controlled all information
and all culture. It published three daily newspapers in Arabic
and one in English. It endlessly spewed out books, plays,
movies, magazines, poems, songs, paintings, sculptures, and
speeches. The great daily deluge told the people that the Jews
were conspiring with the imperialists to destroy Iraq and Islam,
that the Arab renaissance had arrived, that Iraq was a mighty
nation destined for great things. Above all, it told them that the
Leader was omniscient. Certainly he was omnipresent. He was
the president of the republic, chairman of the Council of Ministers, commander in chief of the armed forces, field marshal of
the Iraqi army, chairman of the Revolutionary Command
Council, general secretary of the Regional Command of the
Baath party, chairman of the Supreme Planning Council, and
chairman of the Supreme Agricultural Council. He was the
leader-president, the leader-struggler, the standard-bearer, the

Arab leader, the knight of the Arab nation, the hero of national liberation, the father leader, and the daring and aggressive knight. Saddam's voice and name dominated all radio and television broadcasts, and his every utterance was conveyed to the people as if revealed from the Prophet himself (and, indeed, his official lineage declared him a direct descendant of Muhammad).

The whole city was a monument to the Leader. On every street was a painting of his face. Some of the paintings were thirty or forty feet high. Every office, every shop, every home, even the dashboards of cars were decorated with photographs of the president. There was a Saddam for every occasion, every location. In front of the Ministry of Justice, he wore judicial robes and held a scale; at the Ministry of Housing and Reconstruction, he had rolled up his sleeves to dig the footings of something New; at Firdaws Square in the center of town, he wore a blue overcoat and an astrakhan and, for some reason, looked Oriental; in front of the Ministry of Information and Culture, he worked at a desk, with pen and paper; and at the Ministry of Foreign Affairs he smiled diplomatically in a pinstriped suit. At the Ministry of the Interior, he was dressed in the gold-trimmed black *abaya* of a sheikh; amid the tracts of public housing for the poor in Saddam City, he wore the simple *dishdasha* (shirt-robe) and red-and-white *kaffiyeh* (scarf) of a workingman. There were Saddams smoking cigars and wearing sunglasses like Castro, and Saddams in sparkling white-and-gold parade dress like Prince Charles.

The young Saddam of the the twenty-five-year-old black-and-white photograph that adorns the desks of high-ranking government men has a slim, handsome face, notable for its intelligence and sensitivity. That disappeared soon, though; it is missing from even the Saddams of a few years after. The Saddams of the middle period have harder, coarser faces, but are still handsome, and still human. The latest Saddams, the ones painted in the past few years, are much uglier, with big, fleshy jowls and peculiar tints to the skin. There is, in the middle of the city, a big, full-length Saddam that is one of the newest ones. He is wearing a gangsterish black shirt and dark sunglasses and needs a shave, and he looks more than anything like the photographs of Jim Jones, late of Jonestown, shortly before the night of the Kool-Aid.

At noon, an abundant crowd had gathered for Friday prayers at the Imami al-Adam Abu Hanniffa mosque. The mosque was full when we arrived, and the overflow had spilled out through the arched doorways into the courtyards. Mostly, the young worshipers were men, some in Western suits, some in long gray *dishdashas*, many of them wearing *kaffiyehs* wrapped around their necks or heads. All of them were cloaked in supplication, holding their palms up to God, knocking their heads softly on the ground, resting their buttocks on their naked heels. They knelt shoulder to shoulder on the faded old carpets overlapped on the stone. Inside the mosque, thousands more knelt. They prayed in a tightly focused mass, their lips sliding in easy, practiced unison over the words of the opening *sura* of the Koran, the slippery syllables of spoken Arabic melting into each other, making a soft but powerful murmur, like the water of a good-sized brook.

High on an ornately carved wooden pulpit, twenty feet off the floor, brilliantly lit from great crystal chandeliers, the imam preached in full and fiery throat. The sermon was to the point of the times.

"We are a nation, a nation that wants peace! But we refuse to be dominated! We don't want only a peace! We want a just peace!" He had a great bellow, punctuated by sharp heaving intake sucks of air, almost as if he were sobbing. "Why do the Americans keep medicine from us and milk from our babies? Why? Why? Why do they persecute us?" He promised revenge. "When the war starts, we will be victorious because our God is with us. America is the imperialist and is the antagonist in an unjust aggression, and our God will punish them!" And he promised heaven. "If anyone dies in this war, his death is preordained to be a martyrdom. Those who die will go to paradise!"

Loudspeakers bolted to the corners of the mosque carried his words to the people outside, who seemed to find them good. A man standing next to me wearing a tweed sports coat and pressed slacks and carrying a bulging briefcase of old, worn leather, nodded his head vigorously. "Yes. Yes. Yes," he said, in English, poking at me with his eyeglasses. "Write this down." His name was Taha Hassa, and he was, he said, a professor at the Academy of Fine Arts. As we were talking, a second man came up, and a third, and in a few moments I was at the center of an energetic little scrum of worshipers.

"I think peace is coming because the war would be very bad for the United States," said Taha Hassa. "Iraq is not a nation that loses fights. We taught this to the Iranian people and we will teach this to the Americans. It will be a long war and it will be like Vietnam for the Americans. The Americans will never reach the streets of Baghdad. They will die on the line in Saudi Arabia."

A very old man pushed him aside and took his place in my face. He was short and thick and tough, with creased, furrowed skin that looked as if you couldn't cut it with a knife, a peasant of peasants for five thousand years. He said: "My name is Hamad al-Tarif. By God, I will fight in the streets. I will fight with my teeth"—here he drew back his lips to show an incomplete set of yellow-and-brown stubs. "The enemy comes to my house; I do not go to his. He comes to my country. This is not right. It must not be allowed. By God, none must be left alive! I am seventy years old, but I will fight! If I do not have any weapon, I will tear the enemy to pieces with my teeth and my nails!"

A crone, even more ancient than he, moved to his side. She was a very short woman, coming up to just my shoulders, but as broad as an old tree stump. She wore a black *chador* that covered her from head to toe, as most of the country women do in Iraq. She lifted up her walking stick and waved it in the air, and shouted, "I am an old woman but I will walk in front of the soldiers to fight! How dare Bush come here to attack us? To attack the people of Muhammad?" She beat her chest with her small fists and threw her head back and wailed like a keener at an Irish wake. "Ayah-eeeh! Ayah-eeeh! Saddam Hussein is my son! Saddam Hussein is my son! I will go to my death for Saddam Hussein!"

Now, all around was chaos, everyone pushing forward to get a turn to yell, fists shaking in the air, fingers pointing, bubbling over with anger at this terrible outrage, and all the terrible outrages of the last hundred years.

Up rushed a little man as angry as a boil. "I am a doctor," he said. "I am an educated man. I speak very good English and I have been to America. Listen to me! If America attacks us, they will lose. Mr. Bush must understand that he is dealing with Iraqis here, not Panamanians!"

Well, I will tell him that.

"Yes! You tell him that. And you tell them this thing they are trying to do is not fair. America is not fair! America attacked Hiroshima and Nagasaki with a nuclear bomb. Is this fair? Is this humanity?"

It struck me how oddly intimate the outrage was. Most people did not talk about the United States taking action against Iraq. They talked about George Bush hurting *them*. They were astonished that Bush (Boosh, they pronounced it) was doing this to them. "Why does Boosh attack us? What have we done to him?" the doctor demanded. What did Iraq's taking Kuwait have to do with the United States? With Boosh? Boosh was not an Arab, nor a Muslim, nor any relation to any Kuwaiti. He was not a member of any tribe involved in the affair; nor was his religion involved. It was clear he had no business in this thing at all. He must be fulfilling some secret deal with the Jews, or implementing a scheme to recolonize the Middle East, or perhaps he was simply crazy.

Yet, at the same time, the anger wasn't personal at all. There was a theatricality to it, a sense that the threats, the oaths and imprecations, were in themselves all the results anyone really desired. Certainly, none of the people yelling at me—poking at me, shaking their fists at me—were angry at me personally, or wanted to hurt me. If I had suggested that I was frightened of them (and I was a little, at first, but the lack of harmful intent was so clear that it was impossible to stay scared), they would have been offended. They hated the Iranians and the Israelis with an ancient fierceness, and they were angry still at their former colonial masters, the British. But they liked Americans. They admired American music and clothes and movies and women; at the Babel Cinema downtown, a movie called *Bye Bye Baby* was playing, and the poster advertising it was a succinct, lurid depiction of all the Arab fantasies of the great American life, a busty lipsticked blonde sprawled on a pool table, her arms in front of her to welcome—or was it to fend off?—the man advancing on her. To emigrate to the land of pool tables and blondes was a dream.

At the racetrack near the American embassy, a big Friday-afternoon crowd had gathered, maybe ten thousand men on the hard-packed dirt and the long wooden benches. The names of the horses and their odds were scribbled on chalkboards, and between races the bookies erased the old runners and wrote up the new. It was mostly a poor crowd, and the men had the hot-eyed look that gamblers get when they cannot afford to lose. I arrived between races and watched the bettors in their agony of indecision, studying the form books they clutched like missals, muttering and pacing, and then, just before the windows closed, running off to place their money according to whatever sudden inspiration had seized their minds.

At the top of the grandstand, rich men sat in small boxes, with rickety tables and spindle-shanked chairs of stamped metal and linoleum. With the exception of the hawk-nosed old bedouin chiefs, splendid in long gold-trimmed white *abayas,* the men were all dressed in imitation of the West: Paris double-breasteds, London tweeds, Dallas petrocloth. I spotted a pair mid-range in age and tonnage, two well-fed gents in a box to them-selves. They were men of rolls, tender little ones growing from under the chin, cascading in a series of grander swells to the big tires of their bellies. They were advertisements for lives spent in a pleasant journey from one table to another. The fronts of their vests were spotted with toothsome stains—here a bit of yesterday's *foul madama,* there a smidgen of last night's *kebab,* up in the corner a little patch of aging *hummus.* Boiled and strained, their vestments would have yielded a thin but tasty soup. They both had bottles in front of them (the Islamic prohibition of alcohol is widely ignored in Iraq) and their ashtray was full, and they had settled back in their chairs with an air of beery inertia.

I nodded in greeting, hoping for an invitation, and they stood and ushered me in with elaborate gestures of welcome. The larger of the men lifted the ashtray and, with an expansive gesture, wiped his suit sleeve across the table, pushing a puddle off the edge in a pretty little yellow beerfall. He made a small, quick bow, and introduced himself. His name was Mr. Femi Azzat Saloom, he said. He was the owner of a restaurant near the American embassy, a very good restaurant. I must dine there someday as his guest. He was honored to enjoy my pres-ence in his box. His friend bowed too. He was Mr. Abdul Amir Abut, the owner of a lamp store on Rashid Street, a very fine store. Perhaps I would visit it? We all shook hands.

"A beer for you?" asked Mr. Saloom.

No thank you.

"No, no. Of course you must. It is no trouble. You see, we have a waiter here." Mr. Saloom waved grandly about him, as if to suggest with the sweep of his arm the impossible luxe of if to suggest with the sweep of his arm the impossible luxe of it all. "We only have to call him. We do not have to move a bit. He will bring it to us."

He stood and yelled, and promptly a man came running. He was thin, and his clothes were dirty and ragged, and he was missing half his front teeth, and he had an open sore on his upper lip.

"The waiter," Mr. Saloom announced. He spoke briefly and sharply to him, and the man ran off, in a staggering lope. I think he was crippled, but he might have just been very drunk. He lurched and wobbled back a few minutes later with a bottle of hot beer, which he poured into three glasses.

"It is an honor to have you in our box," said Mr. Saloom, lifting his glass in a toast.

Thank you. I am honored to be here.

"Thank you. You are American?"

Yes.

"Ah! Our enemy!" Both men laughed and so did I.

"Let me tell you something," said Mr. Saloom. "We are not afraid. If there is war, we stay right here, at the races. Ha, ha, ha, ha. We are best friends. We come to the races together every Friday since many years. One day—this is true—one day, we were here, right in these seats, and over there"—he pointed across the track to a point beyond the starting gates on the far side—"over there an Iranian rocket fell down. And it exploded. Boom!"

"Boom!" said Mr. Abut.

"And we stayed right here and watched it and did not move! And they did not stop the races either!" said Mr. Saloom. "And if the American rockets come, I tell you, we will not move again!"

We drank and smoked and sat, the unchanging troika of Arab afternoons (although generally the drink is coffee or tea, not beer), as the sun sank lower in the sky and Mr. Abut and Mr. Saloom lower in their chairs. Down at the track, they were getting ready for the penultimate race of the day. The white Arabians, glowing a soft, very light gold in the waning sun, pawed the ground at the starting gate. They were beautiful, their manes braided with bright-colored ribbons matching their jockeys' silks, their coats glossy and sleek, their hooves painted and polished a fine tuxedo-black.

The master of the course, in scarlet coat and tan jodhpurs, high on a big bay, poked with his riding crop getting the runners in their places. When the gates clanged open and the horses leaped in a line of moving muscle, everyone stood and shouted all at once.

It was a good race. The lead changed three times. Aku Maha held it on the outside for the first third, but lost it to the favorite, Aglun, who took it for most of the rest of the run. Khatar, a big white horse, came in on the inside in the final stretch to win by a nose. After it was over, there was much tearing up of betting slips and cursing and stamping. Mr. Saloom and Mr. Abut had bet on Aglun to win, and had lost forty dinars apiece. They seemed only mildly disappointed. When I left, they were busy with their heads together, huddled over the form book, cheerfully searching for something good in the final run.

THE FOOT AND MOUTH
BRIGADE

THE UNITED STATES OF AMERICA officially departed Iraq on the morning of January 12. The whole press corps turned out to see the good-bye, but it was a sorry show. The acting chief of mission, Joe Wilson, had stayed up late the night before, packing in his office, drinking wine, and ranting about the failure of it all, and this morning he felt ill. He had carefully washed and carefully shaved and carefully dressed himself in a careful dark blue suit, but he looked awful. He walked through the lobby of the airport with tentative, shaky steps, as if he were not sure whether these were his feet or somebody else's entirely, and stopped before the cameras to make brief and forgettable remarks. He wanted to leave then, but the plane wasn't ready, and there wasn't anyplace to go. So he wandered around, and the pack of cameras and microphones followed him, nobody really sure what to do, and every few feet he would stop, and they would stop, and he would unload himself of a few more comments, and they would record them for history, and then he would wander off again. The whole thing had the awkward feel of the dinner-party good-bye that lingers at the front door for half an hour, even though everybody ran out of things to say halfway through dessert.

An old lady came up to Wilson on his travels. She was dressed in unmatched and unfitting clothes and carried a sign in one hand and a bouquet of roses in the other. The sign said, "War Destroys People and the Environment. When Will We Understand That All Our Children Are OUR Children?" She told the cameras her name was Eva Bormann, from Hanover, West Germany, and that she was "very happy today because peace is beginning now. Things are happening very, very quickly and people are beginning to come to an understanding of the new way of nonviolence." Wilson looked at her with polite disbelief, but she gave him the flowers anyway, in an arm-sweeping gesture. He rose exceptionally well to the occasion, accepting the bouquet with thanks. Then, as Eva Bormann walked away, he turned and, with a small, graceful bow, gave the flowers to a pretty French photographer who happened to be standing there.

Wilson finally got off shortly after noon, in a chartered jetliner with forty-three other passengers, including six American officials, seven private American citizens, and an international array of diplomats: six Canadians, five Dutch, two Belgians, one Brazilian, three Norwegians, three Swiss, one Turk, a Finn, and an Algerian. As far as the embassy could figure, approximately 100 American citizens remained in Baghdad, not counting 150 or so journalists and perhaps 100 peace missionaries. Of the great powers, only the Soviet Union (it was still, barely, a union and a great power then), France, and Great Britain retained diplomatic staffs, and of these France and Great Britain would leave soon.

After the departure, Adnan took me to church, the oldest Christian church in Baghdad, he said. It was made of stone, but most of the original walls had been covered with a patchwork of stucco and concrete. Next door was a courtyard, also of stone, and a yellow brick building of some years, although not as many as the church. A thin man with a ring of keys on his belt was sweeping. When I looked down at his broom pushing over the worn old stones, I saw that he was cleaning not a courtyard, but a graveyard. The stones were headstones laid flat, the graves underneath them. The thick walls of the church were likewise studded with the dead. Slots had been hollowed out and bodies filled in like squares in a crossword puzzle. The gravestones were marble, I was pleased to see. In granite, the lines of the words stay sharp and new for too long. Marble decays at a suitable rate, crumbling like the body underneath into ever softer, smaller pieces of itself.

There was minor poetry in the faint old words on the stones.

> Ici Repose
> La Contessa Gabriel asfar
> Née Sebie Tarzi Bache
> à Baghdad le 10 Mai 1846
> Décédée à Baghdad le 5 Avril 1927
> En Votre Nom Soit Sanctifiée
> En Votre Règne Arrivée.

The yellow brick building was once a school, the caretaker said, built in 1737. The church was built three hundred years ago, maybe four hundred, maybe much more; no one really knew. It was called the Church of the Virgin and St. Paul, Egyptian Orthodox. He pushed open the big wooden door and we stepped into the soothing dark. It was a poor church. The walls were unpainted plaster, much cracked, the small stained-glass windows of amateurish design and muddy colors. In front of the altar, on a scrap of frayed red carpet, stood a small fake Christmas tree, made of sparse branches of tinsel, covered with red, yellow, blue, and green lights, blinking on and off in the pleasant gloom. The altar was bare, and I asked the caretaker if he had taken the chalices and the crosses and put them away in a basement or bank vault to protect them from the bombs. "God protects," he said. "God and Maria and the Son protect this church. Not Saddam. Not me. Leave it to God."

The tin rack of candles before the painted plaster statue of Mary was full with burning offerings, their waxes dripping down to make a rolling, lumpy pie of wax. They were not the fat, squat votives familiar to me, but tapers as long and skinny as a lady's fingers. There was a plentiful supply of them, each wrapped in brown tissue, stacked in a wooden box next to a metal box with a jagged-edged slot in the top. I dropped in two coins and selected my candle. Adnan stepped back and turned slightly away as I lighted it; he was very polite, and I think he felt it would have been bad manners to watch me pray.

There had been much hopeful talk in Washington that the economic sanctions imposed by the United Nations would drive Iraq, in hunger, to quit Kuwait, but in Baghdad you could see how silly that notion was. In the city's largest vegetable, bulk-food, and dry-goods market, the dark little alleys were filled with plenty, and the air was sweet and ripe with smells from the overflowing bins. Pistachios, almonds, raisins, sultanas, sunflower seeds, cashews, peanuts. Hills and hummocks of cabbages and lettuces. Huge heads of scarlet radishes with wet green tails three feet long. Mounds of fat ruby tomatoes, ripened on the vine until they were a breath away from dropping. Rows of purple-black eggplants, big white onions, yellow potatoes, turnips, ginger, scallions, dill. Wire baskets full of fresh eggs. Concrete pools filled with live fish (and a fish-delivery man, pushing a wheelbarrow with two big bruisers swimming back and forth in great agitation, battering against the sides as the wheelbarrow bounced along, and the water sloshing all over the place). Sides of mutton and lamb hanging from shiny metal hooks, the dripping blood puddling underneath. Ovens full of flat bread baking. Live ducks and geese and chickens lying on the sidewalk with their feet trussed together. A tray of black, hairy goat heads, eyes rolled upward at the sky.
    And: sweaters, toys, blouses, trousers, children's underwear, ladies' fancy shoes, men's wallets, scarves, pencils, pens, cigarette lighters, knives, writing paper, razors, shaving brushes,

scissors, thread, pots and pans of a cheap and bright aluminum, tea kettles of the same, belts, robes, slippers, shoes, socks (Iraqi men are fond of good hosiery, and in the lowliest of *suqs* you will find superior footgarb, thin, silky coverings with motifs of clocks and diamonds and squares), erasers, brushes, forks, dominoes, buttons, hats, blankets, pillows, bandages.

Stacked crates full of Pepsi and Canada Dry Club Soda, Heineken and Johnny Walker Black, apple juice, orange juice, and grape; mounds of packaged spaghetti and macaroni; piles of plastic-wrapped Ceylon tea; cartons of toilet paper, Marlboro and Winston cigarettes, chocolate bars, cookies, batteries, combs, matches, playing cards; big cans of powdered milk, olive oil, clarified butter, tomato paste; sacks of lollipops and jawbreakers and bubble gum and boxes of McIntosh toffee from England.

Down an unstraight and narrow path, we turned into the warehouse of Mustafa Jemal Abul Giben, wholesaler. He was a big man and had a belly like the old Nast cartoons of robber-baron capitalists, with their stomachs drawn to look like dollar signs. He stood in his own private mountain range of food, the peaks stretching to the rafters: fifty-kilo sacks of sugar, ten-kilo tins of ghee, hundred-kilo sacks of tea, Everests of rice, K-2s of flour, Kilimanjaros of sugar, on and on back into the dim recesses of the shed.

I complimented him on his wealth.

"Oh, I am not rich, I am just careful," he said. "I always store very much in inventory because you never know when there will be trouble, so when the blockade comes, I am ready, and I have this warehouse full to the top to last me through." He smiled, and his lips slipped back from his teeth as if they were buttered.

As we walked out, Adnan laughed out loud in admiration. "What a big liar he is!" he said. "It is all from Kuwait, of course."

In that one market were all the reasons why the economic embargo would never force Iraq out of Kuwait. First of all, Iraq was too fertile a country; it was a net importer of food, but it still produced enough vegetables, meat, poultry, fish, and wheat that it could not easily be starved into submission. Secondly, Iraq could get most of what it did not produce from Jordan. No amount of Western pressure could shut off such a profitable trade route. Thirdly, Iraq had stolen so much from Kuwait that it would take years to empty the warehouses.

Everything was more expensive since the sanctions, of course. The price of everything had increased between two and five times, the shopkeepers said. Except for the ruling class, people were eating less, buying less. Business was slow. I saw only one concern doing a brisk trade, a table set up in the middle of an alley, hemmed in by a large, eager crowd. The man behind the table was selling nothing but masking tape, forty meters for four dinars. "Everybody buys," said Adnan. "For taping up the windows when the bombs come."

I wondered if there were any Englishmen left. The English have a tradition of sticking around in times of trouble. In 1941, when the nationalist Rashid Ali led a small revolution against the prime minister Nuri al-Said (who was Queen Elizabeth's man in Baghdad), British subjects in the city holed up in the embassy for a month, waiting for the Tommies to come up from Basra for the rescue. They made a good, plucky time of it.

"At 6:00 P.M., a bar was opened under the palm trees, and there was an hour of conversation and ease over the glass to which one was rationed, and another gathering immediately after to hear Dr. Sinderson's garrison news, which he succeeded in presenting in rhyme for every day of the month," wrote Freya Stark, who was among the cloistered. "Here in the evening light the Ambassador would stroll out for a game of clock golf on the lawn, or walk up and down with such political officers as had come in. . . . All the garrison were invited to lunch or dinner in turn, and sometimes to bridge afterwards in the drawing room, where fans scarcely cooled the air and sleeping figures slumped on chairs looked like those pictures of tombstones at the Day of Judgement just giving up their dead. The King and Queen, in court dress, full-sized in oils, looked down with a well-bred absence of surprise."

Well, nothing is what it used to be. This time, the British had left along with everyone else, and the embassy was dark and almost empty. The acting chief of mission was the sole remaining diplomat, and he was leaving in a few minutes. His car was waiting in the courtyard. Near it, a woman sat alone in a straight-backed chair, against the wall of the consulate, taking the afternoon sun on her face. She was in her fifties, I guess, and handsome, with a strong jaw and fine brown hair streaked with gray that she had pulled back in a bun. She wore a gray sweater and a tartan skirt, the outfit of a librarian with a sense of style. She was an Iraqi but she had worked for the embassy for many years. When I asked her some small question about her plans, she answered in a kind of bewildered dialogue with herself.

"Where to go? Where to go? It is cold this time of year. You cannot live outside at night. You have to have warmth and comfort. It is okay for those who have relatives outside of town, but what of those who do not? What of me? Everyone is worried. Of course they are. Of course they are. That is human nature. Everyone would rather have peace. Everyone wants to know what will happen. I wish I knew. It is especially difficult for me. I am a chicken really. I hate this."

The first British Club in Baghdad opened its doors in 1919. It was a fine, big place, with a swimming pool and tennis courts and gardens. But the Baathi had taken it for their own use, and the English now drank in a more appropriately postcolonial setting. The New British Club was a smallish concrete building, unmarked by any signs, set behind a stone fence in a residential neighborhood. Inside, it had been tricked up in a halfhearted imitation of a pub back home, with dark wood floors and a dart board by the stand-up bar. The bar was deserted, the dart board unattended, the long-handled Watney's and Bass ale taps immobile. Hanging on one wall was a portrait photograph, slightly crooked, of a dignified middle-aged lady in a blue cloth suit and a modest crown. She was, indeed, looking on with a well-bred absence of surprise.

On the bulletin board in the front hall were the remaindered writings of those who'd left town. There was a pleasant inconsequentiality to them; they gave off a whiff of the way life had been—an odor of mornings spent shuffling paper, afternoons at lawn parties and cricket, and evenings drinking beer and playing darts. "Minutes of the Oasis Club, British Embassy, Baghdad. Meeting 18 June 1990: Minders: Cricket Equipment. Mr. Davies is still making inquiries re acquisition of nets. New Furniture for Club: Mr. Philpot said a firm of local buyers had been located for the existing Club furniture; i.e., sofas, chairs, and tables."

There must have been some bitterness when the invasion of Kuwait bid a good-bye to all that. "Dear Sir," began a letter stuck up with a little red pin. "Under the Emergency Powers Act of 1939, you are hereby notified that you are required to place yourself on standby for possible conscription in the military service in the Gulf conflict. You may shortly be given orders to report to the Queen's Own Conscription of the Third Foot and Mouth Brigade. There may be little time for formal military training before you depart, so you are advised to hire videos of the following films and try to pick up a few pointers as you watch: *The Guns of Navarone, Kelly's Heroes, A Bridge Too Far, The Longest Day, Henry V, Blazing Saddles,* and *The Sound of Music.* Alternatively, any old John Wayne rubbish will do. To mentally prepare yourself for your mission, try reading the works of Wilfred Owen and Robert Graves. This should give you some idea of what may be involved."

In the back room were three men playing billiards. One was

instructing the others. He seemed to regard the ball as a small, cunning animal, and he lay in wait for it, skulking around the edges of the table, then sneaking up, so as to catch it when its guard was down, and then, suddenly, slashing at it with the stick. He demonstrated the dramatic results this produced and watched with satisfaction as his whiplashed ball careered wildly about the felt.

He was the chief barman of the New British Club, George Yakoub, and his students were the assistant barmen. He pointed to the table. "We are teaching ourselves the game. When the English return, we will challenge them to a competition. They will not know we will have mastered the game and we will take them by surprise and beat them." He smiled broadly. "There is nothing else to do anyway. On Fridays, before, we would have maybe three hundred, four hundred people in here. They would come from ten o'clock in the morning and it would go on all day and many people would stay until one o'clock, two o'clock in the morning. Happy time. Times are not happy now. A man who works is happy in his work. He has much to think about. How many people are coming in? How much whiskey is he selling? How much beer? So much to think about. Now there is nothing to think about. Nothing to do."

The club had paid the men three months' wages in advance, so they came to work every day, even though there were no customers. "If the trouble stops, they will come back," said George. "And we will keep this club ready for them. Do you know, we still have a deep freezer full of meat pies and Cornish pastry? So we will be ready for business." He bent over the table again and when I left he was working on the slaughter of a three-cushion shot.

The delusions were beginning to slip away. Each day brought news of this or that failure of diplomacy, and more and more people talked openly of the war as something that really was going to happen, and that was going to be a disaster. You heard all sorts of rumors. On the morning of the 16th, three divisions of American paratroopers would drop on the city. American warplanes would bomb the chemical plants by the river, causing great toxic explosions. Saddam would fire missiles on Israel; the United States would respond by going nuclear against Iraq. By the morning of January 13, the city was in a state of ongoing exodus, the rich heading to country houses and rental villas in the north, the middle class and poor going off to stay with relatives, and the foreign workers packing themselves like volunteer cattle into cars and trucks and buses for the run to the Jordanian border. The most-traveled route of escape was the highway that ran south from Baghdad to the cities of Hilla, Najaf, and Karbala. The latter two were holy cities, home to two of the great shrines of Shia Islam, and the theory was that the Americans wouldn't bomb them. Adnan's wife was going to Hilla on the 14th, and on the 13th he and I drove there. It was a dismal trip. Adnan was glum. His sons had been called back to their units, and he expected to be called up himself any day. We drove, in a cold, sheeting rain, through a dreary landscape of mud fields and factories, and dozens of earth mounds from which the snouts of 130-millimeter howitzers poked up against the flat horizon. In Hilla, two lines of men stood in front of the metal gates of a military barracks, on the edge of a square dominated by a thirty-foot-high plywood Saddam waving a plywood sword. None of the men had umbrellas or raincoats, and the rain was soaking them through, but they stood there as patient as cows. The longer line was made of men in their twenties and thirties. "It is military registration," said Adnan. "They are calling up more and more people, and you must go and register at the offices." The shorter line had only fifteen or twenty men in it, and all of them were crippled. Some were missing an arm, and a few were blind, but the greatest number had lost a leg or two. They were not registering for this war, but had come to the army office to pick up their disability checks earned in the last one. Some of them had metal crutches and modern prostheses, but most stood on homemade wooden crutches, with rags wrapped around the tops for cushions.

On the way back, we passed, about twelve miles from the city, through an area of flat, unfarmed scrubland that the Ministry of Civil Defense had selected as the place for evacuees from the city in the event of severe bombing. Twice in the last month, the ministry had organized drills to show people how to get to the flatlands and set up tents there, but no one except the foreign press had paid much attention, which was the point anyway. The only sign of any real preparation was a few placards on sticks stuck in the mud identifying campsites. There was no water, no tents, no electricity. In the end, at least half of Baghdad's residents would flee the city, but there would never be an organized plan to move large groups of people from the city to live in the dirt fifteen miles from anywhere.

A few miles past the tent sites, a group of soldiers commanded by a young officer had set up a roadblock and were slowing down all vehicles, waving through private cars but signaling buses and taxis to the shoulder. Adnan explained the drill; he had seen it before, in the Iran-Iraq war. It was happening all over the country today, he said. The soldiers stopped the buses and taxis and forced the drivers to hand over their operators' licenses. They then allowed them to continue their run and deposit their passengers. But afterward the drivers would have to return to the soldiers or forfeit their licenses. When they returned, the soldiers would dragoon them and their vehicles and press them into service ferrying troops to the front. It was a quick, free, and fairly effective way to mobilize a lot of men quickly. It was also a portent. What happens in a war in which one side has the power to move half a million troops halfway across the world and the other has to steal buses and taxicabs to move a few thousand soldiers a couple of hundred miles?

*   *   *

On the morning of January 14, the Iraqi Parliament met in extraordinary session to ratify the war. The Parliament building is a large, modern wood hall whose sides come together in a high dome, from which hangs a crystal chandelier that must weigh several tons. It is a fine stage, and on it, from time to time as needed, the farce of representative democracy is played.

A hundred or so journalists showed up for the session. The writers sat down in the seats provided for them, in the front two rows of the assembly hall, and examined the neat little green-covered notepads and the earphones over which the English, German, and French translations of the discussion would be played. The photographers seized the high ground, climbing over and on top of seats and desks and even the speaker of the house's dais, competing with each other to find the most difficult and outlandish spots from which to shoot their pictures.

At ten-fifteen, Speaker of the House Sa'adi Mehdi Seleh took the chair and addressed the 250 members of the Assembly. "Ladies and gentlemen," he said. "We declare from this chair that we are prepared to go into holy war until the dignity and the honor and the dreams of the Arab nation come true. Ladies and gentlemen, this is a historic showdown between the forces of good, justice, and truth brought by Iraq under the leadership of Saddam Hussein on one side and the forces of aggression led by the United States, which has a history of tyranny, aggression, and arrogance, a showdown that has put the entirety of mankind at a crossroads and upon whose consequences the entire world depends."

He read on and on, rarely even looking up from the papers. He was a man doing his job, dutifully. He denounced America, and Israel, and the Arab traitor states of Saudi Arabia, Egypt, and Syria. At the appropriate points, delegates stood and read statements too. Dr. Anwar Kassira recalled George Bush's suggestion that Iraq had "miscalculated" in its deliberations on the ramifications of seizing Kuwait. "Iraq has not miscalculated, thank you very much," he said. "The miscalculations were Mr.

Bush's, in his assessment of Iraq's military power. He miscalculated when he thought that, through threats and intimidation, Iraq would withdraw from Kuwait."

Sa'ed Elde'an Mahmoud spoke of the "Zionist-imperialist plot against Iraq and the Arab nation," and told his fellow members that "Iraq was at a crossroads" and noted that "to be, or not to be, that is the question."

Eventually, Dr. Kassira, who was the chairman of the legal committee, offered a motion: "The National Assembly met in extraordinary session on January 14, 1991, and reviewed all the rapid developments taking place in the Arab Gulf region and in the Arab world, including especially the American threat to launch an aggression. After deliberating and listening to remarks of the members of the National Assembly, the National Assembly declared President Saddam Hussein is authorized to enact all jurisdictional and constitutional powers required by the situation to maintain the rights and dignity of Iraq and the Arab nation." There was a rush of seconding motions.

"Thank you," said the speaker. "Shall we vote for the motion?" They voted by show of hands. "It is approved unanimously," the speaker said.

After that, it was pretty much just housekeeping details. A proposal was made to alter the Iraqi flag to include on it the words *Allahu Akbar* ("God is Great"), the customary battle cry of Islamic warriors on their way to martyrdom. Another motion was approved moving a verse from the Koran from the end of the resolution to the beginning.

As I was getting up to leave, the delegate immediately behind me leaned forward and tapped me on the shoulder. I turned and looked at him, a big man with a particularly large and bushy mustache. To my eye, he was glaring at me.

"Where are you from?" he asked.

The U.S., I said.

"I know that. Where in the U.S.?"

Washington, D.C.

"Washington!" He beamed. "I love Washington! I went to school at Catholic University and my brother went to the University of Maryland, in College Park! Oh, I miss Washington. Such a fine city! I used to like very much Georgetown—very nice. I used to go there on Friday nights. And Rock Creek Park—very lovely." He said he had studied economics at Catholic University. I said my sister Meg had studied drama there. He said he had taught for two years at Virginia Commonwealth University, in Richmond. I said my sister Kate was an alumna of VCU. He offered the opinion that it was a small world. I said it certainly was. He said I must come back and visit him after the war. I said I would be happy to.

ADNAN WEEPS

THE SUNSET OF THE NIGHT the war began was theatrically grand. A thick fog, as white as cotton, had hung almost at ground level for hours that day, and by dusk a fat scarlet ball was burning through a haze that went from gold to dusty rose to purple. I spent the evening wandering the city with an Australian newspaperman named Patrick McGeough, a bearish man with a beard of Biblical proportions.

Adnan drove, and he stuck mostly to side streets to avoid the military checkpoints. The MPs were now stopping all cars and searching them. We parked in the shadows of a tree and watched one checkpoint half a block away, manned by an officer and four or five soldiers. With the first four cars they stopped, the drill was the same: halt, shine the light, a quick look, and a wave on. But when they shone the light in the fifth car, the officer in charge made a sign with his hand and two soldiers with Kalashnikovs at port arms came forward and opened the rear passenger door. A young man climbed out and stood, blinking and nervous, in the pool of streetlight. The officer said something to him, and the young man reached into his pocket and pulled out his identification papers. The officer studied them for a moment and then made another motion with his hand. The soldiers took the young man by the arms and walked him away to the van. They put him inside and shut the door, and the officer waved the stopped car through. Adnan explained. "They are looking for all men under a certain age, maybe twenty-five or thirty, and when they find one who looks that age, they check his identification papers and if he does not have a deferment from the army, they take him away. They have to do this because many men are evading their duty right now and failing to report to their units."

All morning long, our car radio had played love songs, but there had been a programming change sometime in the afternoon, and now it was playing only martial music. "This is a very bad sign," said Adnan. "This is the same thing that happened at the beginning of the war with Iran. Love songs in the morning, then military songs."

At nine o'clock we stopped by the French embassy, where the chargé d'affaires and a few remaining staffers were closing things up and getting ready to leave. The French were the last Western diplomats in the city. The door to the embassy was open, and the light from it made a false moonglow on the cobblestones of the courtyard. The chargé's car was parked by the big double wrought-iron gates, waiting for the drive across the desert to Jordan. Four jerry cans of gasoline stood next to it, ready to be tied onto the back. Through the open door and windows we could see three or four staffers, dressed in T-shirts and shorts, rushing around from desk to desk, filing cabinet to filing cabinet, room to room. They were hunting documents. Whenever one found a cache, he would grab it up and rush it over to the shredder, where a harried woman stood feeding the paper into the maw. There were piles and piles of things to be shredded all around her. Her hair kept falling in her face and she kept trying to blow it back, because she couldn't get a hand free.

After a while, the shredders turned off the lights and walked out the door of the embassy, closing it carefully behind them. We went over to the residence, half a block away, where the chargé, a M. Jenvier, was hosting a farewell reception. He threw

a very nice party, very French. In the dining room a large table
was laid with platters of cheeses, and pâtés, and *saucissons de
Lyon,* and good French bread and miniature pizzas, and various
other small, fancy edibles. To drink, there were two decent
bordeaux, a 1986 Mouton Cadet and a 1987 Château Montagne,
and a blanc de blancs and champagne. The Bordeaux and the
blanc de blancs were on a help-yourself basis, there being a
table full of bottles off to one side, but the champagne was
served properly, from silver salvers by men in white jackets.

In the living room, someone played songs on the grand piano,
and a small group sitting on the long sofa hummed and murmured along. People told ironic little final-days stories to each
other. There was much (generally admiring) talk about one of
the French photographers who had developed a sideline taking
pictures of his fellow journalists. He didn't charge anything; he
was figuring to make his money on the other end, when there
would be a market for the photos to run as illustrations with
obituaries. He called the pictures "necro-shots."

The Golden City, one of the big nightclubs, was still open at
eleven o'clock. A six-piece band was playing hard, even though
it must have been a discouraging evening for them. The singer
wore a black leather raincoat that came down to his knees, and
which he kept tightly belted, giving him the look of a flasher
who had mistakenly wandered onstage. We ordered a couple of
Cokes, and when the waiter came there arrived also two hook-
ers, Egyptians I think, large women in tight, shimmery dresses,
with faces painted across the spectrum of visible light. They
squeezed into the booth, sliding their rumps squeakily over the
vinyl. "Hello. You will buy us whiskey? Champagne?"

The one next to me pulled out a cigarette and looked over.
I made no move for a match. She gave a small, defeated sigh and
pulled out her own lighter. The other one lit up too and they
both sat there for the length of time it took to puff halfway
through the cigarettes, not saying anything. McGeough and I
didn't say anything either. I suppose they would normally have

tried to push the thing further, but it was so clearly hopeless that they abruptly gave it up, and without a word stood and walked away.

At a table right at the front of the dance floor, a strikingly handsome man—tall, with dark, piratical features, and a black beard trimmed in a short square cut—sat with a good-looking woman, ignoring her, slouched in his chair, drinking and smoking. The band was going on in its frenzied way, and it was so painful to listen to that I was about ready to leave, but then the man at the front table stood up suddenly, and with slow, dramatic steps walked to the center of the floor. He danced then, all alone, bathed in the lights reflected off the mirrored ball overhead. It was clearly a traditional dance, and it was full of elegant, precise movements, like flamenco—one arm was held bent at the elbow, close across the torso, the other flung out as he made his neat, sweeping turns. The band played hard for him, and he danced a long time, maybe ten minutes, and was sweating when he made his final, perfect gesture, sunk to one knee, with his hands thrown high and his head bowed.

When the man sat down, we walked over and McGeough asked if we could join him. He shrugged why not. He had a bottle of Johnnie Walker Red in an ice bucket before him, and he hoisted the bottle up and held it by the neck so that it hung there for a moment and we could admire the way the light made it shine yellow as icy water ran down from its sides and splashed on the tablecloth. He brought the bottle down slowly, and then turned it fast, to slosh his glass full. The waiter ran over with glasses for us, and the man sloshed them full too. I loved him for his act. He was playing a rich, old part, the Glorious Drunk, the man who greets the bombs by howling at the moon. McGeough gave him his cue. Why was he here dancing and drinking? Why hadn't he fled town like all the rest? Wasn't he afraid of the bombs? He leaped to his feet. He glared down at McGeough. He tossed back his drink in a single deep pull and held the empty glass up to the light. "You live," he said. "You live, you dance, you die."

At midnight, the sofas in the lobby of the Al Rashid were full of dozing families, bedding down there rather than in their rooms so that they could be close to the bomb shelter. The foreign journalists who had stayed—about a hundred, mostly Europeans—were chatting among themselves and doing small things to get ready. I dropped by the room of a Scottish radio reporter and we had a small glass of whiskey while he arranged a microphone hanging outside the window. He had the microphone hooked up to a tape recorder equipped with a sound-triggered on-off switch, hoping to record the sounds of the attack. I decided to get myself ready too, and went to my room and packed my bag and put it by the door, and made sure I had my notebooks and pens and computer in my shoulder bag.

It was an ineffectual way to prepare for war, but there wasn't really much of anything else to do. It was too late to escape. The airport was closed, and liable to be bombed at any time, so the only practical way out of Iraq was by car to Jordan, and no one wanted to drive across country on the first night of the war. I went up to the CBS offices on the ninth floor and used one of their phones to call my fiancée, Max. She was in Tel Aviv, on assignment as a producer for CBS. It wasn't possible to dial Israel from any Arab country except Egypt, so the call had to be patched through the CBS foreign desk in New York. We had a brief, awkward, unhappy talk.

I spent the next few hours in the CBS offices, sitting in a chair in the corner, on the periphery of a floating conversation. People wandered in, talked a bit, wandered out again. All the talk was about the bombing, of course. Where for days the effort had been to keep such talk low-key and upbeat, tonight it was thoroughly pessimistic—not hysterical, but there was a gloomy satisfaction. It was a kind of inoculation, I think: say the worst you fear out loud and you free yourself a little from the fear. Of course, no one voiced the true worst fear; no one said: We are going to die here. But there were a lot of predictions just a shade less dire. Allen Pizzey, a CBS correspondent, went on at length about the sort of bombs he thought would be dropped on Baghdad—two-thousand-pound penetration bombs, which, he said, were designed to crash their way through successive stories of a building before the final, lethal explosion. I found it unfortunately easy to picture this, and I got an image stuck in my head, like a song, of this two-thousand-pound sharp-nosed beast of a thing rooting and burrowing through floor after floor of the Al Rashid with single-minded malevolent intent, while we sat in the shelter looking upward, waiting for it to find us. It was a cartoon image, and the bomb was a cartoon bomb, big and black with fins, like something Wile E. Coyote would buy from the Acme Bomb Co. to drop on the head of the Road Runner.

The serious rumors began coming in around midnight. Mostly, they came from the television networks, which had arranged with government sources for some sort of tip-off just before the actual attack, so that they could warn their people in Baghdad. An ABC producer said the attack would begin within a few hours. Someone else said it would start at dawn. A BBC producer and a French correspondent came in to report that their sources were also suggesting it would happen soon. A little after one, CBS got its warning, in the form of a coded message telephoned from New York: "Your wife is fine, but your children have developed a cold." It was supposed to mean "The attack is imminent; get out now if you can." It was based on information from within the Pentagon, and it seemed the authoritative word, but at that point it didn't really matter. I stayed in my corner and talked idly with Richard Beeston, a correspondent for *The Times* of London, a young man, fresh and pink and dapper in a blue blazer with gold buttons, over which he wore, with aplomb, a flak jacket. We watched people bustle about and drank whiskey. I got a little bit drunk fast, and was thinking of taking a nap when Beeston had the idea of going over to the American embassy.

We took our bags and the bottle and went downstairs to the front porch to look for a taxi, and were standing there, at 2:35 in the morning, when the war began. I had spent so much time listening to talk of war that I had come to assume vaguely that what had begun with words must continue with words and end with words. The shift to explosions had a sudden, clarifying, and stupefying effect. I stood there on the front steps, staring up at the antiaircraft tracer trails in wonder, a briefcase dangling from one hand, the bottle of whiskey from the other. Beeston was staring too, and together our eyes and mouths made a picture of round, astonished O's.

You would have had to have been blind not to be transfixed. The city was blacked out, and the sky above it was a deep purple, with the silhouettes of the taller buildings just visible as dark-gray edges. Against this the tracer rounds made lines of incandescent beauty, lovely arcing curves and slow S's and parabolas of light. Only every fifth or sixth round was a phosphorescent tracer, and this created the illusion of exaggerated distance between the rounds, giving the trails a look of almost deliberate laziness. The horizontal and vertical tracking movements of the gunners created a second illusion, that the trails were bending as they progressed, as if refracted by passing through something in the sky. The eye could easily take in half a skyful of lines and at the same time see each round by itself, as a discrete, angry red ball, soaring high against the purplish black in a graceful reach, and then, at apogee, exploding in a lacy bright-white starburst.

The guns made a great mess of sound that worked itself out, after a minute or so, into an almost symphonic order, the big 57-millimeters booming with deep bass thuds against a chattering of the lesser artillery. I thought then that the large sounds were bombs, but I read later that this was not so. The first of that sort of explosion did happen while we stood gaping, at 2:38 A.M., when eight American Apache helicopters used missiles and rockets to destroy two radar installations in southwestern Iraq, but these demolitions were much too far from Baghdad for us to hear.

After several minutes, we turned to run inside. I set the bottle down on the top step, and positioned it just so, as if I were leaving it for someone who would be coming along shortly, and who would be annoyed if I didn't arrange things nicely. It seemed to take us a long time to go from the steps to the door. When we got there, I looked back over my shoulder and saw the bottle making a spectacle of itself, winking yellow, red, yellow like a hyperactive stoplight.

To the degree that there can be a good place to be bombed, the Al Rashid is one. It was built in 1982 for a summit of nonaligned nations, and was designed to reassure the delegates that they would not become accidental victims of Iraq's war with Iran, then in its second year. It is a big, thick rectangle of steel and slab concrete rising out of a dull but pleasant garden. The windows are made of inch-thick tempered plate glass and are protected by concrete shields angled downward from the sides of the building so that they may block shrapnel while still affording a slit of a view. In the basement is a large, well-built bomb shelter, the amenity that had drawn the rich locals who made up the bulk of the current guest list.

In the lobby, a moving mass of people—businessmen and children, busboys and maids, government officials—was hurrying to the shelter stairs. Most were dressed in their nightclothes, with coats or blankets atop. One middle-aged man was wearing fine cotton pinstriped pajamas and bedroom slippers and carrying a leather briefcase. He looked like something out of an anxiety dream, the man on his way to work who has forgotten to put on his clothes.

The shelter was through a door at one side of the lobby and two or three flights down a concrete stairway. I hadn't been in it before, and I was comforted to see that it lived up to its billing. It comprised maybe six or seven large rooms, connected by halls. The floors, walls, and ceilings were made of concrete and the doors were made of steel. I stayed down there for several minutes as the fire stuttered and thudded to a stop. After the quiet lasted a minute more, I went back upstairs and made my way, slowly, nervously, through the chaos in the lobby to the outside. The bottle was gone from the steps, and everything was still. On the skyline I could see a few lights. There were no fires or smoke, and when the air-raid sirens came to a wailing stop, the night was utterly quiet.

Pretty soon, the sirens started up again in their peculiarly polite way, a slow-building roar, as if reluctant to interrupt. I watched as the guns began firing, but after a few minutes I was afraid and hurried back toward the shelter. I was near its door when, at about 3:00 A.M., the first explosions of the night came, huge, physical things that filled my ears, and shook me, and made my stomach flutter in liquid waves. What I had heard, I read later, was the result of American Stealth bombers making the first attack on the city itself, dropping penetrator bombs through the roofs of the International Telephone and Telegraph Building and the Tower for Wire and Wireless Communications, both downtown near the river.

The crowd in the shelter quickly stratified itself by class and interest. The hotel staff retired to a section of rooms down the hall from the rest. The journalists staked out the central room and hallways. Some of them worked, the writers scribbling in their notebooks and the TV crews shooting the scene, but most huddled together in groups around shortwave radios, trying to pull in the news from America and England that would make sense out of what was happening over their heads.

The families took the side rooms and carved out small spheres of influence, spreading out blankets and coverlets taken from their beds and marking the perimeters with suitcases. Everyone reverted to primal roles. The children went to sleep, or curled themselves up into balls so nothing bad could happen to them. The mothers folded themselves around and on top of the children, and the fathers stood guard by their patches of space, looking wary and fierce.

We were let out of the shelter just before dawn, at first in groups of two or three and then in a rush, and we wandered in the way of the sleep-befuddled through the lobby. The electricity was out, which was the way it would stay for a long time. I found a bathroom off the lobby and went in, making my way by the last bit of light through the closing door to the urinal on the far side of the room. With the door shut, the windowless room was completely dark, and when I turned to go back out I found I had no idea where the door might be. I walked toward my best guess, but immediately came up against a wall, catching it sharply on the cheekbone. I dropped to my knees, thinking that crawling would be safer, and banged my head on another wall, but I was moving slowly now and it didn't hurt as much. Carefully, I worked my way along the wall, starting at the beginning of the line of sinks, gliding my palms at shoulder height. I made a full circuit of the room without finding anything that felt like a door. I tried again, this time with one hand at shoulder level and one at stomach level, and still couldn't find it. I sat down on the floor to think, and was sitting there a few minutes later when the door opened. I didn't say anything to the man with the flashlight, and he didn't say anything to me.

Adnan showed up for work at his customary time of 7 A.M. and took Beeston and me for a drive around the city, to see what the bombs had done. We drove over roads that were bare of cars and through neighborhoods that were as still as boneyards. By the river, the al-Dora oil refinery, Iraq's second-largest, appeared to have been hit, although not too badly. Downtown, the International Telephone and Telegraph Building was a dead loss. The bombs had trepanned it, punching a neat hole precisely through the center of the roof. The explosions had destroyed the top few stories and knocked out four big holes in various places along its brick sides. The Ministry of Defense complex, the air force headquarters, the Ministry of Justice, and the Ministry of Local Affairs had all been badly damaged. In the direction of the airport, a heavy cloud of black smoke arose. But it was remarkable how precise the destruction was. Except for the buildings hit, Baghdad looked just as it had the day before. I stood for minutes wondering at the sight of the telephone building, a smoking ruin surrounded by untouched buildings in the middle of a crowded neighborhood.

As the day warmed up and the fog cleared, a few people began to appear on the streets. Some hurried along, nervous to be out in the open on whatever errand had been so necessary, but others went about with a show of determined normalcy; the war was new enough that dignity was still affordable. Two city street cleaners, old men, worked with brooms and a trash can on wheels, sweeping the gutters. They moved at (I assumed) their regular plodding pace, the man in front pushing the trash into periodic piles, his colleague bending carefully over to pick each pile up with a dustpan and put it in the barrel. On Rashid Street, a young, handsome man, in slacks and a sport coat, strolled with his girlfriend as if they were taking the air on a Sunday afternoon. He carried his Kalashnikov assault rifle in his left hand, holding it loosely by the stock, and his right arm was twined around the waist of the woman. As they promenaded, there came a sudden outburst of explosions and gunfire, but neither showed the slightest sign of having heard a thing. I waved to them from the car window. The man smiled broadly and gestured with his rifle to the sky. *"Mish-melleh,"* he said. "No problem."

The attacks began again some time after nine-thirty. They were bracketed by long and loud defensive fire, but the bombs themselves were discrete, and almost discreet. Whenever a wave began, Adnan would brake the car slowly, usher Beeston and me out, and lead us hurriedly to whatever nearby building seemed to him to offer the best protection. Then he would return to the middle of the street and stand there, his vast wool cape draped around his shoulders, calling the shots as he heard them. "Antiaircraft fire, maybe five kilometers that way," he would say, pointing to the west. He would listen a moment more and point again, in another direction. "A bomb. A big one, I think. Maybe ten kilometers that way." He told us how to tell the difference between the bursts of bombs and those of the big guns. "The guns you only hear with your ears," he said. "Bombs you feel in your legs."

You might have thought, looking around the city, that the defense of Baghdad was in good shape. By midmorning there were thousands of soldiers out on the streets. At the antiaircraft batteries on rooftops all around town and on top of the big earthwork mounds along the river and highways, the gunners were still at their stations. Four soldiers arrived for relief duty as we were driving by one battery. They came in a taxi, and when they got out, one of them dug into his pocket and paid off the driver, which struck me as admirably conscientious, given the way the day was shaping up. The central bus station was still full of soldiers looking for rides to wherever they were supposed to be, and hitchhiking troops lined the roads out of town. But the battle of Baghdad was already over; the attackers owned the air. They bombed at will, and hit what they aimed at; the *son et lumière* of the antiaircraft batteries seemed not even to exist for them.

The city's defenses, I later learned, were more impressive in terms of theatrics than combat, unable to hit the high-flying Stealths and useless against cruise missiles. Moreover, the coordinated attack of the early morning had included flights of pilotless drone planes programmed to fly to Baghdad and circle it, drawing radar-directed fire from the antiaircraft batteries. American fighter jets flying south of the city launched missiles that homed in on the antiaircraft batteries' radar beams and followed them in to destroy the gun emplacements. By daylight, the Iraqis had lost a number of batteries and had learned that they could not afford to use their defensive radar, leaving them with the choice of firing not at all or firing aimlessly.

That morning I saw the allied forces take out the heart and symbol of Iraq's military forces in ten minutes' work. It was ten-thirty in the morning and Adnan was driving along the Tigris, just across the river from the Ministry of Defense complex. Part of the complex had already been hit, but the building at its center was still untouched. This was an old yellow-brick building, built by the Ottoman Turks, and was not of much practical value as a target. It hadn't been used as a wartime command center in years, but it was, technically, still the citadel of Iraq's armed forces, and I suppose the allied targeters must have felt its destruction would strike a psychological blow. As we were driving by it, I heard—and felt in my legs as Adnan had said I would—a great explosion. The smoke ballooned up instantly in a huge and accelerating cloud, first white and then a roiling, oily black. I thought we had seen a bomb hit, but learned later that this was the work of Tomahawk cruise missiles. We got out of the car to get a better look and were still staring when the second missile smacked home five minutes later, shuddering the ground again. Five minutes later still, the third missile hit.

We drove to within a few blocks of the building, and stopped in case its battering wasn't finished. All we could make out was smoke and fire. The sight depressed and angered Adnan. "There is no one in this building anymore," he said, as we watched it burn. "It is not really a military headquarters. It is like a museum. It is a very special building for us, part of our heritage. Why do they destroy this? It is not necessary."

As we drove away, Saddam Hussein's voice came on the car radio, as boastful and bombastic as ever. "We have been attacked by criminals and they will be punished," he said. He called on the Iraqi soldiers to stand and fight, and he swore that Iraq would keep Kuwait and liberate Palestine.

The debate over the probable outcome of the war would continue for weeks in the United States, but in Baghdad the days of delusion had ended abruptly. Even the minders were shocked into truth-telling. Saddoun al-Genabi, chief of the Ministry of Information minders, sat slumped in a chair in the lobby. His eyes were red. A reporter sat down next to him. "Saddoun, I am leaving," he said. "I will see you when I return."

"You had better say good-bye to me now," said Saddoun. "Because the next time you see me I may be dead. If I am dead, visit my grave."

Another reporter was standing on the hotel lawn when a minder came up to him. He had never even talked to the man before, but the minder suddenly began telling him the story of his life. He was thirty-five, and had spent his adulthood in government work, ten years in the military, followed by service in the Ministry of Information and Culture. He had been an antiaircraft gunner in the Iran-Iraq war and had served all eight years. Once a shell had landed a few feet from him, but had not exploded. Telling this, he suddenly began weeping. He told the reporter he had gotten the word that morning that all the men born in his year must report for active duty. The reporter tried to comfort the minder; he told him that surely, God willing, he would live. "For me, it makes no difference if I live or die," the minder said. He was crying hard. "My life is over. I wasted my life in the army. People I went to school with, and who were able to stay out of the war, have already started businesses. They have gotten good educations, good jobs. Look at me. I am a *minder.*"

All but a handful of reporters left that afternoon. There was a fever to get out before nightfall brought a new round of heavy bombing. The lobby and hallways were busy with rushing and hauling of luggage and packing for the trip to Jordan. Most of the drivers who had been shuttling reporters around for the last couple of weeks had disappeared, and as the afternoon waned the bidding for those who remained grew fierce. For a while, the price stabilized at three thousand dollars, but a group of desperate Spanish reporters drove it up to five thousand. They poached two of the four drivers that the CBS bureau chief, Larry Doyle, had lined up for us, but we still had Adnan and one other, which was enough to accommodate all of us except Nick della Casa, a free-lance cameraman from London who was working for CBS and who wanted to stay. The rest of the CBS people left, and I left with them. We departed just before 4:00 P.M., in two cars, with Adnan driving the lead one.

The highway from Baghdad to the Jordanian border cuts flat and straight through the Syrian Desert, a landscape of powerful ugliness and dullness, mile after mile of dirt. Occasionally, the dirt congregates to aspire to a small hill. There are a few very small villages along the way, most of them bedouin outposts, huddles of lean-tos and tents and pickup trucks, with rude pens of tin and wood scraps strung together for the sheep. Here and there the road has been widened from two lanes to four and

specially marked, for military use as emergency airplane run-
ways.

There was, that day, almost no traffic on the road, except for
military. Three times we passed convoys of mobile Scud missiles heading to the western edge of Iraq to take up their
positions against Israel. It was an odd sensation, fleeing a city
under bombardment to drive by the rockets on their way to
bombard the city where Max was. The Scud convoys moved
along slowly, a jeep in front, with two soldiers manning a
.50-caliber antiaircraft gun, followed by a fuel truck, followed
by a flatbed truck on which was mounted a Soviet-made SAM-6
ground-to-air missile. The Scuds themselves rode on a long
flatbed. They were impressive things, big and fat, with blunt,
ugly, menacing snouts. Two soldiers stood by the SAMs, holding on to them to keep upright when the truck bounced in the
potholes. They didn't even look at us as we passed them. They
were too busy staring at the sky. They were waiting for something to come out of it and blow them into bloody little bits all
over the dirt of the Syrian Desert.

We stopped before dusk by the side of the road for a picnic.
The wind was blowing hard, driving stinging bits of dirt and
pebbles up into our faces, and we huddled together by the back
of Adnan's car. We ate cocktail-party food salvaged from the
CBS stores: little foil packages of smoked almonds and crackers
and a kind of canned cheese made by Kraft, a processed cheddar
that was so rubbery you could hardly cut it, and if you dropped
it, it bounced.

Soon after the picnic we saw the kind of thing the soldiers at
the SAMs were looking for. Fairly low in the sky, about twenty-
five degrees above the horizon, two Iraqi Mirage fighters were
flying in tandem, making slow and lazy sweeps. The sun was
setting red and purple behind them, and they looked as pretty
and as posed as a postcard. But one of them suddenly jinked
hard to the left, wobbled, and dove straight down toward the
desert floor. Nearby, two small white puffs erupted and van-

ished. The other Mirage followed his partner down, and they both, accelerating wildly, shot off to the east, flying so low to the ground it seemed they might plow through one of the dirt hills. High above, we could see the contrails of the allied warplanes that had fired the two missiles that missed. They kept straight; I guess they were en route to bombing something and didn't have time to chase strays.

We stopped for gas at around eight o'clock at the little town of Al Rutba—a few houses, a police building, a gas station, and a pack of dogs. We were about eighty miles from the Jordanian border. A hundred cars or more were already in a chaotic line at the pumps, moving slowly and painfully forward, attended by a nonstop high-pitched and high-decibel argument. The line worked in a very Iraqi way. Civilian cars queued up and waited. Government cars went straight to the front. At the pumps were two teenage soldiers with Kalashnikovs. They enforced order. For every civilian car that got a tankful, a government car was allowed to butt in.

It was raining lightly, but I got out to walk around a bit, and I was idly trying to find a familiar constellation when the soldiers at the pumps started yelling: "Lights out! Lights out! Get away from the petrol!" Everyone seemed to know what to do. They turned off their headlights, switched off their ignitions, and walked away from their cars. There was plenty of time. The attack didn't start for another three or four minutes, and we all stood quiet in the night and listened to the sound that the soldiers had heard first, the faint, growing sound of jet engines high above. The defense began before the bombing, a thunder of antiaircraft fire. Adnan said these were the big 57-millimeter guns. They could fire a hundred shells a minute, and when their rounds exploded they sent shrapnel for a radius of thirty feet. They were capable, with radar guidance, of hitting planes at twenty thousand feet.

Soon, to the south, we saw a string of orange-white explosions. They must have been direct hits on something that was itself explosive; they were some distance away and yet you could see the fireballs well above the horizon. There was a string of them, as neat as a dotted line. Adnan said he guessed the target was the al-Walid air base. The explosions didn't last long, but the antiaircraft fire continued in crazy fear and defiance for an hour or more after the attackers had gone. The gunners were not aiming at anything, just shooting upward. The tracers trailed flaming scarlet and gold against the stars. It looked as if the stars were shooting each other. There were so many stars and so many tracers you could hardly see it all, and I stood gape-mouthed, with my head tilted back in the middle of the gas-station yard, the drizzle falling on my face.

After the all-clear siren sounded, we drove on, with the lights out for fear of another attack, moving slowly, and looking for the right turn back to the highway. We missed it anyway, and found ourselves on a dirt road that petered out at a barbed-wire fence. We had found something military by mistake, and Adnan turned the car around fast. As we moved along, he flicked the headlights on every hundred yards or so and then flicked them off immediately. Other cars were doing the same, compromising between driving completely blind and drawing fire, and you could see them in the dark, flashing on and off like fireflies.

We were nearly back at the main road when two teenage soldiers appeared before us, trapped when the headlights flicked on, pointing their Kalashnikovs at the car and shouting. Adnan stopped and they moved around to the sides of the car, their rifles pointed in the open windows. They were jumpy with nerves, their hands tight on their weapons. They screamed at Adnan, and one of them put his rifle up to within a few inches of his head. He glared at the rifle and at the boy holding it, and spoke sharply. He had not said three sentences when they began to lower their rifles, and in another minute they were saluting him.

As he drove away, Adnan lit up a cigarette, and I could see that his hand was trembling. I asked him what he had said. "I told them I was a general and that you were personal friends of President Saddam and that I had been ordered to escort you to the border and that if they tried anything they would die for it."

Right away, we got lost again. We drove around in fits and starts, first one way and then the other. Every ten seconds or so, Adnan would flash the headlights on and for the briefest of moments illuminate a patch of road and dirt. Everything looked the same. It was like lighting up nothing at all. We were arguing back and forth about which might be the right way to go when, quick as a stroke, we were in the middle of a new attack.

This time the target was much closer to us, maybe ten miles off. The explosions were bigger and louder than any before, one after another, very fast, and they shook the car hard. Worse, we were bracketed by antiaircraft emplacements lining both sides of the road only a hundred yards or so away. The guns started up a terrific defense, their streams of fire arcing up and crossing above us, like a cathedral roof.

Adnan stopped the car dead in the road, and for a moment we all sat there unable to do a thing, then we began talking at once, trying to tell each other which was the best way to go. The problem was that there was no good way to go; there was fire in every direction you could see, and small pieces of burning metal were falling to the ground all around us. My legs were shaking violently, jittering as if I had the chills of a bad fever; I was grateful that it was dark in the car so that no one could see them.

In the end, it was decided that we should at least try to get on the right side of the highway, so that we would be heading out of Iraq. We did that, and drove a little bit, but the barrage kept up unabated. We talked of getting out of the car, but there was nothing—no buildings, or hillsides or trees—that would offer any cover, and at least the car put a metal roof between us and the falling spent rounds. A half mile on, we found a small hill beside the road, and pulled the car up close to that and waited. After another five minutes or so the explosions stopped, and a few minutes after that so did the ground fire. Adnan started up the car and drove on. The rest of us fell almost right away into a very deep sleep, our butts and shoulders bumped comfortingly against one another. I remember thinking as I drifted off that it must be true what they said about great fatigue following a great fear.

We arrived at the Iraq-Jordan border near the town of Trebeil not long after midnight and parked in a long line of cars and trucks. There were hundreds of people there, the beginning of what would soon become a flight of thousands. Most were poor people: Egyptian, Sudanese, and Indian laborers. They had stayed too long because they couldn't afford to leave their jobs, and because it was so hard for them to get out. It is a wretched thing to be even a rich refugee, but incalculably worse to be a poor one. The poor live at the mercy of the state of things, and the state of war is chaos.

The Iraqi border post was a concrete structure, no more than a dozen years old, but already incredibly decrepit. The buildings were half ruined, the windows and doors broken, the walls and floors filthy with ground-in dirt. The land around was nothing but rocks and pockmarked dirt heavily strewn with garbage. It was bitterly cold. There were a couple of skinny dogs prowling about, looking for things to snatch and eat.

It was after noon before we got through customs and arranged the bus ride that would take us across the no-man's-land between the last Iraqi checkpoint and the first Jordanian one. Just before we got on the bus, I said good-bye to Adnan, and Doyle paid him for the drive to the border. He gave him three thousand dollars. When Adnan held the money in his hand, he couldn't speak for nearly a minute. Then he said, "Thank you. My son will be married now." He hugged us both, and cried. He was still crying when the bus pulled away, and his face, with the tears on it, was the last thing I saw in Iraq.

"ONE LIKE YOU
MAKES DREAM COME TRUE"

O N THE JORDANIAN SIDE of the border dozens of swell young
men in uniform were loitering about, a dandy bunch of
dandies, washed and polished and shaved and shined to a top-
hat gloss, Sandhurstian in navy-blue commando sweaters and
knife-pleated trousers and jaunty red berets. They looked badly
out of place and time, gentlemen emissaries from some *époque*
a great deal more *belle* than this, which was more or less what
they were, the remnants of the only good army modern Arabia
ever produced, the British colonial Arab Legion. In the war of
1948, the Arab Legion under the command of the former British
army captain John Bagot Glubb, was the only Arab force to
distinguish itself. The Jordanian army today still dresses, and
struts, like the old Arab Legion, but no one in Jordan thinks it
could last five minutes in a fight against the Jews.

The Jordanian immigration buildings did not provide a suitable milieu for the gentleman soldiers. The buildings were a
bureaucratic slum, begrimed and busted-up, the ground around
them thick with trash and shit. Families of refugees squatted in
the dust by their cardboard suitcases tied with rope and their
plastic trash bags stuffed with blankets and food (the plastic
trash bag has become the universal accessory of the very poor—
carryall, poncho, shoe lining). The officers picked and waded
their way through the unpleasantness with high-stepping care.

78

The CBS people in Jordan had sent two big four-wheel-drive cars to take us across the desert to Amman. The drive was dispiriting. There are pieces of the Arabian wilderness that are like the deserts in boys' dreams and movies—great wind-rippled dunes, towers of rose rock and violet shadows, date palms by the oasis—and the most famous of these is in Jordan, Wadi Rum, in the southern part of the country. There, David Lean's CinemaScope Lawrence, gold skin and blue eyes, gamboled in gold sand and blue skies. The real Lawrence, who was the star of his own boy's movie-dream, knew the filmic quality of Wadi Rum the moment he rode into it: "The hills drew together until only two miles divided them, and then, towering gradually until their parallel parapets must have been a thousand feet above us, ran forward in an avenue for miles. . . . The Arab armies would have been lost in the length and breadth of it, and within the walls a squadron of planes could have wheeled in formation. Our little caravan grew self-conscious, and fell dead quiet, ashamed and afraid to flaunt its smallness in the presence of the stupendous hills."

But mostly, deserts are horrible, bleak places of dirt and rock, unremittingly hostile to life. Those few animals that can survive in them—the camel, the bustard, the desert fox, the gazelle, the hare, and various rats, snakes, and lizards—do so by living in fierce parsimony. The only humans who can stand the struggle for any length of time are the hard brown bedouin, and those wanderers are like the scrub grass and the lizards, winkling every morsel of value from their food and their water and their energy.

The land between the border and Amman was an especially morbid piece of desert, flat and black and as bald as a banker. There was water in only one spot, at the oasis at Azraq, and the wells of the Amman waterworks had so aggressively plumbed Azraq's underground streams that the marshes had shrunk to a single, muddy pool, and the great flocks of birds that used to stop en route from Africa to Europe now flew on to the Sea of

Galilee. The surface was neither soil nor sand, but a thin gruel
of the two, with rocks of volcanic basalt, round and smooth and
covering the ground as tight as cobblestones; not even the
smallest shoot of green could eke its way between them.

Here and there were the black goat-hair tents of the bedouin.
These were congregated most thickly near the border, close to
the smuggling activity that was a mainstay of the bedouin
economy. Desert smugglers work just as maritime ones do,
off-loading goods from big trucks (ships) standing out of inter-
diction's way, and transferring them into pickup trucks (boats)
for a quick run in. The pickups of the Iraq-Jordan border plied
back and forth across the no-man's-land carrying whatever the
market was currently demanding—these days, cigarettes or
whiskey into Iraq, dates and sheepskins and videocassette re-
corders the other way. The smuggling of VCRs surprised me,
and I inquired about it. We live, as the editorialists say, in an
interconnected world. Jordan placed a high tariff on foreign
electronic goods, but Iraq did not, which led the merchants of
Amman to swift, shadowy encounters with the merchants of
Baghdad, which led the bedouin bouncing from rock to gully in
their Ford 4 × 4's, to a spot in the sand where sat a pile of boxes
marked Sharp and GoldStar, as the border guards looked carefully heavenward and calculated their rake-offs; all of this un-
changed, except for the trucks replacing camels and the VCRs
replacing spices, from the days of everybody's great-great-
grandfathers, who lived also in an interconnected world.

When not smuggling, the bedouin drove their flocks of
skinny goats and sheep looking for sustenance out on the basalt
sea. The shepherds had divided up the fields of stone so that
each had his own little plot of rock, and to mark the boundaries
they built piles of stones, cairns and steeples and pyramids.
There were many thousands of these, all over the desert. Some
piles hewed strictly to the vertical line, one stone on top of
another until the toppling point, three or four feet above the

ground. Others were constructed on broader lines, and these managed to climb to greater heights, but by only a few feet.

The road through this desolation was only one lane in each direction, and it lay as light as a passing fancy, a thin little strip of tarmac, heavily potholed and cracked, and aged far beyond its years. In many spots it was so worn that it hardly existed, the desert poking through the sparse coat of tar and gravel, gnawing at the roadway and crumbling it more day by day. Some of the potholes were so deep that the impact of hitting them could lift you off the seat and knock your head against the ceiling, and there were a couple of miles-long stretches where the asphalt had given up completely and the roadway existed only out of force of habit and memory of better times. In these parts, our driver was obliged to slow considerably, but otherwise he pushed forward as if pursued by Type A fiends, hunched with intense concentration over the wheel that the jolts threatened to tear from his grasp. He was a wild-looking man, with flyaway hair and a grin that was all gaps and red gums, and a week's beard that had sprouted in varied patches of brown and gray and red, like the fur of a mongrel cat. The car was equipped with an electronic nagger, and whenever the needle on the speedometer topped sixty-five kilometers an hour it emitted a steady, high-pitched squeal, which obliged him to turn up the volume of the cassette player, so the moans of the Egyptian singer joined, but did not drown, the buzz.

He drove mostly in the incoming traffic lane, which brought us into conflict with the trucks. They were big semis, sixty tons fully loaded, carrying oil from Iraq and food and dry goods from Amman, driven at thundering speed by dead-eyed hired hands—Palestinian, Sudanese, Thai, and Filipino—who stayed behind the wheel for twenty hours at a time to earn their $40 per month. They came at us at regular, unnerving intervals. Our madman would swerve to the right side of the road with twitching, clucking annoyance at the penultimate moment. Often the margin of the miss was, it seemed to me, as narrow as could have been hoped for. We passed by the abundant evidence of others' less successful calculations, the charred, spidery skeletons of trucks and cars. The remains of the crashed oil tankers looked like giant aerosol cans exploded in a campfire, long black cylinders with jagged holes punched here and there through their thin skins. I never saw evidence that all the carnage suggested to anyone who used the road that any of this could be avoided by driving in the proper lane. It was as if the law of cause and effect hadn't been invented yet.

The Jordan Intercontinental Hotel in Amman was the sort of place journalists like, being large, and luxe, and possessed of minibars and direct-dial telephones. Except for a few faint touches of local color—a brass pot of Arabic coffee cooking on a coal brazier in the lobby, *hummus* with the croissants at breakfast, etc.—it could have been the Marriott in Geneva or the Sheraton in Jakarta or the Hyatt in Toledo (Ohio or Spain).

There was a small store in the lobby with a selection of two-day-old newspapers and an unexpectedly large feast of books; Barbara Cartland and Henry Fielding and Somerset Maugham side by side. I bought a Penguin paperback of Maugham's short stories, a fawning biography of King Hussein, an even more toadying life of Saddam, a *Practical Guide to Jordan with a Classified Telephone Directory and Maps,* and various issues of *The Jordan Times, The International Herald Tribune, The Times* of London, and *The Independent.* As I was hauling my load to the cashier's table, I noticed a shelf of books—above the travel and geography section and below the thrillers and bodice rippers— devoted to a particular genre, the presence of which was one of those small signs that informed the guest that he was, after all, in Amman. I thumbed through one of the better-known works, *The Protocols of the Elders of Zion,* that old elaborate fantasy of the Czar's forgers.

"The GOYS are like a flock of sheep—we are wolves. Do you know what happens to sheep when wolves get into the fold?" I read in the *Protocols.* "God has given us, his chosen people, the power to scatter, and what to all appears to be our weakness, has proved to be our strength, and has now brought us to the threshold of universal rule."

The cashier did not take her cigarette from her mouth—she had lips like the clasp of a change purse—when I asked her the price. "The price is inside the cover," she said. "It is a good book. A very old book. It will tell you the true secrets of the Jews."

Amman was obsessed with the Jews, which was only natural. The city was, in an unhappy and accidental way, the Jews' creation. In 1921, when the Emir Abdullah, grandfather of the current king, anointed the ancient village of Rabbath Amman as the capital of the new British-made entity of Transjordan, almost the only people who lived there were a couple of thousand blue-eyed, fair-haired Circassians, who had come from the Caucasus mountains in the 1870s. The first Arab-Israeli war, in 1948, sent a million Palestinians across the river and doubled Jordan's population. The war of 1967 added another several hundred thousand refugees and cost Jordan Jerusalem and the West Bank, creating an Israeli-occupied territory that became an engine for continued emigration. By 1991, Amman had become a crowded, growing metropolis, built and shaped by the Palestinians who made up almost 70 percent of the population. It was a hustler's city, a talker's delight of a place, full of cocktail chatter and arguments. The talk quite often came back to the subject of the Jews. For a long time, it had been a depressing and frustrating conversation. Saddam Hussein changed that for a little while.

The first salvo of Iraqi missiles to hit Israel, eight crudely modified Soviet Scud B's, landed early in the morning of Janu-

ary 18, while I was sleeping at the Iraqi border and Max was
staring at the sky in Tel Aviv, and by the time we arrived in
Amman the city hummed with a mean joy. At last someone was
killing the Jews. The Scuds (the Jordanians told themselves)
would force Israel into the war, and that would break the
West-Arab coalition, and Saddam would rise like Salah al-Din
to lead a mighty Arab army that would drive the Israelis into
the sea. "The Arab peoples, who are already pregnant with
hatred of the United States, will deliver painful strokes to the
American interests all over the world," wrote the cheerfully
bloodthirsty Dr. A. H. Malhas in a column in *The Jordan Times*.
"Protective chest vests may become standard American underwear." This was, in truth, a senile, old, toothless wreck of a
dream, doddering and wheezing and buckling at the knees, a
balding retread of the dreams of '48 and '67 and '73. But Saddam
had given it voice again, and Amman loved him for at least
pretending to requite its passion.

Downtown, in the blocks around the old al-Hussein mosque,
was a *suq* that was the great gathering place of the city. Every
bit of it was filled with people—young men in pleated slacks,
bedu soldiers in olive drab, giggling girls and shy-faced boys,
old women in black *chadors* and old men in long, tunic-like gray
thobes—but no one seemed to get in the way of anyone else. The
serious shoppers and the casual strollers all somehow managed
to occupy the same space at the same time without collision,
eliding the space between them to just a shave of air, and gliding
by each other so close that every passing had the *frisson* of
almost-touch. There was much to buy: pistachio nuts, peanuts,
walnuts, almonds, and raisins; saccharine-sweet white custard
dished up from a big tub by the bowl, with honey dripped on
top; *schwarma*, the sandwich of shaved lamb, with chopped
tomatoes and sweet onions wrapped in greased hot pita bread
(the lamb is layered in vast circles on a vertical spit which

rotates before a vertical broiler, and the *schwarma* man splits a piece of fresh hot flat bread open, sops up some of the fat that drips down to the pan, and presses that for a few seconds against the broiler screen, which grills the inner bread just a little, in a flurry of sparks); roast young chicken, also on the spit, served with raw onions, chilies, and a little *hummus* on the side; fresh fruit milkshakes and sweet, strong black Turkish coffee by the cup; knock-off Marlbril cigarettes, novelty-brand radios, strong perfumes; clocks, socks, hats, sandals, ladies' hosiery.

One afternoon, a few days after my arrival in Amman, the bustle was particularly lively around a particular plot of entrepreneurial turf. In front of the al-Afghani Company a camera crew was videotaping, and a dozen passersby had stopped to watch. Inside, the store was a narrow little space, no more than twenty feet long and twelve feet wide. Its ceilings and walls were hung with items of the tourist trade, brass coffee pots and tin scimitars encrusted with glass jewels and madonnas hewed from olive wood. Three reporters—an Englishman, a German, and a Dutchman—elbowed and hip-nudged each other for space. They had come for the same reason I had, to catch a small piece of ugly vox pop.

The little work space had been converted to a rough assembly line. At the counter next to the front door, one man was breaking down a stamped, engraved sheet of metal into component pieces; the pieces were shaped like tiny missiles. At the next counter, another man was working with two fine paintbrushes and two small pots of paint, applying first a white background, then the red details. At the back counter, a third man was filing the rough edges, polishing the painted pieces, and attaching them to cheap key chains. The work was simple and swift. Not counting the time it took for the paint to dry, the whole process of converting a piece of metal to a facsimile of a Scud missile did not take more than ten minutes.

The al-Afghani Company also sold buttons. They came in Arabic and English, and it was a sampling of buttons stuck up on the front door that the television crew was shooting. The buttons were big and shiny and all variations on the same unpleasant theme. "East or West, SCUD is best," said one that had a picture of Scuds raining down on a dead man wearing a skullcap. "Saddam, One Like You Makes Dream Come True," said another, the words running next to a drawing of a speeding Scud missile. A third showed two Scuds bearing down on a man lying on a beach underneath a sign: "Israel." Next to the man's fat stomach, a Star of David lay, and the caption read: "Wherever you hide, al-Hussein 'Scud' is going to FIND." The last button I looked at was the most virulent: "Israel is a Cancer and Scud is the answer."

Fouad Afghani, the owner of the store, came up to me while I was looking at the button. He had the happily harried air of a shopkeeper selling out his stock. "This is very true, of course," he said. "Israel is indeed a cancer and Scud is indeed the answer."

Yes?

"Oh my, yes. Israel is a land of people who don't belong among the Arab peoples. They come from the outside and have been put on the inside. They have never mixed. There will never be peace as long as they are here. We know this is true from the Koran. Since old time, there has always been fighting between Jewish and Arab people. The Jews have always killed. Since a very old time, this has been going on.

"Arabs are pure in heart. But these people are different, because of their religion, you see. Jews all the time kill their own prophets. This is known. Now, what do you call a man who kills his own prophet? Maybe you say he is a bastard? Of course you do."

Fouad Afghani was born in the ancient Arab seaport of Jaffa, next door to Tel Aviv, in 1947. His father owned a store there; the Afghanis were mildly well-off. When Fouad was six months old, the first war began, and the Afghani family crossed the bridge. "I will not return as long as there is an Israeli soldier at the border who stops me and searches me and gives me permission to go and visit my own home," Fouad Afghani said. "Who could accept such a thing?"

At first, the war had hurt business. "It was very bad," Fouad Afghani said. "No tourists at all. But then we began a Saddam line, first with buttons, then watches, now with Scud key chains, buttons. And, God is with us, this business is very good."

Clearing a space on the glass countertop, he laid out three trays of watches. In the most important respect they were all identical, the face of each decorated with a color photograph of the smiling Saddam, but beyond that there were many differences. Some were basic, Timex-like jobs that offered a straightforward clock face with a second hand and maybe a date box, set in a stainless-steel bezel, with a simple leather or plastic strap. But there were a number of styles tricked up with bezels and bands of fool's gold and designs of tiny rhinestones set in or around the face. Fouad Afghani saw that I admired these.

"Very nice, these are. Top of the line. The price is between ten and eighty dinars per watch, depending on your fancy. You want one of these plain watches with a plastic band and nothing else, it is not so expensive. But what kind of watch is that for your wife? You would be ashamed to give that to her, no?"

I'm not married.

"A girlfriend, I am sure."

Yes.

"Well now, even better. Before you are married, you must show your girlfriend—"

Really, fiancée. We got engaged last summer.

"Well! So you must bring her back from your trip to Amman something very special, something that says 'I love you forever.' "

A Saddam watch would say that, you think?

"The lady's model in gold with the diamonds on the edges, yes. The cheap watch, no."

He had sold five hundred Saddam watches, a very nice run

of business. The really big sellers, of course, were the cheaper items. "Saddam buttons, you can wear, you know, on your shirt. We have sold three hundred thousand since August. Very good. Very steady. This is our number one item."

The al-Afghani Company brought out its first Scud item, a button, only two days after the first missile fell on Israel, and they had sold two thousand in the two weeks since, he said. Of the Scud key chains, on the market only six days, he had moved, as near as he could figure, at least three thousand; of the Scud buttons, at least two thousand.

In fact, business was so good that Fouad Afghani could no longer afford to sell to just anybody. "Some Jordanians want to buy Scud key chains, because they do not cost as much as the Saddam watches, but I do not sell to them. They only want to buy one or two and we have too much trouble keeping up with the rush for that. We only take the bigger orders, ten pieces or more." He showed me. The big orders were pinned on scraps of paper on the back wall: Peter Svenson, Intercontinental, Room 70—10 Scuds. Ingrid Tonquist, Marriott, Room 8287 —20 Scuds. CNN—5 Iraqi maps and 5 Scuds. TV-Spain—10 Scuds.

The big customers are all journalists? I said.

"Oh yes, of course," said Fouad Afghani. "About eighty percent of our sales, maybe more, are to journalists. They are the number one customers. It is much better for me to sell ten pieces to one person than one piece to ten persons. Maybe later, we will sell to Jordanians. Right now, to journalists. That is where the business is."

He was right. I bought eight Saddam watches, five Scud key chains, and seven buttons. I got a discount for volume, 10 percent off.

Amman is built on *jebels,* hills, seven major ones and six lesser, and it rambles from one hilltop to another, and up and down the sides, strung together by streets that wander in confused fashion through traffic circles around which the cars whirl dervishly. No one bothers with street addresses, because hardly any of the streets are marked with signs, and most have several names anyway. Location is by hill and by circle; invited to dinner, you are told to come to Jebel Amman, First Circle, second left, go two blocks, or something like that. The hills stratify the city's social structure, each hill having its place in the pecking order. The grandest hill is Jebel Amman, where the Intercontinental stands, surrounded by embassies, restaurants, boutiques, banks, and the better sort of villas. The richest Palestinians, the bankers and merchants and import-export hustlers, live here.

Their houses stand in testimony to the newness of the money that built them. Many are only a few years old, and a lot are still, or perhaps permanently, under construction. They are peacocks of buildings, creatures of playfulness and vanity. The best of them seem to have been made up as the job went along, without any fussiness about architectural drawings and with the happy assurance that nothing succeeds like excess. If one porch is good, five are better; if three balconies, ten; if columns, a colonnade. They are houses that are entirely open to suggestion. By all means, a dome painted blue, a portico faced in marble, a fence of arabesques in iron, mosaic on one wall and stucco on another. They do not bother with conventions of uniformity, but grow in a multiplicity of shapes—squares and circles and rectangles and triangles all unconcernedly jumbled together. In matters of height as well they are nonconformists, setting a new roofline with every new section. A single house might have four sections of distinctly different shape and height, the central hall being, say, square and squat, while the east wing is taller and round and the west wing taller still in a skinny rectangle. And within these sections there might be still further parsings of style and deviations of height and shape, additions popping up like musings.

A house I particularly admired had four different styles of

arches gracing its doors and windows. I drew pictures of them in my notebook and looked them up later, and found that in this one structure were half the arches of the world. The front entranceway was crowned with a broad, slightly spatulate arch called a basket handle. Another doorframe was an example of the horseshoe arch, and the windows were variously done in the trefoil—modeled after the trifoliate leaf, fatter at the bottom, pinched at the middle, and spreading out again towards the top, like a fat woman in a girdle—or the graceful ogee, the sides of which describe a gentle reverse curve near the apex, so the arch as a whole resembles two elongated inverted S's joined at the head. It is a pity the builder stopped when he did. With another wing, he could have found opportunities for the round arch, the lancet, and the Tudor, and made a clean sweep of every arch known to man.

The main shopping street in Amman is on Jebel Amman, a street formally called Abu Bakr al-Sadiq Street, known popularly as Rainbow Street. It does look rainbowesque, with its bright shop windows filled with silks and gold. The stores of Jebel Amman are filled with the Best, and it is a notable thing that the Best in Amman is always from somewhere else. At the Twang Music Center, just off Rainbow Street, I could buy a Gibson guitar from America or a Steinway piano from Germany or a Roland synthesizer from Japan. The Romeo + Juliette Gift Gallery would sell me Cuban cigars or a gold cigarette lighter or a pair of Gucci shoes or Fabergé perfume. The Fa Sha ("Your Taste of Good Life") Shop offered eighteen different lines in luxuries for the table, including Baccarat, Wedgwood, Royal Copenhagen, Spode, Waterford, Aynsley, and, changing the topic slightly, Neuhaus Belgian Chocolate. IBM and Wang both had set up shop. At H. Zananiri & Sons, I could buy a Sub-Zero refrigerator, or a Krups coffeepot, or an entire kitchen from Poggenpohl.

The best food in Amman is from somewhere else too. Under Restaurants in my copy of *A Practical Guide to Jordan with a*

Classified Telephone Directory: Amigo Nabil, Chen's Chinese Restaurant, the Chicken Chalet, the Chili House, Corfu Greek Taverna, Golden Fried Chicken, La Terrasse, Leonardo da Vinci, L'Olivier, McBurger Restaurant (two locations), New York New York Deli, Pizza Hut, the Restaurant China, and the Turkish Restaurant.

A hundred years ago, even fifty or twenty-five years ago, cities like Amman didn't exist in the Middle East. Now they are everywhere, and everywhere the same, the new Big, Fast Money towns, with hot deals going down every evening in every dim and padded corner of every lobby bar, and the sound of construction always in the ear. There are twenty-eight banks in Amman, twelve more than there are women's clothing stores, twenty-two more than there are cinemas. The blue-and-white sign of Citibank crowns the arch of Rainbow Street on the very top of Jebel Amman.

Seeing the rich Palestinians grazing from shop to shop on Rainbow Street, it was hard to think of them as refugees, or even Palestinians. They were part of a subset of the universal brotherhood of man, the international shoppers, a people the same everywhere. Whether from Tokyo in Paris or from Paris in Manhattan or from Manhattan in Milan, they are well-made, well fed, and well put together, not apparently plump but with a buttery softness to their skin, and beveled edges to their curves.

Apart from the shops and shoppers of Rainbow Street, though, it is easy to see Amman for what it is, the capital of the New Diaspora, the home, as the writer Jonathan Raban put it, of the twentieth century's Wandering Jew, the Palestinians.

Most of the Palestinians live crowded on the lower sides and narrow valleys of the *jebels,* in bareboned squares of space— boxy little stone houses with flat roofs, scaled-down warehouses stacked on top of each other and against each other and out over the edge of where the land drops away, like an overdone Escher print. There are occasional spaces between the squares for patches of scrabby, scrawny green, but Amman is largely, Escher-like, colorless. Most of the houses are unpainted, left the natural noncolor of concrete, and their windows and doors are frameless, curtainless squares. The sole concession to ornamentation on most of them is an outsized TV antenna, built in imitation of the Eiffel Tower. These thousands and thousands of little *Tours d'Eiffel* share the skyline with a forest of skinny, scaly, rusting sticks of steel. It is the Arab custom that as a man gets richer he builds additional stories upon his house, and to make easier the addition of the eventual next story, builders often leave the job started, by extending the steel reinforcing rods from the last story up five feet or so above the roofline. It rained most of the month I was in Amman, day after day of freezing, sleeting sheets of gray wet, and the sight of that skyline of steel rods waving stiffly in the wind through a curtain of rain set my teeth on edge.

One night, in the Wahdat refugee camp, the Wahdat Social and Sports Club held an auction. The thing ostensibly for sale was a piece of metal cowling that, it was claimed, was part of the wing of an American F-16 jet shot down over Iraq near the Jordanian border and given to the club by Saddam Hussein in thanks for previous donations of food and money. The real thing for sale was not the thing itself, but the chance to look at the thing, the chance for a smidgen of *faux* revenge.

It was a piece of metal about four feet long and a foot and a half wide, painted olive green with a yellow stripe. On it was painted in white a sleek, slippery slide of Arabic script, the translation of which was: "This is a part of an American plane. Made in New York. Funded by Saudi Arabia. Shot down in Trebeil by the Iraqis."

The auction had a peculiarity that made it really more of a fund-raiser. To up the ante, a bidder had to actually pay the amount by which he was raising the old price—say five dinars, to bid 1,135 over 1,130 dinars. The average bid that night was between three and five dinars. The average salary of the wage earners in the Wahdat camp ran to about five dinars a day, making the auction a very expensive evening out. Yet the chance to actually see evidence of the destruction of the enemy—it was understood that America was only the enemy by proxy, the stand-in for the Jews—was such a draw that the clubhouse was packed with four or five thousand men and boys, and the bidding lasted for hours.

The men settled in a loosely gathered circle while the club officials set up two big wooden tables as a platform and arranged on it themselves, the piece of metal, and a microphone stand. A banner for the club's football team hung over the scene. The team was called the Palestines, and its symbol, as depicted in the banner, was a soccer ball surmounted by the mosque of al-Aqsr in Jerusalem, where, not long before, rioting Palestinians, perhaps driven by rumors that a militant Jewish group was marching on al-Aqsr to lay a cornerstone for the Third Temple, rained stones on Jews praying below, and Israeli soldier-police shot at least twenty-one of the Palestinians dead.

The bidding began a little after seven o'clock, opening at one thousand Jordanian dinars, or about $1,600. The auctioneer was a prominent used-car salesman named Abdullah Abdelhamid, a big, heavy man, flashily dressed in a long leather coat buttoned tight around the tummy. He was energetic and he had a fast, hard, professional line of patter. He spoke through a microphone, which he held with one pinkie extended and used as a pointer and prop, like a lounge singer. His spiel bellowed from two giant speakers, one on each side of him. The amplifier had been cranked up to earsplitting, so loud that the timid held their hands cupped over their ears.

The money was passed hand to hand through the crowd, and the auctioneer made a production out of each note, holding it up high in the air as he announced the name of the bidder and then depositing it with a sweeping flourish into a two-handled silver victory cup. He was practiced and ceaseless in his exhortations, driving the bids slowly upward with the ease of a man used to moving the merchandise. "Everybody pay something now," he would say. "Pay what you can afford. Come, come, my friends, keep what you must but give what you can."

"Victory is so sweet with the help of God!" the young men screamed. "Mubarak is an ass! Mubarak is an ass!"

After a slow start—1,125 dinars, 1,130, 1,135—the money began to flow. Pretty soon it was up to 1,200. Someone bid a U.S. dollar, and that got lots of laughs and whistles and catcalls. Someone else bid an Iraqi dinar; that got lots of cheers.

. . . 13,690, 13,700, 13,810 . . . A new wrinkle: a small boy named Orayeb Darwich was passed overhead, hand to hand, person to person, to reach the silver cup and give ten dinars to Abdullah Abdelhamid. Everyone cheered a great deal over this, and patted Orayeb Darwich, and soon there was a traffic jam of small children moving through the air. I noticed one very pretty, very prissy little girl with a red ribbon in her pigtails being handed along; she wore a neat red cloth coat with gold buttons and little red pumps, and it was like watching a miniature Republican National Committeewoman sail slowly through space. She gave ten dinars.

Abdullah Abdelhamid had a big voice and made the woofers and tweeters vibrate with every syllable. He shrieked up to falsetto and dipped to basso profundo, with much trumpeting and rolling of R's: "Make way for the people in the back! Make waaaay for the peeeeeeple in the back!" Even the smallest utterances were in his mouth Great Expectorations. "This is for the support of Irrrraq! This is for the support of the children! Oh! Let us praise the young men of Iraq! Oh! Let us praise Saddam Hussein!" . . . 14,041, 14,051, 14,056, 14,061, 14,066, 14,086 . . . At 14,179 he stopped to drain a glass of water. At 14,485, the Wahdat Social and Sports Club succumbed to its own pitch and kicked in the whopper bid, five thousand dinars. "More! More! More! More!" shouted Abdullah Abdelhamid.

The money was coming in so fast now he had a hard time keeping up with it, but he still waved each note in the air with a flutter of the hand before dropping it in the cup.

By 19,490, everyone had dropped out except for two men, Walid al-Khatib and the father of Orayeb Darwich. They went back and forth for a long time, topping each other in increments of five dinars. Abdullah Abdelhamid worked them like a revival preacher. "Oh God bless you. God bless you. God bless you all." 19,875. "Oh, Orayeb Darwich! Orayeb Darwich!" At about nine-thirty, the microphone broke, and everything stopped amid yelling and confusion. By this time I was drained by the heat and the excitement, and I left in exhaustion. I read in *The Jordan Times* the next morning that Walid al-Khatib had ended up the winner.

Walking back through the dark mud streets to the car, Mona, the young Jordanian woman I had hired as a translator for the evening, said she was nervous. "It is very dangerous to be here at night. The people here are thieves." She was a Palestinian, but lived far removed from the refugee camps, indeed had never been to one before. Her father was a rich businessman, and the family lived in a large new villa in a large new suburb. She had been educated in a convent school, and she took her holidays in London and Paris. She wore a cashmere blazer, silk shirt, ironed blue jeans, and cowboy boots. She picked her way through the muck and trash of Wahdat with care not to dirty herself.

I asked her, as we were getting in the car, what she had thought of the auction, and she shrugged. She wasn't very interested in the kind of people she had seen this night, the shrug seemed to say. She had her own plans for revenge. The day before, she and several of her girlfriends had driven to a recruiting center for the People's Army and signed up for training. "This is the fight of our lives," she explained. I could see her face in the streetlights, and she was very animated. "The talk is over. This is the great battle between our people and the

Israelis. We must fight, and we will win. I will myself shoot the enemy."

The People's Army numbered about 200,000, and its stated purpose was to back up the real army in case of war with Israel. Its unstated purpose was to give young Palestinians an outlet for their martial ardor other than trying to kill the king, as they had tried to do on several occasions. The soldiers of the People's Army were not allowed access to weapons.

There was a demonstration every Friday or so at the Baqua'a refugee camp, on the edge of the city, and one day I went to take a look. The taxi that took me there enjoyed a rich inner life. The rear window ledge was bewigged in some sort of acrylic hair, shocking pink and waving whispery-wild in the slipstream from the open windows. The dashboard and the rearview mirror were outlined with a profusion of dangling little scarlet balls, orphreys on the chasuble of Bishop Liberace. The facing of the dash was covered with a paper that was faceted and mirrored and iridescent with various shimmering blues and greens and reds. The effect of the whole was overpowering and improbable, like going for a ride in a Fabergé egg, and when I stepped out from this into the rain and mud and general drear of Baqua'a, I had to walk several blocks, wobbling like a sailor on shore leave, to get my sensibilities back.

Baqua'a, home to eighty thousand people, is a maze of narrow mud streets lined on both sides with little square concrete houses, one or two stories high, with corrugated-metal roofs. The houses are crowded upon each other and upon the tiny shops and tea stalls and cheap restaurants. Here and there are houses that are larger, and fancier, with courtyards and rooftop television antennas. Foreign cars are parked in front of their steel gates. These belong to men who have grown up in Baqua'a, and who have made enough money to leave, but who still live there, as a statement of politics and identity, and because they feel more secure inside Baqua'a's fence than outside.

As I walked along, with the pungent smell of cooking in close quarters, the streets full of children and old men and mothers and daughters walking arm in arm, I remembered something Jonathan Raban had written. It was no wonder that even some who could afford to leave the camp stayed. The second Semitic diaspora had spun out two million people from the same old places whence had come the people of the first one—Jerusalem and Bethlehem and Jericho and Jaffa—with the same results. Palestinians lived all over the world, hundreds of thousands of them in the Gulf states alone, and wherever they went, their intelligence and hard work and ambition made them welcome, but everywhere the Palestinian went was a way station. He could adopt the culture of the land, but it would not adopt him, and it might at any moment turn on him. It was a feeling any Jew would know in his bones.

At the previous Friday's demonstration at Baqua'a, the crowd had thrown rocks and roughed up a couple of photographers, which made for good stories and pictures of Palestinian Rage, so this week's affair drew a press contingent of a hundred or more. The cameramen got there early to stake out good places, and as I neared the mosque I saw some of them had gotten up on the rooftops and were, with their stork-legged tripods, silhouetted against the gray sky. In the mud street, reporters and photographers almost outnumbered residents. Most of the European journalists wore red-and-white *kaffiyehs,* to show that they were one with the Palestinian cause. At the mosque, the prayers were just ending. The overflow of faithful were kneeling in the streets, knocking their heads on scraps of carpet spread out in the mud, a line of small, shabby brown men. In front of them were the photographers, with Nikons and Sony Betacams to their eyes, a line of big, staring white men. A couple of the correspondents stood in front of the men at prayer, with their backs to them, using them as scenery for their standups: "Friday is a day of prayer in Amman, a day of communion with the God of Islam. But not this Friday. This Friday was a day of rage. . . ."

Really, it was a day of sodden, soggy sorriness. The demonstration had an air of profound familiarity. The posters were all in English or French, and were for the benefit of television audiences in Washington and Paris: "Death to America" and "France, Savez Vos Enfants de la Mort dans le Golfe," "Morte a l'Amérique" and "Down with the Imperialist Aggression Against Iraq." It was all reflex language, weak and flabby and used-up. An Arab politician puts Imperialist before Aggression as automatically as his American counterpart puts Patriotic before Duty. The pictures, too, hewed strictly to timeworn themes. A banner of a strong young *intifada* fighter with broken shackles dangling from his wrists, stabbing a writhing Uncle Sam through the abdomen with a bloody, dripping spear. A poster of brown hands waving Kalashnikovs, rampant, over the Israeli flag torn in the dirt. Reflex art.

The marchers trudged through the rain, their feet in plastic sandals slogging in the mud. I fell in with a man in his thirties. He introduced himself, amiably enough: Muhammad Asanit, genetic engineer, educated in India, holder of two graduate degrees, unemployed. He was dressed like a poor man, but clean, in thin tan slacks and a blue nylon windbreaker over his shirt. We talked about nothing of consequence at first. He gave me a synopsis of his schooling in India; I chatted about my trip to Baghdad. He was a careful, calm man who chose his words slowly and spoke quietly. "Saddam Hussein is the greatest hero of the Arab nation," he said. "He will remain a hero even if he loses. Indeed, Saddam is not a man. He is greater than that. He is a great hero because he is the first man since Nasser to stand up to the occupiers."

The occupiers?

"The Jews. And their American servants. Today, the Scud missiles will hit Israel; tomorrow, they will hit America."

The curious thing was that he said this without any animation that might suggest he believed what he was saying. It was Friday afternoon at the demo, and the foreign press had come. There were certain things the foreign press expected to hear.

Around a corner from the demonstrators and down a mud alley, I came across a small pack of boys. They saw me at the same time, and as I started toward them they scurried about picking up stones from the ground, and then, with impressive speed, lined up and began winging their rocks at me. They had mastered the form of the *intifada*—a couple of running steps forward for momentum's sake, the right arm cocked back, left leg extended and planted, and a wide, full-armed throw—but they were a pretty long way from me and pretty small boys, so none of their missiles did any harm, although one hit me weakly in the back as I turned and walked away. They didn't pursue, and as I rounded the corner I peeked over my shoulder and saw that they were already moving off in the other direction. I had the odd feeling they had stoned me for form's sake, much as the man I had just spoken to had done his job as an interview subject. It was Friday afternoon at the demo, and someone was supposed to peg a rock or two.

As the month wore on, Amman fell from elation to funk to a bad city-wide case of nervous depression, brought on by dawning reality. It was becoming obvious that the Jews were not really suffering so much after all. The Scuds were all sound and fury; they blew apart buildings, but they did not kill many people. And what if a Scud, one tipped with a chemical warhead perhaps, did succeed in producing a more satisfying kill count? Israel would doubtless enter the war. That was supposed to be the beginning of the dream scenario, leading on to the breakup of the Arab coalition against Iraq, to *jihad* and to the defeat of the Jews, but the more people thought about this the more they suffered doubts. Jordan's history of wars with Israel did not lend itself to optimism.

The Jordanians wanted too much. They wanted to encourage the Iraqis to kill the Israelis, but they didn't want the Israelis to take offense at this. They wanted to help Iraq but to be treated still as neutrals by America. They wanted to be heroes in the great fight for Palestine, but they didn't want to get hurt. There were no brigades of Jordanian volunteers rushing to fight in Kuwait, no terror-bombers running off to answer Saddam's radio pleas that American targets be struck. The only people who seemed to have any heart for the whole thing were the truckers running the economic blockade of Iraq to bring oil in tankers up the road from Al Khanem, the refinery in western Iraq. Amman celebrated the truckers, in newspaper features and speeches and television newscasts, as great heroes, and that was true enough. With the pipeline from Saudi Arabia cut off, 80 percent of Jordan's oil came from Iraq, and without it the economy would have collapsed. The danger the truckers faced bringing in the Iraqi crude was terrific. The trip from Amman to the oil-pumping stations in western Iraq and back took forty-eight hours over roads also used by mobile Scud launchers and regarded by American and British bombers as legitimate targets. By the end of the first week in February, allied raids had killed fourteen truckers, wounded twenty-six more, and damaged or destroyed fifty trucks. There was no cover from the raids on the desert highway, and no defense.

On a run down to the border one day to collect stories from incoming refugees, I stopped to talk to a group of truckers just coming out of Iraq. A man named Mahmoud Ismail Zeidan, a big-stomached, big-shouldered bruiser with a mustache like an old-fashioned circus strongman, said he had made the trip sixteen times in the past thirty days, and had been bombed every time, which was probably a couple of at least slight exaggerations. "They have been bombing us on a daily basis since the 25th of January," he said. "It's very hard to get in and get out. There is constant bombardment, and there is no medical care, so even if a person is hit only a little bit he will probably die. The main reason is the lack of ambulances. They usually arrive one or two days after an attack. So people who are hit often die from loss of blood before they get there. There were some people hit near Al Khanem, and they remained where they were hit for two days before an ambulance got there, and they were dead."

The previous night, he said, there had been four attacks just in the stretch of road between Al Rutba and the border crossing at Trebeil. "The planes come down very low and bomb at random. No one is hurt. We all run from the trucks every time and hide. Two trucks are destroyed. One from a bomb and one from driving into a big crater." He said he wasn't scared because his life was in Allah's hands. The driver next to him said he, personally, was scared. "No, you are not scared. No one is scared," Zeidan corrected him. "We are men. We do what we must for Jordan."

Most of the vehicles coming through the border that afternoon, and most afternoons, were full of refugees. They came over the line in buses and trucks, which disgorged them near the camps the government and the Red Cross had set up. I watched as a new bunch staggered through the mud with American Touristers and Hefty Cinch-Sacks on their heads, clutching the charity-issue gray felt blankets and bottles of water, making their way to whatever tents they were assigned to. Almost all of them were foreign workers—Indians, Iranians, Filipinos, Egyptians, and a Sudanese the color of a Kalamata olive in a tartan-check raincoat. A dump truck pulled up with twenty more Indians; they climbed down and stood there stiffly, shivering, wet, their skins going faintly green with the cold. It had been a hard crossing, they said. Four Sudanese had died of exposure. "It was very cold. They went one by one." A woman was sitting by herself, holding a baby in her lap and weeping steadily. A reporter who saw this wrote her up in his story as crying for joy at having escaped Iraq. It turned out this was a mistake. She was crying because the baby in her lap was dead.

THE BLITZ OF
TEL AVIV

ISRAEL OCCUPIED A SCHIZOPHRENIC POSITION in the official Arab mind; it was the devil-state and, simultaneously, it did not exist. You could not arrange direct travel to Israel from any country except Egypt, and no Arab country except Egypt would allow entry to anyone whose passport bore an Israeli entry or exit stamp. Most regular Middle East travelers carried two passports, one for the world at large and one stamped "Valid only for travel to Egypt and Israel." The dual-passport system was part of an elaborate construct designed to get around the ban on travel. It was a matter of observing the proprieties. A customs official in Dubai looking at a passport that showed the traveler had flown to Dubai from Cairo but did not show how he entered Cairo in the first place would know that the traveler must have somewhere a second passport, which showed that he had come into Egypt from Israel—but he would not act on that knowledge as long as nothing before his eyes obliged him to. The traveler coming from Israel, for his part, took care not to put anything before the guard's eyes. Before leaving Israel, he searched through his belongings, getting rid of all things Israeli—money, newspapers or magazines, Hebrew laundry markings on shirts dry-cleaned by a hotel in Tel Aviv, the label in a sports coat purchased in Jerusalem, a tube of toothpaste purchased in Haifa, a matchbook from a restaurant in Jaffa, whatever. Inside Arabia, he took care never to say anything that might betray his visit to the nonexistent devil-land. In conversation among reporters, Israel was "Dixie," a dodge I thought was silly and transparent, but used nontheless.

Transparent dodges were what kept the whole thing going. People traveled from Amman to Tel Aviv every day, but everyone pretended they were going to or coming from somewhere else. Most went under the pretense of going to the West Bank, the land between Jerusalem and the Jordan River that Israel has occupied since 1967. They went by bus across the western Jordanian desert to the Allenby Bridge, walked across the bridge, then boarded another bus for the ride through the desert on the other side, skirting Jericho and Salt (where the local tour guides every year designate a natural mineral formation as Lot's wife and make a nice business of delighting the gullible with the sight of God's handiwork, still standing after all these years), en route to Jerusalem, and from there to Tel Aviv. The entire excursion took about five hours and was an elegant example of how things can be made to work by a judicious averting of the eyes. It rested on a violation of the laws of nature; the traveler eyeing Lot's wife was a body occupying two places at once: he was in Jordan, and in Israel. Jordan had no objection to anyone visiting the West Bank, since that was, as far as Jordan was concerned, part of Jordan, not Israel. Once across the bridge, the traveler was, as far as the Israelis were concerned, in Israel, and could go anywhere in the country. Later, there would be no problem in returning to Jordan, the traveler having never, in the Jordanian view, really left the country. Israeli border guards liked to confide how young King Hussein used to slip over to the discos of Tel Aviv, dance for the night, and make it back to Amman by the next day, no harm done.

There were, among the travel agents of Amman, specialists at arranging trips to the nonexisting devil-state. I went to one around the corner from the hotel, the Guiding Star Agency, which occupied a tiny office on Prince Muhammad Street. The proprietor sat perched on a chair wedged into the well of her desk, hemmed in by hills of paper, piles tumbling from the desk and rising from the floor, burying boxes and chairs and filing cabinets. She had a telephone receiver to her ear, and the coiled cord burrowed to someplace within the pile. On one corner of the desk I could see the edge of a fax machine poking out under a layer of brochures and invoices and government forms. She was herself as cluttered as her desk, with a pen in her hand and a pencil tucked behind her right ear, and her henna-red hair arranged in a halfhearted bouffant that sagged in the middle like a falling soufflé. The pockets of her cardigan sweater overflowed with paper; they were misshapen from hands jamming into them all day, shoving in this piece of paper, searching for that one.

When I told her I wanted to go to Israel right away, she put a look on her face of exaggerated dismay, to convey the depth of the impossibility of what I asked.

"It is not good now," she said mournfully. "The bridge is closed."

Why?

"Who knows?" A shrug. The bridge closed often, and unpredictably, although most often in times of obvious tension. Sometimes the Israelis shut it, sometimes the Jordanians.

When will it open?

"The day after tomorrow, I think."

I'll go then.

"No, you cannot go then. It will take three days to get the permit from the Ministry of the Interior."

So long?

"It is the rules."

I don't want to wait three days.

"What can you do? It is the rules."

There must be another way.

"There is no other way. There is nothing I can do for you. But wait, let me think." She frowned deeply and looked wor-

ried, and I knew I was fine, that there was some other way to
Tel Aviv, and that she would tell it to me in her own time, after
she had impressed upon me the unsuitablity of my request and
the heroic efforts that must be made to satisfy it. She frowned
some more, and dug into her papers, and after several minutes,
found an airline guide, which she studied. Eventually she spoke.

"You are very fortunate. I have found another way. It is very
difficult to arrange, but I can do it."

The other way was the regular, if slightly circular, air service.
I would fly from Amman over Syria and Lebanon, avoiding
Israeli airspace, to Larnaca, on the island of Cyprus, 175 miles
northwest of Israel's coast, where I would be admitted under a
transit visa, change planes, and fly to Tel Aviv. I must remember only to change passports, she reminded me. I would use the
all-purpose passport for the arrival to and departure from Cyprus, but switch to the Israel-only passport for the arrival in Tel
Aviv. When, later, I left Israel for Egypt, where I would pick up
a visa for Saudi Arabia, I would use the Israeli passport again,
but then when I entered Saudi Arabia I would switch back to
the global passport. She ran through the routine twice, so I
would fix it in my mind. She would fax the airline in Cyprus,
and she would also fax her cousin in Jerusalem to request that
he arrange with the Israelis permission for my return to Amman
via the Allenby Bridge, just in case I might want to do that. Did
I need a hotel room in Tel Aviv? She could arrange that by fax
as well. "It is very simple," she said. "I have a cousin in New
York who has a fax on a line that is set up to call-forward to my
cousin in Jerusalem. So I fax a note saying here is what I need
done in Israel, and my fax goes from Amman to Brooklyn to
Jerusalem—and it is done." The flight to Cyprus left in three
hours, she said, so I must hurry.

When you get to Cyprus, the Guiding Star lady had said, go to
the Lufthansa counter, near the cafeteria, and you will find

some chairs. Sit in one of those chairs and wait, and a man will come find you and take care of you.

Two or three other men waited with me, and, camped nearby was a family of unhappy Russians who, I dimly gathered from their conversation, had been stuck there for more than a day already and was awaiting an Aeroflot flight that might or might not exist. The grandmother was gnawing on what appeared to be a pickled foot of some sort. I smoked and read, and after two hours, the door to the airfield opened, and I could see that the plane, a small, twin-engine propeller job, had landed and was parked there. A man had come off it and was walking toward us. He was dressed stylishly, in good slacks and a zipped-up black vinyl jacket and sunglasses, and he could have been a graduate student. At the same moment, the door to the street opened and another man came through. He was wearing a sports coat and an open-collar shirt and jeans, and he could have been a young lawyer on the weekend. Both men were, of course, from the government. The security forces of Israel are interested in everyone who flies in or out of Israel, but they are profoundly interested in anyone coming from an Arab country. The questioners were polite, but as insistent as homicide detectives.

Why are you coming to Israel?

Journalist? Who do you work for? Do you have any identification proving you are a journalist?

Have you been to Israel before? Have you been to the West Bank? When?

How long were you in Amman?

And where were you before that?

Iraq? Why were you in Iraq?

Did you bring anything you purchased, or anything that was given to you, from Iraq to Amman?

Are you now carrying anything you purchased in Amman?

Did anyone in Amman give you anything to carry, to bring with you?

No? Nothing at all? A book, a magazine, even a letter? A gift for a friend?

Who packed your bags?

Who carried them?

Have they been out of your sight?

Did you make any new friends in Amman?

Did you visit any people in their homes?

And so on, and on, the three of us standing there in a fluorescent frieze in the big empty room, until, eventually, the men made one of those silent decisions policemen make, and it was done.

You could walk backward in time in Tel Aviv, peeling the onion of the years as you went, going from a group of 1980s seafront villas, all sharp-edged lines and glass brick, to a curvilinear and peculiarly organic 1960s hotel (a kidney-shaped pool and liver-shaped garden, with a duodenal path from one to the other) to a cluster of 1940s Bauhausian apartment blocks, to the Cairene-Parisian mansions and town houses of the 1920s (crumbling brick and flaking stucco, massive wood shutters and wrought-iron balconies of ladylike curves and frills), to a tangle of dark Arab streets where were crowded together mud-adobe hovels from Allah knows when and centuries-old brick mansions built around secret gardens of dates and figs and fountains.

Or you could stay perfectly still in time. Tel Aviv is a beach town, a place of bikini stores and cafés and ice-cream stands, and it has the beach-town quality of seeming to be always living vaguely in some past summer. The air is full of salt and ozone and atomized Bain de Soleil. The broad stretches of white sand running the length of the city are filled with tanners and swimmers and Windsurfers. The cafés along the waterfront and the downtown nightclubs go into the early-morning hours, except on Fridays, with locals and tourists and kids in from the countryside mixing together. There is, all over, the tang of sex, the young men on motorcycles and the young women promenading in a beach-town way, hard and brown and fit, and cheerfully obvious. The men wear tight jeans and shirts open to their bellies, the women wear short skirts and tight tops and jewelry as outsized as adolescent ego.

I had been in Israel in November, two months before the war began, and the country then had been in a sulk. The stone-throwers of the *intifada* had graduated to stabbing people in the street. Religious nuttism was on the ascendancy. No one knew what to expect of Saddam's Scuds, and so expected the worst. There had been a sense of futility and fatigue.

One afternoon I went to the battered, bloody ruin of the Gaza Strip, where 800,000 people live their short, nasty, brutish lives in chicken-coop squalor and rage. It requires the Israeli Defense Forces a full and heavily armed division to keep a similitude of peace in Gaza. The soldiers of the Givati Brigade live on the edge of the Shati refugee camp, the worst place in Gaza, in the concrete shell of an empty apartment block they guard with heavy machine guns and concertina wire. Except for twice-daily patrols into Shati, they scarcely dare show their faces on the streets. They live under siege by those they be-siege; "the enemy," one soldier said to me, "is the population."

They took me on an afternoon patrol. It was an unhappy, dangerous business, the armored trucks and jeeps careering through the narrow dirt streets, scattering the people up against the walls of their hovels, the stone-throwers pegging sharp, jagged missiles at our heads as we whipped by, the sudden, shrieking stops and fierce, mostly futile foot chases. The soldiers were very young, as soldiers mostly are, and I could see they were frightened. I thought they were right to be. They were armed and outfitted for combat of the late twentieth century and their opponents, with their rocks and knives and hatchets, were hardly better equipped than Iron Age warriors, but the population of Shati outnumbered the patrol a thousand to one, and closed all around it with malevolent desire. The patrol

managed only one arrest, that of a skinny, scruffy, shoeless man
who may or may not have pegged a rock. As they threw him
into the back of the jeep a woman—his wife, I guess—rushed
up, screaming, arms flailing. The captain leading the patrol
punched her square in the face with a right jab that traveled no
more than twelve inches, and she sat down hard, wailing.

Afterward, I talked with the captain in the bare, windowless
box in which he lived. His name was Alon Alporvitch, he was
twenty-three years old, and this was his third four-month tour
of duty in the Gaza Strip. He hated it. "I don't think the work
is good," he said. "Not for me, not for the army. . . . I know from
the history of the U.S. in Vietnam that this cannot work. I want
peace more than anyone, but it will not be the army that
achieves it. It is clear to everyone." When I asked him why he
had hit the woman in the face, he said, "I didn't hit the woman."

I saw you, I said.

"I didn't hit her. She came at one of my soldiers to claw him
and he threw her away from him and then she came at me, and
I pushed her away, in the face."

I asked him if it bothered him to treat a woman like that.

"Yes. A lot. But the thing that bothers me most is the children."

The first signs that things were different now was the blue-and-
white Israeli flags that flew everywhere. The taxi that took me
from the airport to the Tel Aviv Hilton, where Max was living,
sported four: a cloth one fluttering from the radio antenna, two
paper decals plastered on the rear window, and a small one
crowning the dashboard. Every street we drove on was filled
with flags, flag posters, flag stickers, hanging from wires strung
across the road, flying from apartment windows, on the lapels
of pedestrians and the bumpers of cars.

After I checked into the hotel (the man at the front desk gave
me a gas mask along with my room key), I took a shower and

read, while waiting for Max to get off work, a month's worth of *The Jerusalem Post*. There was something about them that seemed strangely old-fashioned, and after several weeks' worth, I realized what it was. They reminded me, in their mood and style, of old magazines and newspapers from the Second World War, the Good War:

"Fly the Flag of Israel on every house, on every business, on every vehicle."

"Remember to take your GAS MASK."

"To our Beloved Soldiers in Israel's armed forces. G-d Bless You and Guard You."

"Karen Hayesod extends a hearty welcome to the participants of Solidarity Mission of the Leadership of the Jewish Community of Mexico. Your presence at this time adds strength to our people."

"Sir, We arrived in Israel on January 7. . . . As we sit in the sealed room with our gas masks on, having placed the two babies in their *mamatim*, we cannot help but reflect on all that we have seen around us. We stand in awe at the courage and determination of the Israeli public. We see life during the day going on as near to normal as possible. We salute Israel for the fortitude shown under conditions that would devastate most nations, and we are proud to be among you at this time. Henny and Herb Margoshes, Boston."

"Sir, I am horrified to learn that observant Jews with beards are being supplied with gas masks which were intended for small children, at a time when there are not enough to equip the children. . . . Every Jew, having received dispensation from not shaving from the highest rabbinical authorities in the country, must shave or at least trim his beard so that a regular mask can be efficiently used. Not to do so constitutes the sin of endangering life."

*   *   *

Israel's war was London in the blitz, speeded up as everything was now, and colorized, but still the stuff of the late-night movies, the best of the good war, when everyone, not just soldiers, could be part of a brave and important stand simply by not running away. It was entirely a war of air raids. By this time, thirty-three Scud missiles had landed, almost all of them in greater Tel Aviv. The rockets had destroyed 148 homes or apartments, damaged another 3,991, caused 1,644 families to be evacuated, wounded 273 people; 518 people had been treated for anxiety reactions and 220 for the ill effects of mistakenly injecting themselves with atropine, the antidote for nerve gas. Fourteen people had died, two from the impact of missiles and twelve others of heart failure or in accidents relating to protective equipment.

Those who stayed for the blitz saw the war as the great test—of Israel and Israelis in general, and also of every single, specific person. What did you do in the war? would be the dividing question for fifty years. In fact, it was already. The question was a multipart one, an exercise in gradations. Who left the country completely? Who stayed in the country but left Tel Aviv for Jerusalem or some other safer place? Who stayed in Tel Aviv during the day but fled for Jerusalem at nightfall? Who stayed in Tel Aviv all the time but stayed in a sealed room at night?

For Max's birthday, we went out to dinner to a place we had been to once before, the Italiano de Montefiore, a small white room with a garden attached. It was a popular place, and in December, when we had last been there, it had been filled with people. This time, when we walked in, we saw two people—the bartender, polishing a glass, and the owner, watching the TV on a shelf over the bartender's head. The owner jumped up and led us to the best table, in front of a large window looking out on the empty street. He brought us a bottle of good Yarden cabernet sauvignon and sat down to join us for a drink. He was a thick, square man, the sort who automatically sighs when he sits.

He drank a can of diet Coke. "I would like a glass of wine, but my daughter has put me on a diet," he said. Sigh. "Forty-eight years old, on a diet." When I said there had been a lot more people in his restaurant the last time I came, he said one sour, terse thing—"Scuds"—and made a purse-lipped noise of disgust, like the fat detective Nero Wolfe's sound: pfui. "Pfui. This is not a war. No, it is not a war. It is something to scare people but it is not a war. As far as I am concerned, since you ask me, the government made a big mistake. It should not have closed everything up, made everyone stay at home. What has happened that is so bad? Nothing. But everybody hides at home like children afraid of the dark."

It was not the Israeli way. "I remember the first war, the war of independence. I was five years old. I lived five hundred yards from one of the big battles in Jaffa. They were fighting in the streets all around us, but my family never left. Now, everybody runs away from a few rockets. This is not right. We must fight. If you have a war, you do something about it. You don't just stay at home."

He drank some of his diet Coke, and it didn't help his mood. "Israel never wins in this kind of thing. You will see. When Iraq is gone, it will start again with Egypt, with Syria. It never changes. I do not trust any of them. We will have to give something, and no matter what we give it will not be what they want. Because you know what they want?"

What? I said, although I knew the answer.

"They want to kill us. They want to drive us into the sea."

He had fought in '67 and '73, driving tanks. "It is not the same spirit as it was then. People have changed in this country, they are not what they were. Israel is not what it was. All they care about now is earning enough money to buy a new car or something. They have forgotten the way we were. We have started to become like Americans, less patriotic, more materialistic, less willing to sacrifice for the country, more ambitious for the self. When the Scud attacks started, friends of mine left Tel

Aviv and went to Jerusalem or Eilat. I am talking about *men*." He shook his head.

"I really do not understand that. I understand a mother with her children doing that. She has no choice. But I do not understand men doing this. In the old days, men stayed in their places and did what they had to do. Now—pfui. I do not understand my friends. After the war is over, I will judge them forever in a different way. But I will not do anything about it. I will just tell myself I know them better now for what they are. Their children, I think, will judge them differently too. They will go to school and the children of those who stayed will say things to them, say, 'Why did your father leave?' And they will come home and look at their fathers and wonder."

He waved around at the empty tables. "For four weeks we closed at night completely because there was no one out at all. On Monday we opened up again at night for the first time since the attacks began. No one came, not one customer. Tuesday night no one came. Wednesday night no one came. On Thursday one man came. Tonight, you are the only ones. The people of Tel Aviv have become afraid of the dark."

They don't want to die, I said. You can't blame them for that.

"Listen. My parents came from Russia in 1926. They risked their lives every day to build a home. They lived through riots. They lived through three wars. They never ran away. That is the way we used to live. We said to ourselves, 'It is our country and you do what you have to do.' Now, suddenly, it is a different way. People run away. We always want to think about ourselves that we are different from other people. That in other countries people run from danger but not here. Now we have people running away every day. It is not good for the country. I don't understand it."

We left him not understanding it. I told an Israeli friend about this conversation. He was in his thirties, and he had a wife and daughter. "He says he doesn't understand?" my friend said. "I don't understand *him*. People leave because they are afraid for their family. How can you criticize a person with children who leaves the city? These old people, they only talk like this because they do not have young children still, and they have forgotten what it is like. Why should anyone be expected to subject their children to Saddam's missiles? It will not help win the war any faster if somebody's ten-year-old daughter is killed."

For all his talk, though, my friend had not left the city himself, and his wife and daughter were also in Tel Aviv. "It is funny," he said. "When the war started, my wife left the city with our daughter, Gaby, and went to a kibbutz. They stayed for one week and then came back. They were unhappy and Gaby was bored. Now they are back and it is better. They are staying at the Sheraton and Gaby can ride up and down in the elevators. And last week, school started again, so it is almost like normal times. It is funny how the longer it goes on the more you get so you don't worry about it anymore. If anyone had told me two years ago I would stay in Tel Aviv with my wife and child during a missile attack, I would have said, 'Are you crazy?' But it turned out to be different from what I thought. It turned out to be something you just end up doing."

The thirty-fourth and thirty-fifth missiles arrived at about ten o'clock at night on February 14, catching me on the seventeenth floor of the Tel Aviv Hilton, in the Executive Lounge, stirring a Campari and orange juice. I had just made it, in the little kitchen at one end of the room, and I was walking out again, paying attention to the way the Campari muddied the orange juice in a pleasingly purplish way, when everyone stood up all at once, and put down their drinks, and picked up their gas masks. Now that I listened, I could hear the air-raid sirens in the distance. They were surprisingly discreet, hardly rising above the level of the hubbub in the room. Still, everyone else had heard their first notes. I suppose it was a sound you developed a sensitivity for. I put down the drink and picked up my mask and went out to the hall, and got into an open elevator. The rules were that you were supposed to go to the bomb shelter, but I hoped to see a Patriot interception, so I pushed the button for the eighth floor, where CBS had a corner suite that offered a view of the city skyline and sea. There were two other people in the elevator, a beautiful couple. She looked like Daryl Hannah and he looked like money and tennis. They asked me where I was going, and when I told them they wanted to come too. "We were going to the shelter, but we'd much rather be where the action is," the woman said, nodding her head fast with excitement, making the light shiver in her big yellow hair.

She was wearing a little dress that scooped low over her breasts and rose high on her legs, and she had slung over one shoulder, casually as you would a blazer, a gas kit. The gas kits were issued by the government and each kit contained one gas mask, one syringe of atropine and one container of fuller's earth, which is a kind of powdery clay and was meant to be dusted on the skin to absorb mustard gas. In their pure government-issue form, the gas kits were not attractive—awkward rectangular boxes of heavy-duty brown cardboard with official writing all over the sides. But Tel Aviv is as fashion-conscious as Paris, and deplores the utilitarian. Women immediately began to remake the kits at home, covering them with fabric and attaching to them pieces of braid or ribbon or metal chain so they could be swung from the shoulder, like a purse. Within a couple of weeks, stores were selling commercially made coverings in bright-colored nylon, and by the time I arrived in Israel, a lot of women owned several—one or two nylon numbers for the day and a fancier job for evening wear. The woman in the elevator had one of emerald green, densely decorated with glossy black squiggles that looked Japanese. I had seen only one I liked better, carried by a pretty young woman I had walked behind on Dizengoff Street the evening before. She wore a tiny, tight black velvet skirt, black leather boots that came up over her knees, and a black satin bustier. Her gas kit hung from one shoulder, and it was in the same black velvet as her skirt, studded with rhinestones that flirted in the streetlight's shine.

On the balcony of the CBS office, I could see clearly enough through the eyepieces of the gas mask, but in every direction there was nothing to see, none of the brilliant-white flashes in the sky that every television viewer knew, just the black Mediterranean and the India-ink skyline and the gray-purple sky. It was, except for the subdued wailing of the sirens, a peaceful scene, nothing like the hysteria of Baghdad. It was over very quickly, and it ended not with any bangs that I could hear, but with the whimper of sirens moaning to a halt.

After the all clear, I went downstairs to hear Nachman Shai. He was a brigadier in the Israeli Defense Forces, and after an attack, it was his job to tell the country what had happened, in a limited way. The briefings were carried live on television and radio, and Shai had become a much-admired national figure. Schoolgirls wrote to him asking for autographs. Women named babies after him. On Dizengoff Street, the city's great boulevard of shops and cafés, I had seen, in a store called Zoom, a Nachman Shai poster for sale, hanging up in the front window with Paul Newman as poolroom hustler and James Dean as pouting youth. In the poster, Shai held a red phone to his ear and he was sweating slightly and looking haggard but mildly handsome.

In person, he seemed an unlikely heartthrob. He was a slight, smallish man with sloping shoulders and mousy brown hair that fell in a thick and unruly shock over his forehead. He had a modest, pleasant smile and wore wire-frame aviator-style eyeglasses and a green uniform that was, in the Israeli fashion, purposely casual—no jacket, no tie, the sleeves rolled up. He walked into the room in a hurry, sweating a little, his hair slightly messy, no makeup. He rested his hands on the edges of the podium that stood against a backdrop of three Israeli flags, and went immediately, without any flourishes, to the matter.

"Good evening. Tonight we have had our fourteenth attack.

Altogether, this brings to thirty-five the number of missiles that have been launched into Israel by Iraq." He pronounced his th's as z's, so "with" came out "wiz." He shortened and thickened his vowels too; "sealed rooms" was "sid rhums." He passed out his information in small, dry bits, lubricated by the thinnest coating of wit.

"Can you confirm that one missile landed in an industrial estate?"

"I can confirm that one landed in the south of Israel. That is all I can confirm on that subject."

"Can you speculate on why the missiles landed where they landed?"

"Why? Why not?"

"General, I know that you can't be specific about locations, but you said one missile landed in the south. Can you confirm that another one landed in the north?"

"Well, there's not much left to choose from, is there? We only have north, south, east and west." A faint laugh. "But I would not like to be more specific. No doubt Saddam Hussein is launching different missiles to hit different locations and we do not wish to give him more information than he may get from other sources."

And that was pretty much that. At first I could not see his appeal, but as I thought about it, I began to see why people liked him so much. A flashier type would have made everyone nervous, but by his very blandness and reticence, Nachman Shai reassured. His nightly appearances fixed his image with that of the government he represented, suggesting that the men in charge of everyone's fate were also unexcitable, calm, intelligent, and nice. That was a comforting thought to take to bed, and people were grateful to Nachman Shai for providing it.

On Dizengoff Street the war was *la mode.* At the Comme Il Faut store, the mannequins in the window wore dresses made of the clear plastic sheeting used to seal rooms against gas attacks. Loops and bows of shiny black ribbon connected and accentuated the pieces of plastic, and the design was cleverly arranged so that the pieces overlapped each other to make strategic areas a little less than fully transparent. At a bridal store, the four bride mannequins were accessorized for attack. Each wore a gas mask, spray-painted white, and gloves and veil made of the plastic sheeting. The veils were decorated with little white and green and yellow atropine needles.

Dizengoff's cheaper clothes stores, the ones geared to tourists and teenagers, offered a range of war-related T-shirts. Some offered simple, explicit statements of personal courage: "I survived Israel in 1991." Others, more pointed, made explicit the accusatory question that hovered in the Israeli air. "I survived the Gulf War in Israel. Where Were You?" Some were exuberantly, exultantly boastful. In a tiny grocery store bedecked with Israeli flags, I found a bunch of shirts that crowed their derision of Saddam and their confidence in victory: "Saddam, Wanted Dead or Alive, $100 Reward" "Americans, Don't Worry. Israel Is Behind You." The most abusive had no words but needed none—a drawing of Saddam Hussein sitting, surrounded by destruction, naked in the desert, shitting in his helmet.

The shopkeepers said the most popular shirt was none of these, though. It depicted, in a series of drawings, the successful resolution of a Scud raid. The first drawing was of a snake, with the words underneath it that were broadcast on the radio to signal an attack: *Nahash Tsefa*—viper. The second drawing showed a family sitting calmly in a sealed room, with a little baby in a little sealed box. The third drawing showed the undamaged, peaceful skyline of the city. *"Sharav Kaved"* was the caption. "All clear." People found the shirts soothing, the shopkeeper said.

At the Guavanam art gallery, the front window was dominated by a print of a Magritte painting, a big blue puff-clouded sky over surf, with a large black rock hanging between the two.

A photograph of Saddam's head had been pasted under the rock. The owner of the shop said he had sold three of the prints, at a good price of 120 shekels each. "I put the Saddam face in there just for a joke, you understand, and put it in the window to make people laugh," he said. "So, to my surprise, this man comes in and says he wants to buy it. I say, 'Okay, I will take out the Saddam face and sell it to you.' He says, 'No, no, no, I want it only with Saddam.' So, fine, the customer is always right. I made up a second one, and it sold too, and then a third one. Now, this is the fourth."

America and Americans were the passion of the city. The Israelis were astonished and delighted that for the first time in two thousand years, somebody was willing to stand up and fight for the Jews. Every day, there were ads in the newspapers thanking America—on February 14: "The publisher, editor, and staff of *The Jerusalem Post* wish the U.S. Patriot crews in Israel a Happy—and not too homesick—Valentine's Day"—and there were several billboards around town with the same messages. Norman Schwarzkopf imitators performed in television comedy skits and the general's smiling red face appeared in a newspaper advertisement for Old Virginia cigarettes. That ad, more than anything else, recalled the mood of an earlier war. It could have come out of *Life* magazine in 1945. *"Take a jouncing Jeep, a Johnny Doughboy—an 'I'd walk a mile' grin—add 'em all up and you get CAMEL—the fighting man's cigarette."*

Walking by the hotel pool one sunny day, I wandered into a picnic hosted by local dignitaries for the Patriot crews. American flags flew over the swimming pool, the tables were done up in red, white, and blue, and Stars and Stripes bunting festooned the diving board. Flanking the entranceway were painted plywood statues of George Bush, with his hand outstretched for a handshake, and the Marlboro Man. To my surprise, the artist had perfectly captured Bush's smile—that nervous, kick-me grimace of an unsure son. By unkind contrast, the Marlboro Man stood with an air of laconic assurance. He sported a six-gun on his hip, and a cigarette dangled, Bogartly, from one corner of his mouth.

The colors of the flags strung on wires across the pool mixed fractals of red and blue among the diamonds of white Mediterranean sun in the turquoise water. Lunch was over, and the young soldiers were lying about on plastic lounge chairs by the pool. It was a surprise to see how big they were. The Arab soldiers I had become accustomed to seeing were skinny; these boys bulged out of their clothes in bunches of muscle and thick padding.

Major Michael Woods, a public information officer for the 322nd Army Air Defense Command, intercepted me as I was walking over to talk to a group of the soldiers. He surprised me, talking about the reception the Americans had received, by speaking in his own voice, not the official one.

"I've been in the army for sixteen years, and I'll tell you, I've never been to a country that welcomed me like this. The generosity and warmth have just been unbelievable. You know what is amazing? People bring us cakes and cookies. On Valentine's Day we all got cards. We've had comedians and singers come perform for us in our barracks. I'm not kidding."

I didn't think he was kidding, but I didn't blame him for assuming that I did. It was amazing. In his lifetime—in mine, too—American soldiers were more often figures of vilification than adulation. This kind of thing was something a soldier of Major Woods's generation had only read about, or seen pictures of—the nurse kissing the sailor in Times Square, the mademoiselles in the glorious spring of Paris's liberation. It was not something that happened anymore. "We get invitations from private citizens to come stay at their homes for the weekend, to come swim at their pools or visit their beach houses," he was going on. "When we walk down the street, shopkeepers come out and give us candy and nuts. We were all invited to dinner

at a kibbutz one Saturday and some famous Israeli singer came
up to sing for us. When we got up to leave, the people ap-
plauded us. You know, soldiers are not used to people applaud-
ing them. It's, you know, like almost overwhelming."

He thought of something else. "I mean, have you seen those
huge billboards they've put up? 'Salute to the Patriots.' Good
grief. I mean, it's like we are the cool thing or something. Did
you know fatigues are the height of fashion? It's true. I've had
people walk up to me and offer me money for my hat. I tell
them that they can get one just like it in an army surplus store,
but they want to buy it off the head of an American. Amazing."

At about this point, something caught the attention of a
group of five soldiers lounging by the far end of the pool, and
they suddenly stirred themselves, sitting up in their chairs. In
a moment, they were on their feet, waving to someone high in
the hotel. Looking up, I could see a small female form standing
on a balcony on one of the top floors, waving in return. Encouraged, the soldiers began lifting up their T-shirts, exposing their
chests, to encourage the woman in the hotel to do the same, and
I was looking up, hoping with them that she would, when Major
Woods saw what was going on. "You don't want to do that,
mister!" he said, and the soldiers sat glumly back down. By
chance, I later talked to the woman on the balcony. She said she
had understood the nature of the soldiers' request, but had been
inhibited by the sight of several television cameras videotaping
the lunch. Too bad, she said, she would have liked to oblige.

Late on Max's birthday night, the television networks threw a
party in a ballroom in the hotel. When we got there a little
before twelve, it was already a half hour old. The timing of the
party's start suggested its point. Most Scuds landed between
2:00 and 3:00 A.M.; to dance and drink in the hours before and
including the peak danger time was a nice bit of nose-thumbing
at Saddam's missiles, and, for that matter, at death.

We danced for three hours. Everyone did, hundreds of people, jammed in so close to each other that you weren't dancing with one person but half a dozen around you, sliding, sweaty touches of skin every time you moved. The disc jockey played good old music—"Twist and Shout," "Johnny B. Goode," "Back in the USSR." Sometimes he crooned a mantra of American icon names over the music. "Marlon Brando," he murmured into the microphone. "Marilyn Monroe, James Dean, Robert Redford, Paul Newman, Eddie Murphy, Mickey Rooney, Sean Penn, Fred Astaire, Kim Basinger, Sylvester Stallone, James Dean, Marilyn Monroe, Paul Newman."

Fifty-year-old men danced with beer bottles in their hands, grinning and sweating, as if they were back on a last spring Saturday night, soft, light air and everyone young and hard-bellied, at the best frat party of the year. They danced with the local girls, the young women all wild hair and red lipstick and big hoop earrings, like Jersey beach girls, except prettier, shaking and shimmering in skirts that were itsy-bitsy bands of thigh-stretched black no more than eighteen inches from waistline to hem, scoop-neck T-shirts and leather boots with stiletto heels, tube tops and tank tops and spaghetti straps and black leather and rhinestones, and not a pair of pantyhose in the room. The baby spotlight bounced from body to body, picking up the shine of sweat on skin. On the stereo, Madonna was singing a request that someone spank her. I saw a soldier dancing in his uniform, an American TV correspondent dancing with a cellular phone in his back pocket, a videotape editor dancing with a neck brace on his head, like a turban. On the stereo, Frank Sinatra was saying that if you could make it in New York, you could make it anywhere; everyone was singing along in agreement. "The chairman of the board!" the disc jockey was yelling. "Mr. Old Blue Eyes!"

At quarter to two in the morning, the music stopped with an abrupt scrape of needle, and as everyone stopped with it, the sound of the air-raid siren began. For a moment, everything in the room was as still as ice, and then, at once, we all surged forward in the direction of the door, and then we all stopped in the same at-once way, as we heard the disc jockey laughing and the music starting up again. It was such a good party no one even got angry. At two-thirty, the last song played, and everyone sang along with it, a moment of crystalline weirdness, standing in a basement in a city that was in the middle of the latest evolution of a fight that had been going on for forty-three years (or five thousand years, if you took the long view), singing the faintly embarrassing words of a children's dream. "Harmony and understanding, sympathy and trust abounding, no more falsehoods or derisions, golden living dreams of visions, mystic crystal revelation, and the world's true liberation, Aquarius, Aquarius!"

The singers spun out up the elevators and through the halls, drunk and happy, to smaller parties and private pairings; no one wanted the night to stop, the best party of the war.

I went out on one of the balconies of the CBS offices to sit and drink a last beer. Past the surf and the breakwater off the shore, I could see the patrol boats of the Israeli Defense Forces bobbing softly. Inside, a boom box was playing Springsteen. On the other end of the balcony, a camera was locked down, the lens pointing at the skyline, the machine doing its silent work of copying the unchanging picture, so that if a Scud suddenly came across the sky, or if the skyline blew to flinders, the picture would be captured.

AN UNPROMISING LAND

I LEFT ISRAEL two days after the party, and in the same round-about, slightly skulking fashion as I had entered. In the early morning, I caught a taxi in front of the hotel, like a man going to breakfast instead of another country, and it took me out of Tel Aviv. We drove south for several hours, following the coastline, past the old towns of Jaffa and Ashkelon and the barbed-wire frontiers of Gaza.

In midmorning, we arrived at a spot on the map called Rafa, the crossing from Israel into Egypt, from Judea to Arabia. The Israeli customs shed was a clean white building of air condition-ing and fluorescent light, bordered by judiciously watered grasses and flowers, set in the middle of sand. It was Israel in miniature, an isolated creation of modernity in an environment that was naturally and unremittingly hostile; if the staff did not come every day and sweep out the place, and water the plants, and feed the generators, the sand would soon drift into the buildings, choke out the grass, and grind the gears of the ma-chinery to a halt.

The Israeli border agent, a pleasant and efficient woman, pleasantly and efficiently stamped my Israel/Egypt-Only pass-port and ushered me through a gate in a wire fence where a blue bus waited on the tarmac. In a few minutes the driver came out and started it up, and off we drove, with the door open to catch the breeze. I was the only passenger, and I felt a little absurd, sitting in the seat behind the driver with my bags on my lap, wondering if anyone else had passed through the crossing that morning, or if the entire mechanism of state had been cranked up for me. The bus went down the road and through a short stretch of sand and disgorged me at another fence and another building, the immigration and customs hall on the Egyptian side of the line.

There are moments in travel when you can actually feel the shock of culture shock, when, passing from one world to another, the change is so sharp and deep as to stagger the senses. As I walked into the immigration and customs building, Egypt suffused me, getting in my eyes and nostrils and ears. The air was different: dustier, mustier, older, thick with scents that battled each other in the nose—the sharp-sour smoke of Turkish tobacco and the saccharine-flower miasma that lurks in places where perfume is easier to come by than showers; from the food counter in the corner, meat cooking and tea brewing; wafting up from the linoleum, a mélange of old wax and fresh flake soap.

Time, sped up to Western Standard by Israel, decelerated so abruptly that I was nearly nauseated, as if struck down with the horological bends. Everything was thick and slow and drowsing—the feel of the file room of the Department of Weights and Measures on a Wednesday afternoon. Nothing was white, all was again shadows and shades of old yellow, gray-green, and brown. On one end of a long, smooth, butt-worn wooden bench sat a white-whiskered man in a gray robe, reading a book, the cloth cover of which was creased and darkened with palm grease. At the other end a family of four sat in sleepy silence, the squat, bulky mother, the thin, consumptive father, even the children all dragged half under the narcoleptic currents.

Along one side of the room, a wood partition divided the waiting area from the work space of the Egyptian immigration officials. The wall was punctuated with metal-barred windows, like a line of tellers' openings in an old-fashioned bank. I put down my bag, sending a little puff of dust motes in the air, and went to the first window. There was no one there, but I waited (contentedly enough: I was already lulled deep back into Arab time), and eventually one of the many men sitting at the many desks came up and asked for my passport. He went through it page by page, studying each with deep and leisurely care. In time, he spoke. I must wait, he said. The supervisor would have to see me.

I sat on an old iron handcart that had been parked, probably by Ptolemy, in a corner. After half an hour I got up and walked over to the food counter to watch the tea brew, and then to the rear wall, to study a travel poster of the Nile and another of the Sphinx, and then back to the luggage cart. Thirty minutes later, I made the circuit again, more slowly, and fifteen minutes after that the man who had taken my passport appeared in front of me and told me to follow him. We went through a door, down a short hall, and into a room where a man with the air of being in charge of things sat behind a desk. Two lesser bureaucrats sat in front of him, one on the sofa and one on a chair. The man behind the desk was holding forth, and the minions were listening, and all were sipping from little glasses of tea that sent tendrils of steam snaking up around their faces.

In a Western office, I would have thought that I was interrupting a meeting, and would have backed out with apologies, but I knew by now that in Arabia office life was patterned after an older rhythm. An official in his government room received visitors in much the same fashion as his grandfather had in his courtyard—casually, endlessly, and with a good deal of overlapping, since no one was ever in any particular hurry. The love of talk and the love of manners dictated against hurrying into any matter at hand, and conversation proceeded to its destination like a bus on a back-country run. At times, with particularly polite or amiable hosts, it seemed like the terminus might never be reached, but once I got used to it, it struck me as a sensible enough way to do things. It was the Great Circle Route of talk; the line between points A and B looked to be curving far out of its way, but was actually straight and direct. In the furbelows and folderol of the chat between the first cup of tea and the second, and between the guest accepting one of the host's cigarettes and the host accepting one of the guest's, there was much accomplished. Each man sniffed out, from the small signals that encode the way a glass of tea is stirred and sipped or the offer of a match, enough about the other so that when the time came for business, both knew better than before how best to proceed.

When the particular cycle I had interrupted came to its natural end, we all stood for elaborate good-byes, and then the chief bureaucrat and I sat down again, and I accepted a cigarette, and more tea arrived, and we muddled the sugar with small spoons of stamped aluminum and drank elaborately cautious first slurps together, and then he spoke:

So, I had been in Israel?

I had.

What did I think of Israel?

It was an interesting country.

Um. What did I think of the Israelis?

An interesting people.

Um. What did I think of the Scuds?

They did not seem to be having their desired effect.

Um. And the Patriots, what did I think of those?

They, on the contrary, did seem to be having their desired effect.

Um. And this war, what did I think of that?

Well, it was difficult to say.

Um. Um. Saddam Hussein, what did I think of him? Mr. Bush said he was a crazy man, a bad man. Did I think he was crazy and bad?

Well, at the moment, that too was difficult to say.

I was all nerves at stepping wrong; Egypt was allied with America against Iraq, but the newspapers in Amman said the

man in the Egyptian street secretly loved Saddam. This might
be true, or it might not; who knew? And who knew the feelings
of this particular man? I essayed a careful turning of tables.
What did he think of Mr. Bush's remarks?

A break for the imbibing of tea and the lighting of cigarettes.
Please, try one of mine. Then:

"I think it is a bad war, very bad, crazy. Mr. Bush is right. He
is a bad man. This is well known."

That is exactly what I was going to say, I said. It is difficult
to say, as I said, but it is the truth, and, as you are right to point
out, well known.

"Yes, of course. It is strange that we find ourselves again in
this. You know, we prefer peace. We have made our peace with
Israel. Do you think that is a good thing?"

I took a flier, and said yes, I thought so.

"I think so as well."

We both settled back, well satisfied, and finished our tea, the
Great Circle Route between East and West safely navigated
once again. He returned me my passport and ushered me out,
and a few minutes later it was stamped, my bags were gently
searched, and I was standing in the sand.

Cairo was 220 miles away, across the Sinai Desert. Three or
four taxis were parked outside the immigration building, and I
chose one of the drivers, or rather he chose me by grabbing my
bags and putting them in the trunk of his car. It was a dubious
sort of car. It had been born, some years back, a green Plymouth,
but it was now a machine of all nations. The right front side
panel was blue and possibly of Citroën origin. A door was red,
and of a Volvo look. The front hood had certainly belonged to
a Mercedes-Benz. I thought of a story I had heard in Tel Aviv.
As the Camp David deadline neared for Israel to return to
Egypt the Sinai (taken in the 1967 war), some Tel Aviv and
some Sinai men of business hit upon an innovation in smug-

gling: don't cross the border, let the border cross you. The bedouin drove a fleet of new Mercedes-Benzes from Tel Aviv to the Sinai, wrapped them up, and buried them in the sand. When the Sinai was returned, the cars were suddenly in Egypt, without a shilling of tariff paid. The car-farmers dug them up, dusted them off, and drove them to Cairo. I hoped I was sitting in a car that owed part of itself to the great Mercedes crop of Camp David.

The driver got behind the wheel, full of competent intent to get us moving, and we did actually start moving, but stopped immediately. One of the customs agents was chasing us, a suit-case in his hand. He needed, it developed, to visit his mother in Cairo, and would I mind if he hitched a ride with us? Not at all. The driver put his suitcase in the trunk and got back behind the wheel, and we started off again. And stopped.

A woman was chasing us now, and she had a suitcase too. She was in her late thirties, her coarse, handsome face heavily rouged and powdered, and she was one of those women who look large, yet are larger than they look. From bosom to bottom to ankle, she was pinched and squeezed and channeled and choked to make out of her something less than she was. Her shiny black skirt strained and stretched from hip to hip, a confinement of bombazine, allowing her almost no leeway in movement, so that her nyloned thighs rasped against each other with every shift or step. Her big feet blossomed over the tops of glossy (but dusty) little patent-leather pumps that tapered, in heels of cantilevered improbability, to pencil-necked shafts, upon which the whole of her depended; a fair-minded judge would have divorced her from those shoes on grounds of mental and physical cruelty and inadequate means of support. Between the suitcase banging her in the knees, the skirt hobbling her at the hips, and the heels wobbling in the gravel underfoot, she could scarcely walk at all. There was a sudden, sharp crack, and she lurched to the side and down, with a little *Oh*, the suitcase skidding from her hand away in the dirt. A heel had succumbed to its inadequacy and lay broken on its side. We ran to help her, and the driver hauled her slowly to her feet, and by the time she had dusted herself down and settled things in their proper places, her suitcase was somehow in the trunk, and we were four to Cairo. As the only paying member of the expedition, I got the front passenger seat.

We drove first along the sea, the little blacktop road cutting between the sand of the desert on one hand and the sand of the dunes on the other. There was a pause at a resort hotel that stood all by itself on a beach that was empty on either side for as far as you could see. The water was shallow, with a surf that could barely raise the energy for a few scant ripples and a weak froth, actual waves being beyond its ambitions. The only vegetation was a tiny strip of irrigated grass around the edge of the hotel. The sun shone down out of a blue and cloudless sky, and it was hot enough to raise a sweat even in February. In the summer, it must have been something close to torture to lie out there in the hundred-degree white light.

The driver was a gregarious man, and he bustled us all into the hotel to meet the manager, who was a friend of his and who, he said, would no doubt arrange for us a fine lunch. But the manager was sorry to say that lunch was off this month. The cook was only doing dinner, on account of the fact that there wasn't a single guest registered in the hotel. "It is the war," the manager said dolefully. "Everybody is afraid to come."

He must not have had much to do, managing an empty hotel, for he had plenty of time for us. He showed us around the place for a full and mildly depressing fifteen minutes. "Here is the swimming pool. As you can see it is empty at the moment and we are painting it. But the workmen are not working today. It is very hard to make them work. They are lazy. Here is the Ping-Pong room, but it is padlocked and I left the keys at the desk. Here is the terrace for lunch, very nice, but of course we have no lunch." I admired him, though. It must have been a temptation for him to let standards slip, but he was still running a tight ship. The lobby floor was waxed and polished, the grass was watered, and he himself was dressed, elaborately and flaw-lessly, in a dove-gray morning suit, with striped pants and a cutaway coat. He walked us to the door and we left him stand-ing there, alone by the road in the sand, looking like a groom who had gotten impossibly lost.

At the town of El Arish, we stopped to buy a bag of oranges, a bag of dates, and a bag of pistachio nuts before turning south-west onto the two-lane blacktop that would take us across the Sinai proper. We proceeded in an extraordinary clatter, the radio endlessly wailing of lost love, the conversation between the driver and the two in the back conducted in a series of yells atop that, the car itself a feast of engine whine and grinding gears and rattling steel, all the windows open (because of the heat) and the wind whistling through. At first the talk was in English, out of politeness to me, but I was sleepily unresponsive, so it switched to Arabic, picked up speed and volume, and washed on around and over me. I woke for lunch, a movable snack, as we passed around the bag of pistachios and the oranges. I worked my way through a small hill of nuts, tossing the shells in periodic handfuls out the window. The oranges were small and fresh, with their dark-green leaves still attached, and unusually sweet and good. They left my hands sticky, and the tissue pressed upon me to dry them stuck in bits of fluff and fiber to the sugar on my fingers.

We occasionally passed a bedouin tent, and even more rarely a few small houses, but it was all in all too mean a place for life; of baked, cracked dirt and stone, cut at rare intervals with the dry gulch of a *wadi*. It rained here only in the period from November through March, and then sparsely; the average an-nual rainfall was five inches a year. It was the sort of land that easily defeated efforts to make something of it. In the excited years after 1948, when dreams seemed more reachable, the

Israelis had tried to make the desert on their side of the border bloom, but it had not, and they had mostly quit trying. Unyielding to man, the land was unchanging. It was the same now as when Moses led the children of Israel (a large and unwieldy family: 604,550 men of fighting age, and their families) out of the pharaoh's Egypt and into the wilderness. Driving through the bleakness and dust, I pitied the wanderers. What a grinding awfulness it must have been. Three thousand years later, the pain of a people chosen by a difficult God for an impossible task leaps fresh from the pages.

"Would to God we had died by the hand of the Lord in the land of Egypt, when we sat over the flesh pots, and ate bread to the full!" the people cried. "Why have you made us come up out of Egypt, and have brought us into this wretched place which cannot be sowed; nor bring forth figs, nor vines, nor pomegranates, nor water to drink?" They salivated for the food they had left behind. "We remember the fish that we ate in Egypt free of cost. The cucumbers come into our mind, and the melons, and the leeks, and the onions and the garlic."

God gave them water and manna, which every morning lay "like unto hoar frost on the ground." The manna was white, and resembled coriander seed, and tasted of flour and honey. "And the people went about, and, gathering it, ground it in a mill, and boiled it in a pot; and made cakes thereof of the taste of bread tempered with oil." Still, they felt strongly that man doth not live by bread alone, and said, "Who shall give us flesh to eat?"

God's behavior must have made forty years in the Sinai even more of a trial than it would normally be. He was quick to anger and, as he often reminded the Israelites, terrible in his wrath. When a man was found gathering sticks on the Sabbath, "the Lord said to Moses: Let that man die. Let all the multitude stone him without the camp." When Core, son of Issar, son of Caath, son of Levi, led a group in unwise challenge of Moses, God had the earth swallow them. "And they went down alive into hell, the ground closing upon them: and they perished from among the people." When some of the fellows committed fornication with the daughters of Moab, and flirted with the religion of Beelphegor, God fixed it so "there were slain four and twenty thousand men."

And so on, throughout Exodus, Leviticus, Numbers, and Deuteronomy, an unending torment of the same. From Succoth to Pi-hahiroth, through the desert of Etham to Mara, to Elim, to the Red Sea and across it, to the desert of Sin, to Daphca, to Alus, to Rephidim, to Mount Sinai, to Hazeroth, to Rethma, to Remmomphares, to Lebna, to Ressa, to Ceelatha, to Mount Sepher, to Arada, to Maceloth, to Thahath, to Thare, to Methca, to Hesmona, to Moseroth, to Benejaacan, to Mount Gadgad, to Jetebatha, to Hebrona, to Asiongaber, to the desert of Sin (again), to Mount Hor, to Salmona, to Phunon, to Botoh, to Ijeabarim, to Dibongab, to Helmondeblathaim, to the mountains of Abarim, to the plains of Moab, to the river Jordan, across that, and, finally, to Jericho in the land of Canaan—every step of the way was hell, and he who survived the heat and the beasts and the perishing thirst might just as easily fall afoul of the God who brooked no nonsense. I doubted if I would have made it as far as Rephidim.

Somewhere in the middle of all this empty, we had a flat. Any one of the tires could have gone—they were all as bald as good lies—but it was the left rear that chose to blow, in a pop like a backfire that segued into the flap-flap-flap of rubber slapping the road. The driver stopped, we all got out, and I went to the trunk, to start taking out the bags so we could get at the spare, but that, the driver said, wasn't necessary; there was no spare. I doubted if there was a gas station, or even a house, in fifty miles, but he was not concerned, and he was right. We leaned against the car, smoking, and after five minutes or so a car came along, and the driver stood in the middle of the road, and it stopped. There were five or six men in the car, and they all got out to see the flat. When everyone had had his say about this, the driver of the other car gave the driver of our car his spare tire, and all the men gave advice to help the jacking and changing operation along. As we were setting off again, I said I was surprised that this stranger had been willing to give up his only spare tire.

"Oh, it is not a problem," the driver said. "He tells me he lives in El Salhiya, and I tell him I have a cousin in El Salhiya, so next week I will visit my cousin and bring this man his tire back."

But, I said, by giving the spare to you, he left himself without one.

"He doesn't need it. He has no flat."

But what if he does develop a flat?

"Then of course he will stop another car and borrow a tire from some other man."

The Sinai Peninsula is a fat triangle, whose base is the seacoast and whose sides are formed by the Gulf of Aqaba, which separates Egypt from Saudi Arabia, and the Red Sea, which separates western from eastern Egypt and (more grandly) Asia from Africa. The Suez Canal continues the line of water from the Red Sea jutting up between the Sinai and the rest of Egypt to the Mediterranean. We crossed the Suez at a point near the city of Ismailia, on an old and lumbering ferry low in the water from the cars that filled it. I wanted the canal to be a great sight, reflecting its importance in the world. Ferdinand de Lesseps's work was the first of the great modern canals and one of man's all-time feats in the imposition of will over nature: 120 miles long, 328 to 383 yards wide, thirty-three feet deep, a decade in the digging. In political terms the canal was important too. It was for the sake of the Suez that England occupied Egypt in 1882, beginning the scramble for Africa that would see the

European states carve up an entire continent in twenty years, and it was for the sake of the Suez—and the vanished power that it represented—that England and France attacked Egypt in 1956, after Gamal Abdel Nasser nationalized the canal. Nasser's audacious and ultimately successful play was an epochal event. To an entire generation of young Arab nationalists, it suggested a sweeping truth: the imperialists' days were over. Age had caught up with the colonial masters, and they were toothless and frail; in the future, the Arab states would do what they wanted and take what they wanted, and the West would do nothing. Saddam Hussein was nineteen years old when Nasser won his great victory; he joined the Baath Party a few months later.

But there was not much in the actual sight of the Suez that stirred the heart or mind. A great canal is at least as impressive a creation as a great bridge or a great skyscraper, but it is all work and no play, the dull boy of engineering. A suspension bridge, with its sky-reaching towers, great looping cables, and spaghetti straps lifting up the roadway, is a magic trick in steel: what holds up that which holds up the bridge? A great sky-scraper is, as Louis Sullivan said, "every inch a proud and soaring thing, rising in sheer exultation." A canal, even a great canal, is a ditch filled with still water.

There was one thing of interest: on the far side of the canal, scattered here and there along the edge, were rusting steel pontoons. They were a kind of monument to the Arab world's sole quasi-victory against Israel, the remains of the temporary bridges the Egyptian engineers threw across the Suez for the tanks to roll over into what was then Jewish land, in 1973. That war had not been exactly won, but it had not been disastrously lost either, and the Arabs, gathering flowers where they might, took it as a triumph. "It was a very fine thing," the driver said, as we rolled off the ferry and past the metal hulks. "The engineers put up the bridges, and the tanks went across, and we made the Jews run."

Almost as soon as we crossed the canal, the world outside the window changed. At one moment, all was still sand, at the next, green—grass, and palm trees, and fields of vegetables, cotton, wheat, rice, barley, and maize. This was the beginning of the fertile delta of Lower Egypt, created by the silt-rich floods of the Nile. Life erupted, sprang forth from the green—bullocks in the fields, dogs by the road, hens and roosters among the mud houses, cormorants, and ibises wheeling above the flats by the water's edge. It was a childhood history lesson revealed as real: civilization began in the Fertile Crescent, in the land of the Nile and the Euphrates and the Tigris. Coming into the green of that from the parchment land of the Sinai, it seemed such an obvious fact. It was possible to live here.

After the fastness of the desert and the fields of the delta, Cairo overwhelmed, loomed up and sprawled out all at once, all over everything. Most cities, approached by road, reveal themselves gradually and in concentric stages, going from exurbia to suburbia to urbia, from scattered houses to housing developments to apartment houses. But twelve million people live in Cairo, and it has become as dense as a black hole. We passed abruptly from countryside into the cliffs and canyons of apartment towers. It was past dusk when we arrived, but the construction sites were lighted and the work was unstopping, everywhere you looked.

I had only three simple chores to do here: pick up my visa from the Saudi Arabian consulate, buy an airplane ticket that would take me to the sheikhdom of Bahrain, and arrange for a car to take me from Bahrain across the causeway to Dhahran, the Saudi Arabian oil city that was the jumping-off place for the ground war. The next morning I left the Cairo Marriott Hotel and Casino and hired Cairo Travellers, Transport & Tourism, Inc., which was a man and a taxicab, to take me to the Saudis.

"Maddening" is an ill-used word. People say some situation

is maddening when really they mean it is infuriating or frustrating. Cairo was actually maddening: trying to get something done in it made me feel, in no time at all, as if I was losing my mind. The Marriott was a big, old, pleasant hotel, situated in gardens across the street from the right bank of the Nile, overlooking that attractive river's placid sweep. Being in the hotel created an illusion of calm and order, one that vanished the second the car left the driveway and nosed into the traffic stream, and immediately stopped. The cars—an insane number of cars, driven at insane speeds, at insanely small distances from one another, honking insanely—swept us up and carried us over freeways, down highways, past byways, around circles, under overpasses and over underpasses, moving us deeper and deeper into the thing, slower and slower all the time, until we were inching along streets no bigger than goat paths, crawling along in a vast jam of cars, buses, horses, donkeys, camels, wagons, bicycles, motorcycles, pushcarts, dogs, cats, and humans. The millions of automobile engines made a waterfall roar, over which yammered the beeps and honks of the horns, through which rumbled the sound of twelve million people interrupting each other. The fumes from the mingled exhausts made the air a mixture of gasoline and diesel and oil so thick that it seemed possible the stuff could be recycled, gathered and refined to produce a new generation of petroleum products. We moved through the fog of this at a pace generally slower than a walk. The Saudi consulate was about four kilometers away, the driver said, and we should be there within the hour. He was only a little off; it took an hour and a quarter.

The driver parked the car, wedging it in a half-space, leaving its tail stuck out, blocking the narrow street. Instantly, two policemen appeared.

"They are here to watch the car for us so that these bad boys around here do not damage it," the driver said. "You must give them two pounds."

I put my hand in my pocket, and the driver looked shocked.

"Not now! They have not done anything for you yet. When you come back." I left the two guardians of the car chatting and smoking with the driver. There were indeed many bad boys around, or at least dirty boys, and they settled on me like a cloud as I walked up the street, mistering me for money, until I gave them each a coin and they ran off. The street was no wider than a car and a half, with narrow, broken sidewalks, but there wasn't a bit of space not claimed by some hustler or huckster or hawker. On the far curb, a scribe had set up a chair and an upended box for a table, and was hammering out a letter on an old portable Olympia. Next to him, a tea seller with his blackened urn and stacked glasses on a rough wooden cart; next, a legless pencil seller; down the block a bit, a pistachio man; working the middle of the street, a teenager with a bundle of newspapers. They all hustled and hollered in a world of dust. Apart from the cars and the noise, it was the dust that most impressed me about Cairo. I had thought highly of the dust of Baghdad, but I saw now that I had been overly impressionable. Cairo made Baghdad look as if it had just been scrubbed by Dutch hausfraus. A mixture of dirt, dust, and soot covered every surface, and it was impossible to stay clean for more than a few minutes. I had dressed in clothes suited to a visiting diplomat, leather shoes and white shirt and blue blazer, and I had been clean when I stepped from the car, but by the time I reached the consulate gates I was covered with the same scurf as the dirty boys and the vendors, a sort of brown dandruff that settled on and around me in a cloud, and moved with me.

In the waiting room of the Saudis, a large man behind a desk gave me a number and said to wait until it was called. There was no one else waiting in the room. At the end of the first hour, the large man said it might be another hour, and at the end of that, he said it was, alas, too late to do anything today, and perhaps I could return tomorrow.

The next morning I went back to the consulate, took a new number, and waited. After two hours, a sub-underling appeared to summon me to his office, where he took my passport and gave me, before he disappeared, two long forms to fill out, asking the Jew-catching questions that are usual in Arab-nation entry forms: name, original name, father's name, mother's name, mother's original name. After an hour, he came back to bring me into the larger room of an uber-underling, who silently examined my passport and the forms I had filled out, and did not offer tea or a cigarette. After a while, he waved me away, and after a while more, the telex from Washington arrived, and I was shuttled back to the waiting room, where I passed some more time studying the painting of King Fahd ibn Abdul Aziz and thinking what a mean, dissolute bastard he looked.

I was, although I didn't know it, having a fairly typical introduction to Saudi Arabia, and a fairly typical reaction. It was not fair, of course, I reminded myself. The Saudis were not used to dealing with foreign visitors; before the threat from Iraq obliged them to act otherwise, they had let almost no Westerners in. They were an isolated people. The heart of their country, the semi-desert Nejd, was cut off by mountains to the west and deserts to the east, south, and north. Their version of Islam, stemming from the eighteenth-century fundamentalist revival led by the Nejd sheikh Muhammad ibn Abd al-Wahab, was exceedingly puritanical and fiercely anti-Western. Theirs was an ancient, poor land that had, in just the last fifty years, become a rich nation. All these things would naturally make a folk somewhat xenophobic, somewhat arrogant, somewhat difficult. Nevertheless, they were the first really rude people I had met since I left New York, and I didn't like them.

At 1:00 P.M. I was called for a last time and the underling handed me my passport with a visa stamp from the Royal Embassy of Saudi Arabia beautiful in its splendor. At 2:00 P.M. I was at the Cairo airport, with a Gulf Air ticket for the 3:00 flight to Abu Dhabi, connecting to Bahrain. On the way to the gate, I saw one of those big plastic bowls charities put in international airports with a sign urging travelers to toss in their odd pieces of foreign currency. It was half filled with money, and I noticed a great many of the bills were Israeli shekels. I checked my wallet and found three or four one-shekel notes there. I jettisoned my last souvenirs of the devil-state, and tossed those into the bowl.

The car company I had called from Cairo had sent a driver to pick me up in Bahrain and bring me over the causeway to Saudi Arabia. He was a college student, nineteen years old, cheerful and chatty. He loaded my bags in the back and me in the front and wheeled around out of the airport. Instead of turning onto the causeway, however, he drove only a short way down the road and turned to pull into the parking lot of a Holiday Inn hotel. "Why are we going here?" I said.

He gave me an understanding look. "I thought you might like a drink or two, sir."

I did not want a drink, I said, a little stiffly.

He was surprised. "But I always stop here. All the gentlemen of the press prefer a drink before they go into Saudi Arabia."

The parking lot had the exciting air of excess about it. It was filled with Mercedes-Benzes and BMWs. The people coming and going were dressed for a high occasion, the men in shiny silk double-breasted suits with peaked lapels, padded shoulders, and pinched waists. Even the fatter men had their coats buttoned tight around their middles; if one can no longer show off the trim figure of youth, one can show off the corpulence of wealth. The women seemed divided in preference between exaggerated tartiness and exaggerated girlishness, but quite a few had combined both, with results that were almost literally stunning; the full sight was enough to rock you back on your heels. You might see, for instance, a pink ball gown with a tight satin top and a swirling, flouncing skirt, with a red sequined bolero jacket overtop it, and black-lace-and-rhinestone stockings underneath. Their makeup was a many-splendored thing, each face its own palette, each eyelid its own sunset.

I would have liked to stop and stare at this longer, but I had climbed on such a high horse in my original response to the suggestion of a drink that I could not see a way to climb down gracefully, so I told the driver to go on, onto the finest highway in the world. Driving on the causeway between Bahrain and Saudi Arabia is what it must have been like back in the palmy days of the late 1950s in America, when we had all the money there was and the amazing interstate system was sparkling new and the idea of bumper-to-bumper traffic from the Baltimore Harbor Tunnel to the George Washington Bridge was still just a twinkle in Detroit's eye. The road was three lanes in each direction, as smooth and as well lighted as a pool table in a good hall, and as straight as a cue.

THE HUNDRED-HOUR
ROUT

D HAHRAN IS A CITY of such overwhelming falsity that it
barely exists. Indeed, it did *not* exist until quite recently,
but was built, relatively speaking, all at once, in the space of a
few decades, in the abundance of wealth that came with oil. The
place where the city is, on the edge of the Persian Gulf, is
surrounded by oil fields, and the Arabian American Oil Company (ARAMCO, it is universally called), the inspired product
of nationalism and capitalism that handles the job of pumping
and shipping out the product of those fields, is the soul of
Dhahran.

The twenty thousand or so people working for ARAMCO
live in a city of their own, within the larger city of Dhahran,
behind a metal fence, apart not only in space but in time, apart
not only from Arabia but from the late twentieth century. The
ARAMCO city was built by company engineers and construction crews, largely in the 1950s and 1960s, and has remained
perfectly of that era, a model of a model suburban American
community of the days of Eisenhower and order and decent
living. It is as neat and precise as if it were put up by Seabees.
The roads are all laid out in a proper grid, except for the regular
insertions of culs-de-sac to break the monotony of planned
straight lines with the monotony of planned curved lines. Modest, neat houses line these roads, and each house has a lawn, just

as it would if it were back home and not in this waterless hellhole. (The coastal strip where Dhahran was built gets more rain than the rest of Saudi Arabia, but the rest gets none at all. The annual average waterfall of the country amounts to less than four inches, and the vast desert of the Rub al-Khali, or Empty Quarter, often gets no moisture whatsoever in an entire year.) Everything is resolutely American. There are softball fields and civic centers and American-style schools. The children leave their plastic pink-and-green Big Wheels out on the lawns overnight.

The Saudi attitude toward the Americans necessarily in their midst is roughly analogous to the nineteenth-century Chinese view of the British—that they are smelly, ugly, hairy barbarians, whose mere presence is corruptive of any civilized society— and so, by the choice and insistence of the Saudis, there is as little contact as possible between ARAMCO and Arabia. For the American women, this is particularly so. As Saudi law forbids women to drive, the ARAMCO wives may leave their model city only if someone is willing to take them. Most of the ARAMCO wives don't work—mores are also of a fifties-ish sort—and so hardly ever get out of the place. One wife I met told me that the worst of it was when you had a fight with your husband and stormed out of the house. All you could do was drive around inside the gates, she said, so that is what you did. Just drive up and down the grid pattern until the anger numbed itself away. I had a vision of evening time in ARAMCO, with the husbands home from work and the children home from school, and dozens of wives speeding aimlessly about, whizzing around corners and down empty streets, muttering and grinding their teeth behind their steering wheels.

The city that the Saudis built around ARAMCO is the embodiment of the great shift in culture that oil brought to the Arab world. The cities built before oil—cities like Baghdad and Cairo—have an onionlike layering to them, with cores of ancient, Islamic Arabia surmounted by layers of French or British colonialism, with a layer of twentieth-century American on top. The boom towns of the Gulf, former fishing villages transformed by oil, are nearly pure modern American, sprawling expanses celebrating the latest, cleanest way of life. They are modeled, perhaps consciously, on the great capital of oil, Houston, Texas. Like Houston, they are not so much cities as series of high-speed roads going from one cluster of tall, glassy, air-conditioned buildings to another. Dhahran is perhaps the purest expression of all such cities, an edge city that is not even on the edge of anything. Most of its streets are freeways. The roadbeds are as black and smooth as oil itself, and when the big Mercedes saloons and lean red Ferraris tear down them, their fat radial tires make a low, long silky whisper that trails after them like a scarf in the breeze.

Dhahran is the city as convenience store, a place where it seems almost nothing is older than the day before yesterday. Its most common building is not the mosque. It is the gas station. There are gas stations everywhere, and they are beauties of their genre, big, fluorescent-bright jobs, with huge plastic-and-aluminum canopies over a dozen shining pumps. The gas costs pennies. Foreigners pump it; they cost pennies too. In between the gas stations are other large and small buildings of similar construction, dispensing forms of fast food. There are hamburger places, fried-chicken places, and even a pizza place. Also banks, hotels, supermarkets, boutiques, and department stores. Everything is as clean as it could possibly be.

This was the place where most of the American reporters assigned to cover the allied counterinvasion of Kuwait lived and worked, not because there was any war here, but because, in ARAMCO fashion, Dhahran had become a sort of central depository and pumping station of war stories. The locus of activity was the International Hotel on the edge of the airfield, five or six miles from ARAMCO. The hotel was full to the roof with reporters and officers of the censor's brigade, which was called, in an Orwellian way, the Joint Information Bureau. The Joint

Information Bureau controlled the CENTCOM media pool system, the only approved structure for covering the ground war.

I went to the Joint Information Bureau—the JIB, everyone called it—my first morning in Dhahran. It was set up in an office next to a large common area on the second floor. In the center of the common area was a set of tables and desks that was the headquarters of the CENTCOM media pool system, and a television set. The television set received both the U.S. Armed Forces Radio Television Services Network and CNN, so that a reporter might easily record from the sofas in front of it all that was said in the daily military briefings held in Riyadh and Washington. At the pool coordinating desk was the other great source of information, a large binder filled with reports filed by the few reporters belonging to the CENTCOM media pool system who were actually in the presence of troops.

The pool system had been organized by the U.S. Central Command (hence, CENTCOM) after six months of meetings with American media bosses, and it worked like this: the journalists in each medium—print, television, radio—chose from among their number a coordinator who then chose journalists for assignment to various military units. The pool journalists were accompanied by public affairs escort officers and subject to Department of Defense rules and orders. They filed reports that were sent back by military carriers to Dhahran, were censored by the Joint Information Bureau, and then became common material available to all members of the pool.

A major at the Joint Information Bureau office gave me several typed sheets that explained the rules of the system in more detail:

"To the extent that individuals in the news media seek access to the U.S. area of operations, the following rules apply: Prior to or upon commencement of hostilities, media pools will be established to provide initial combat coverage of U.S. forces. U.S. news media personnel present in Saudi Arabia will be given the opportunity to join CENTCOM media pools, providing they agree to pool their products. News media personnel who are not members of the official CENTCOM media pools will not be permitted into forward areas. Reporters are strongly discouraged from attempting to link up on their own with combat units. U.S. commanders will maintain extremely tight security throughout the operational area and will exclude from the area of operation all unauthorized individuals. . . .

"In the event of hostilities, pool products will be subject to review before release to determine if they contain sensitive information about military plans, capabilities, operations or vulnerabilities (see attached ground rules) that would jeopardize the outcome of an operation or the safety of U.S. or coalition forces. Material will be examined solely for its conformance to the attached ground rules, not for its potential to express criticism or cause embarrassment. The public affairs escort officer on scene will review pool reports, discuss ground rule problems with the reporter, and in the limited circumstances when no agreement can be reached with a reporter about disputed materials, immediately send the disputed materials to JIB Dhahran for review by the JIB Director and the appropriate news media representative. If no agreement can be reached, the issue will be immediately forwarded to OASD(PA) for review with the appropriate bureau chief. . . ."

It took two days to get organized enough to get out of this. I found a partner first, Dan Fesperman, a reporter for the *Baltimore Sun*, a newspaper I had worked for a few years earlier. We rented a four-wheel-drive Nissan Safari in good condition except for a driver's-side window that would not roll up. We needed clothes that might help us get past the military checkpoints that were supposed to keep non-pool reporters away from the war, and a well-outfitted friend gave us some of his spares: a soldier's shirt and pants, in the tan-and-brown desert camouflage pattern the soldiers called chocolate chip, a cap and overcoat in khaki, and an oversized parka and overalls made of a light felt material; this was supposed to ward off the kinds of chemical gases that could be absorbed through the skin, mustard and nerve gases, principally. I already had the gas mask I had picked up in Tel Aviv and my little kit that contained a syringe full of atropine. Somewhere, I had gotten a small booklet entitled "Paper Chemical Agent Detector (3-Way Liquid, Adhesive-Backed)," which was filled with leaves of a paper treated with some chemicals that, it was claimed, would react to the presence of various gases, turning brown for one species of nerve gas, green for another, and red for blister gas. I also had a pair of much-too-big rubber boots that were supposed to keep gas off the feet, and several pairs of gasproof rubber gloves, and a large mitt—like those used by cooks handling hot pots—impregnated with fuller's earth. Dan had a gas mask too, and a pretty good map.

At six-thirty on the 24th, Dan and I met at his hotel. The ground war was two and a half hours old, having begun with a feint by the Saudi 8th and 10th Mechanized Brigades attacking Iraqi positions along the Kuwait coast while the 1st and 2nd Marine Divisions, the main attack, punched through the Iraqi line thirty to forty miles inland. We divided up our military garb, the khaki cap and overcoat for Dan and the shirt and pants for me. Of the felt antigas suit, he took the overalls and I took the parka. We pasted strips of the adhesive gas-detection paper on the exterior rearview mirrors of the Nissan. U.S. Army vehicles had inverted Vs painted on their sides and hoods, as signals to checkpoints to allow them through, so we made some for our car too, out of masking tape colored with black Magic Marker. For food, we went last-minute shopping in a large, fluorescent-bright supermarket as American as a Piggly Wiggly in Tallahassee.

*   *   *

The road from Dhahran to Hafar al-Batin—a garrison town on the Saudi-Iraq border that was the jumping-off point to the front—had been the main route, over the past six months, of the largest supply operation since the invasion of Normandy. The soldiers called it Suicide Alley, and the wrecks of overturned trucks and oil tankers, pushed off to the sand, dotted its length. The endless supply train was still moving that morning, and we drove in it, nervous frauds among squat Humvees, trucks filled with tires and boxes and soldiers, oil tankers and gigantic armored bulldozers. Overhead, in the wide, smoke-black sky, flew fat-bellied C-130s, medevac helicopters with red crosses on their sides, refueling planes—their gas-pump booms improbably trailing them—and, low and fearsome, a grouping of four A-10 Warthog attack planes, their terrible Gatling guns protruding from their sharky snouts.

I don't imagine the road had ever been much of a highway, and it was hopelessly chewed up now, cracked and potholed and disappearing for one long cross-country stretch completely. It was one-thirty in the afternoon, the war already over nine hours old, before we made it to Al Qaysuma, about ten miles southeast of Hafar al-Batin. We stopped at the hospital camp of a British medevac unit, thinking there might be a first-day story there in interviewing the doctors about the extent of the injuries and those of the wounded who could talk about what they had seen. We drove off the road to get to the camp, through an array of man-made dunes, and parked at the edge of a wide and long field of tents. We found, not a story, but the first sign of how the war would go: we were in a ghost town. The hundreds of tents stood open and empty. The helicopter pad was bare. The white ambulances stood unused in a low line. A few MPs could be seen standing guard, red-and-white *kaffiyehs* wrapped around their necks and faces to keep out the stinging sand driven by a hard, cold wind. We stopped to talk to one. "Not really had any casualties yet," he said. "Some POWs came in, but that's all."

We looked into the chaplain's tent; empty. In the big command tent, a couple of doctors were drinking tea.

Outside Hafar al-Batin, the allied forces had cut roads through the desert, tracks in the sand marked by rough signs with terse American names: MSR Orange, MSR Peach, MSR Dodge. The one we chose took us for a long time through desert, with no one else around, and we concluded we were lost. We turned back, and tried a second road, with no better results, and then drove cross-country, banging along in growing darkness and despair. It is discouraging not to be able to find a war. When night fell, we gave up, and drove back across the desert and into town.

It was raining hard, and the streets were mud. We braked at the outskirts of town for a sheep that had bounced out of the pickup truck in front of us. The driver got out and picked up the sheep and put it back in. The hotels were full of soldiers, but we found, eventually, a place on the outskirts called the Al Shamral Hotel that had a few rooms left, and checked in there. I drew a room next to a makeshift barracks of Saudi soldiers. The walls had been painted in a pattern that alternated splatters of black and red paint on grimy white, suggesting a flypaper on which thousands had met violent ends. The ceiling suffered from psoriasis, the paint steadily drizzling down in small gray flakes. The bed managed somehow to be both hard and sagging and was as narrow as the rich man's path to heaven. A few feet from its iron frame, a door led to the tiny bathroom. The toilet was a hole set in porcelain in the floor, with the shower occupying the same place, and the sink a few feet away, so that while washing up it was impossible to escape the fumes arising from the depths. The tile floor was perpetually, slimily wet.

The rain lasted all night and the next morning it was still coming down with a hard, cold, driving force. We drove through the brown swamps of the streets to a store—Fhaid al-Braheem al-Sa'ab, Sales, Building & Electric Materials—where I bought some plastic trash bags on the theory that I could make from them some sort of shield that would keep the rain from lashing through the broken window. Then we followed a road north to the border town of Al Ruqi, thinking we might find a way to the front. The plastic in the window didn't last a mile before it pulled out and began flapping like a shroud in the wind. When I stopped to tear it down, I noticed some pieces of orange plastic lying by the side of the road. We had seen yesterday that some of the American supply trucks and jeeps had taken to decorating themselves with pieces of orange cloth tied to the hood or roof, as some sort of an additional marking to the inverted V's. I decided, in one of those inspirations that are born of desperation, that I should cut up some of this orange plastic to mimic the orange cloth and add to our disguise. The material was from a busted-up highway safety cone, and very thick. I had to balance it on the bumper to try to cut it, and with the rain driving down my collar, I was wet to the skin by the time I had managed to hack off one irregular piece about three inches by eight inches. This, in lunatic fashion, I wrestled and wedged into the front grille; another five minutes in the rain. When I stepped back to look at it, I could see that it didn't look anything like an official marking. It looked like a piece of highway cone stuck in the grille. I got back in the car, breathing heavily. "There," I said to Dan. "That should help." We hadn't driven any distance at all before the plastic worked its way free and went hurtling off back down the road. Dan sat there with the air of a spouse who can see that it isn't even necessary to say anything.

At the edge of Al Ruqi, there was a checkpoint. It wasn't much of a barrier, just two miserably wet soldiers and a bar across the road made of a plank of wood between two oil drums. I slowed down and waved and made to drive around it, as if we had pressing business ahead, but it didn't work. Several more soldiers came running out of a small building by the side of the road, and one of them leveled his rifle in a meaningful way and yelled something, and we stopped.

"Where?" said the man with the rifle.

Ahead, I said. We have important business. We must deliver a message to Captain Henry of the U.S. Marines.

"No."

Yes.

"*Sahafi?* Journalist?"

Yes.

"Cards?" We handed over our press credentials, and he looked at them briefly and contemptuously, and gave them back.

"No. Go back to Hafar al-Batin."

We turned the car around and drove back four miles until we were just about out of the line of sight of the checkpoint, then stopped, put the car in four-wheel drive, and turned onto the sand. We were at a point that had clearly once been the front line of the Saudi defenses. The ground was scored with trenches, and at points earthworks had been built up on three sides to make shields behind which tanks could hide and shoot. We drove across this, perpendicular to the road, for three or four miles, until we could see the buildings near the checkpoint only as small bumps on the horizon; we turned back in the direction of the border, but angling away from the road, so that we were still increasing the distance away from the checkpoint. If the soldiers at the checkpoint cared to, they could of course still see us with binoculars, discover we were trying to get by them, and chase us, but they had not looked so dedicated to discomfort and duty as all that.

I drove fast anyway, bouncing over hillocks and swerving to avoid trenches and foxholes. In the distance, ahead, we could, at last, make out the first sounds of battle, the whup-whupping of helicopters and the distant thump of shelling. After twenty minutes or so, we came to an earthen berm ten feet high that marked what had been the outer edge of the Iraqi lines, breached the afternoon before. Five miles beyond that, we crossed a battered, cratered strip of asphalt that Dan's map suggested was the east-west highway running to Kuwait City, just inside Kuwait. A bit farther on, we ran into an army, or at least a big piece of one.

The piece belonged to the support column of the 4th Mechanized Division of the Egyptian army, and consisted of six half-tracks, two armored personnel carriers, four supply trucks, a tow truck, and a couple of dozen troops sitting around in the sand. An officer said there was a battle going on up ahead, a duel between Iraqis with multiple rocket launchers and Egyptians with 155-millimeter howitzers. The howitzers were what we had been hearing. They made an impressive sound going off, like the blast of a small bomb, and in the farther distance you could hear the sound of their shells striking home with a curiously homey and harmless sound, just like the thump of a boot stamping on solid earth. The Egyptian supply and support troops were waiting out the shelling, which had been going on since seven in the morning. Under its cover, the officer said, advance troops were cutting through the defenses and pushing forward the point of an attack that would move north through the Iraqi and Kuwaiti desert and east to the city of Jahra, some twenty miles or so west of Kuwait City. (The Egyptians, I learned later, were leading the Arab elements of the allied attack; they had broken through the lines near the Wadi al-Batin, at the juncture of Iraq, Kuwait, and Saudi Arabia in the late afternoon of the previous day. At the same time, the U.S. Army's VII Corps and the 1st British Armored Division, massed to the west, had moved forward in the main attack into Iraq. To the west of that, the U.S. 24th Mechanized Division had pushed through Iraqi lines and was heading north, and the 101st Airborne, which had the previous day established a forward field and ammunition base deep within Iraq, was moving on toward the Euphrates River.)

We drove on and soon were in the middle of a division

moving slowly ahead across the vast, flat plain, driving on rough roads that armored bulldozers had scraped out of the dirt. Four supply lines stretched out across the horizon. One line comprised only tanks, and it was in the lead. To the east, and shielded by the tanks, were the three lines of supply trucks, jeeps, half-tracks, armored personnel carriers, ambulances, oil trucks, and so on. The third and fourth lines were a mixed bunch of troop carriers of one sort or another and big guns. The procession moved with a stately deliberation, five miles an hour at most, with frequent stops. At first we tried to stay with it, but soon we found that we didn't need to try to hide our presence; the Egyptians didn't care whether we were there or not, and we cut to the side of the convoy and made better speed.

Eventually, we arrived at a field of howitzers, a couple of hundred guns, all with their great barrels elevated for maximum range, silhouetted against the sky. The artillery formed a huge bow, spread out in textbook fashion over a distance of a dozen miles across, with the front of the salient closest to the Iraqi lines and the sides curving back on the eastern and western flanks. They had been firing all morning, and by now, shortly after noon, many of them were silent, but some were still firing. Mixed in among them were portable missile batteries, and these were firing too.

You could sometimes hear the flight of missiles in between the howitzers' booms, a soft, sibilant, sexy whistle that was gone from the ear almost as soon as it came.

At the front of the firing field, we came across a scene of injury. A young soldier was lying in the mud, screaming and thrashing about. Three men were holding him down while a medic cut away his pants legs to get at the wounds. Another three soldiers, also wounded but not as badly, were sitting or lying nearby, awaiting treatment. The injuries, the ambulance driver said, were not due to Iraqi fire. A missile had misfired, turning on its tail and crashing back down to ground near the battery, exploding and injuring the men who had sent it off.

Nearby, a howitzer crew was taking a break, the gunner lying in the sand with his back up against the wheel of his gun. "We have fired forty-six shots and hit many Iraqi targets. Seven hits!" Nobody had shot a thing at him. "Happy, happy, happy," he said. "My heart is happy!" He had two sparkling sterling teeth in the front of his mouth, and when he beamed, they winked silver light.

Still following the tanks, we came, in midafternoon, to the Iraqi front lines, the Saddam Line that had been such a cause of concern. It was breached and deserted. There was another wall of earth, but much smaller than the first berm, only four or five feet tall. Bulldozers had plowed a road through it. Three miles past that was a tangle of barbed wire setting off a place where the road went through a wide patch of ground that was charred, as if the invading army had adopted, literally, a scorched-earth policy. This denoted a minefield, exploded by the curious contraption of armored bulldozers equipped with great lengths of steel chain, flung out in advance to land on the ground and detonate the mines. The road cut through that too.

Just beyond was a ditch, about ten feet deep and five feet across, with three feet of thick black crude oil in the bottom. This had been a much-feared feature of the Saddam Line—the burning trenches of oil that would trap and kill men and tanks. But along this stretch at least, no one had bothered to light it. It was hardly an obstacle at all. The bulldozers had filled it with dirt and moved on. On the other side of the oil ditch, the road passed through a second, larger minefield and through a nasty brier patch of shining concertina wire. A few hundred yards farther were the trenches and earthworks of the line itself.

I saw later, deeper inside Iraq and in Kuwait, superb earth-work fortifications, and I read of some on the front line that were impressive, but these were pathetic affairs, a double line of trenches no more than four feet deep and so narrow that two men could not pass each other without squeezing by like passengers in the aisle of a jetliner. At intervals the trenches wid-

ened into bunkers, little more than glorified foxholes, four to
five feet deep. They were strong enough to withstand a fairly
heavy barrage (because earth is an amazingly effective armor
and because the force of an explosion dissipates so quickly), but
only if the defenders stayed hunkered underground, unable to
fight or even move beyond a few inches in any direction. One
we peered into was only five feet deep by eight feet across and
five feet wide, a hole in the ground. A command bunker nearby
was better, with cinder-block walls and a roof of ten-inch-thick
reinforced concrete. But inside there was still hardly any room
at all. The two sodden, muddy sleeping pallets overlapped each
other and butted right up to the edges.

The men in the bunkers had shared their space with live ammunition; crates of machine-gun rounds and rocket-propelled
grenades were piled in them, and loose rounds and old-fashioned pineapple grenades littered the floor. The trench lines
between the bunkers ran straight and uninterrupted for lengths
of a hundred yards or more, so that their defenders would be
vulnerable to enfilading fire as soon as attacking ground forces
gained a small portion of the line. They were hardly better than
the slit-trench works of the First World War.

The defenders of this sorry position had not even tried to fight.
They stood lined up in the rain, wet and shivering, their hands
folded on the tops of their heads, the Egyptians prodding and
poking them about. They had given up only a few minutes
before, and were still busy with the first ritual of prison life, the
stripping of self. Each man emptied his pockets. Their belongings hardly made a pile in the mud, a sad litter of cheap plastic
combs, letters from home, empty wallets, matches and the occasional cigarette, a few coins. In the background two Iraqis lay
dead, one covered with a coat thrown over his head and shoulders, but the other bare under the rain, bleeding still from the
holes in his chest and back.

I remember one sharp, small scene. Several prisoners sig-
naled to one of the Egyptian officers that they had to urinate.
With a beckoning wave of his pistol, he moved them forward to
the edge of the trench that had been theirs to defend. Motioning
downward with the pistol he had them kneel in the mud. I
thought for a horrible moment that he was going to execute
them so that their bodies would tumble into the trench, but the
Iraqis knew what he wanted. Together on their knees in line,
they unzipped their pants and sent their streams into the ditch.

Behind them, the others of their unit were now, as the Egyptians directed, taking off their boots. It is a difficult thing to take
off a shoe with one hand remaining on your head. Some
managed to balance on one leg, but most fell into a clumsy sit
when they tried it. They pitched their boots into a pile, and the
guards motioned them up again and herded them into two
groups, the enlisted men in one, the officers in another, and they
all sat down in the mud. A few feet away a .50-caliber machine
gun had been set up on a tripod to guard them, and the young
soldier who manned it watched with eager intent for the first
sign of trouble, but he might have been assigned to cover a
group of nuns for all the need there was of his services. The
prisoners sat silent and unmoving.

An Egyptian officer with a walrus mustache bustled about,
waving his pistol and shouting. When we told him we wished
to interview him for our newspapers, he was quite pleased. He
was a major, named Ahmed Morsi, a signal officer of the 10th
Brigade of the Egyptian Third Army. He had at hand, he said,
530 enlisted prisoners and twenty-five officers. Another five
hundred had been taken in the lines just to the rear of these and
were on their way to this point. It was a complete triumph. The
need to stop and gather prisoners was the only thing holding up
the forward march of the attack; there was hardly any resistance
from Iraqi troops anywhere up or down the line. "At first, they
tried to maintain a defense," the major said. "But as soon as we
began our attack in earnest they surrendered. We attacked at six

A.M., with about ten thousand troops, of the 10th Brigade and the 222nd. We attacked without even air support. We were supposed to have air support from the Americans, but we got nothing, because of the clouds. So we attacked without it, and because of this it took us longer than it should have to get through the Iraqi defenses."

This was false modesty. The major was really bragging, in a polite way. His unit had breached the Saddam Line, moved twenty-four kilometers through enemy territory, and taken nearly six hundred prisoners, and had done so without any help from the Americans. They had suffered almost no casualties, and had even managed to avoid killing very many of the enemy.

The Iraqi officers sat in a huddle a little way apart from the larger group of enlisted men. We squatted with one, and I gave him a cigarette, which he tried to light, but could not, for the shaking in his hands. I lit it for him. He was a young man, a first lieutenant of the Iraqi army's 20th Division, he said, and he had been in these trenches for four and a half months. He wanted to talk, and did, in a stuttering, shivering anguish.

"From the beginning of the war, I didn't agree with the ideas of the president at all, but we were obliged to stay in the war because if we tried to desert they would hang our families. Our wives, sisters, brothers. They did this many times, I am serious." He looked around at the other officers, and they all nodded in confirmation. "Saddam, he is a criminal, and he is killing us. We have no choice but to do what he says. We are a poor people, and he has sent us here to face a great army and die."

The man sitting next to him joined in. "It is true, he is a criminal. We do not wish to be here."

"We had no wish to be attacked," said the lieutenant. "When we saw that we were safe, that was enough; we gave up as soon as we saw that we would not be killed. We do not wish to fight. I personally do not wish to at all, and I did not, not one bit. And my company, I ordered them not to fight too, and they all agreed. Why to fight? For what?" He made a short sweep with his arm at the mud and dirt around him. "For this? For Kuwait?"

He began weeping, shoulders shaking. "Listen to me. I have my wife. She is a teacher. I think that I will never see her again." He grabbed my hand. "I am afraid they are going to kill us," he said. "Please do not let them kill us, that is all I ask."

I said I was sure no one would kill him although I was not.

"Thank you. Thank you." He snuffled and whimpered a little, like a child, and talked some more. "I am a teacher too, and an educated man, but I think I have forgotten everything because I have spent so much time in the army. Six years I have been in. They do not release us, ever. It is always the same. Fight in Iran, fight in Kuwait, fight in Iraq. And for what? We Iraqi people, we have nothing in our lives, just killing and nothing more."

Pretty soon the major came back and yelled some orders, and the guards waved their rifles about and yelled too, and all the Iraqis stood up and began moving to the trucks—six big vehicles with high, vertically slatted wood walls, the sort used for hauling animals to the abbatoir. Already they walked with the universal two-step of the imprisoned. It is a slow and humble little shuffle, calculated to send a message to the guards: I am not trouble; there is no need to hurt me. The major walked along and fired his pistol in the air over their heads to encourage them, and in five minutes both trucks were filled to bursting, the prisoners jammed face to face, shoulder to shoulder. Those who had the good fortune to end up at the sides of the truck turned their faces to the slats and peered out between them. The space between the slats was just wide enough to frame the eyes, creating a Dalí-esque effect: the slats a long series of vertical lines, the staring eyeballs a long horizontal one.

After they were all aboard, and there did not seem any room left, there were still the wounded. One had his shoulder and right arm in a sling, the other had a bloody bandage around a bootless foot. The major loosed off a couple of shots and the bodies in the trucks surged back, and there appeared a few feet of space, and the hurt men were pushed and pulled in. After that, there were still two more prisoners; the dead were loaded last. It didn't seem there could possibly be any more space, but the major fired again and again, and in the end, each truck made grudging way for the dead, one body's worth, laid out on the wood floor at the very edge of the edge. I was close to one of the trucks and watched as the body was lifted up and laid home and the gate was bolted shut. He was, by his insignia, a lieutenant. He had caught a bullet in the chest. He lay on his back, bare feet all around his face, his eyes open to the gray sky and his mouth open to the rain falling in. He was not much messed up. If not for the red patch on the left side of his chest that was spreading to his armpit and his back, you would have thought he was sleeping off a deep drunk. His pallbearers turned away, but then the major yelled, and they opened the gate of the truck up again. They had forgotten to search him. They rifled roughly through his pockets, threw the scraps they found in the dirt, and then shut the gate again, and the trucks belched and roared and lurched away.

We headed back across the lines before it became too dark, to return to Hafar al-Batin, where we could dictate stories over the hotel telephone. There were, everywhere, in every direction, still lines of men and matériel stretching back to the southern horizon. There were a variety of vehicles; war is a highly specialized affair. It requires tanks to shoot other tanks, howitzers (self-propelled and towed) to shoot towns and trenches, mortars to do the same thing in a cruder fashion, antiaircraft guns to shoot enemy planes, armored personnel carriers to bring small groups of troops to the front of the front, trucks and jeeps to bring the vast rest up to support positions, supply trucks carrying everything from food to portable bridges, tankers to supply the fuel that keeps everything moving, motorcycles to carry messengers, ambulances to carry the wounded away, trucks or buses to haul off prisoners, and so on.

All of this was moving forward through the dusk in a tremendous racket, part the clanking of treads, part the grinding of gears, part the heavy whining roar of the huge diesel engines. A light rain began to fall, and the breeze carried a mixture of desert and diesel. The troops moving forward waved their hands in V-for-victory signs, and whistled and honked and cheered, so that this was part of the racket too.

The next morning, we went up the same route again and were soon back at the front, which was no longer the front. The Iraqis were all gone to jail and the Egyptians had moved on. A few miles farther along, we caught up with the tail end of the move forward, in the form of the newest prisoner depot. About a thousand of them were sitting on the ground waiting for buses. The man in charge of guarding them was annoyed. "Really," he said, with an exasperated sigh. "Everywhere we go, we collect Iraqis. Collect, collect, collect. It is all we have time to do. They just walk up to us. No shooting, just give themselves up."

By eleven-fifteen in the morning, we were thirty-four miles inside Kuwait, about twenty-two miles farther than our farthest point of the day before. The supply line now stretched sixty unbroken miles. We scooted along to one or the other side of it, trying to keep pretty close to the path, to minimize the chance of hitting mines, but it was easy to make mistakes. Coming to a new berm blocking the way, we turned into the first opening and were about to head across what looked like open space when soldiers, waving and hollering, stopped us. This was, they said, the beginning of a path through an as yet uncleared minefield—a bad place to drive. One of them kindly drew a small map in my notebook, showing that we should follow the berm for three kilometers and then turn right onto a path that had been cleared across the field. We did, and headed on, in a more or less northeasterly direction. Around noon, we caught up with an Egyptian armored column, a dozen miles of tanks, armored personnel carriers, and jeeps, and drove along up the side of it until we got to the lead.

The column had stopped, all the tanks sitting heavily in the sand, chugging out oily black diesel smoke. Ahead, there were no trails or pointers, just desert. Next to the tanks were a couple of armored personnel carriers, and next to them, squatting in a little semicircle so their backs faced the blowing sand, sat a general and a couple of other high-ranking officers, drawing lines in the dirt. The general had a pointer, but the other two just used their fingers. They were arguing about the lines they were drawing, scratching out each other's lines, shaking their sticks at each other, shouting. One of them stomped off in the sand and got a Very gun from inside the APC and fired off three flares, one red, one green, and one white, into the air. While he was standing there, looking up at the sky for some sort of answer that might give him a clue where he was taking his army, we talked to him a bit. He introduced himself; Mustafa Kamad, commander of the 222nd Brigade of the 3rd Division. "We are a little confused," he said. "We got lost." It would have embarrassed me to be leading ten thousand men and get lost, but it didn't seem to faze Mustafa Kamad. "We know where we are, sort of," he said. "We are about a hundred kilometers to the west of Kuwait City. But we are not sure how far north we are." He took us inside one of the APCs, which was outfitted as a command post. One wall was covered with a big, detailed map, and the map made clear the Egyptian's problem. The Allied forces were denoted with red lines and the Iraqi forces were marked with blue. The red lines and the blue began at the familiar juncture of the Kuwait-Saudi-Iraq borders near the Wadi al-Batin, and then took off north and east, in a series of advancing red lines and retreating blue ones. The red lines had started out as neat, small bows making up a larger bowed front, but as they moved up and across the map, the bows were getting longer and longer and less and less neat. The Iraqi lines didn't have any neat pattern at all, except that they were all heading in one direction, back into Iraq. The red and blue together looked like order chasing chaos. "The problem, you can see," the commander said, "is that the Iraqis are retreating too fast. To keep up with them, we must move very rapidly, and we are getting too spread out, and losing our places where we are on the map." His men, he said, could hardly keep up with the job of routing. In two days, they had shot a dozen tanks and taken thirteen hundred prisoners. They had gone so far so fast that they had gone off the edge of their known world. "If you want to see something," he said, pointing to the west. "Go that way, ten kilometers maybe. They are capturing Al Abraq over there."

Al Abraq was a garrison town in the middle of nothing: half a dozen square blocks of small houses of concrete, mud brick, and tin, a couple of barracks and office buildings, a vegetable garden, a grove of date palms, and a graveyard. On the edge of town, there had been a radio station, whose two metal towers had been, I would think, the tallest things between here and Hafar al-Batin. A paved one-lane road circled the town, and inside that circle ran another circle of steel, a cyclone fence with a barbed-wire top. Even in its prime, Al Abraq had been as welcoming as a penitentiary.

Now, it was an advertisement for the power of modern high explosives. It had been bombed, rocketed, and shelled, and there wasn't a bit of it that hadn't been smashed and burned, not a building left intact. The radio-station complex had been of a pretty good size, with a base of a two-thousand-square-foot square cinder-block building. Now, to trace its dimensions was a job for an archaeologist, piecing together the outlines from the rubble of the walls and fallen ceilings that remained. A sheet of corrugated tin that had been the roof lay crumpled like a paper bag off to one side on the sand. The spindly steel towers hadn't stood up at all, of course. The explosions had knocked them apex over base, and they lay on the ground in a tangle of spindly legs, twisted and bent. To get to them we had to walk through a double ring of trenches and bunkers, what had been the town's first line of defenses. The ground was thick with odd pieces of soldiers' gear—gas masks, helmets, canteens, and web belts. A lot of the helmets had rested on their tops and were half filled with rainwater, but we each found one that was dry enough and put them on our heads. They were Second World War helmets, and I don't suppose they would have been much real help in stopping a bullet from a Kalashnikov or an M-16, but it was nonetheless comforting to feel one on top of the head.

The bunkers the Iraqis had built here were more impressive than those on the front line, with corrugated-tin roofs covered by sandbags piled six layers high and great piles of dirt on top of that. If the attackers had tried to take Al Abraq with ground forces directly, without a month's bombing first, the bunkers would have been formidable obstacles. The Iraqis could have stayed inside, safe under a ton of dirt, for days and even weeks, shooting whoever popped a head above the flat sand horizon. But it must have been awful to live in them, trapped by the bombs. I climbed down the stairs into one. Inside, it ran about ten feet long by three feet wide and three and a half feet tall. It had held two men. They had left a lot behind: both their canteens, a two-way radio, a shaving brush with a tiger stenciled on it, various pots, pans, and blankets, and a toothbrush.

Nearby was an example of what must have most frightened them, a direct hit from a big bomb. The bomb had fallen on what had been a small concrete building. All that was left was a surprisingly neat crater. It was thirty feet deep and thirty feet across and its sides sloped in to a point, making as precise a funnel as you could want. The bottom and sides of the funnel and the ground all around the edges of the crater were covered with hunks of concrete and ripped pieces of tin. There had been eight or nine buildings in this little complex, and they had all been bombed down to ground level, pounded flat as thoroughly as if with a hammer. Near one was a bomb casing, a long, green half-cylinder. It appeared to have come from a cluster bomb, of the sort in which the external canister of the bomb splits open shortly before hitting the ground and releasing several hundred bomblets.

We wandered through the torn and shattered buildings. Many had nothing left standing except a few odd pieces of cinder-block wall. The rest was trash. None of it could be rebuilt. If Al Abraq existed again, it would be a new Al Abraq. The bulldozers would shove all this off to one side, and the drifting sand would eventually cover it.

Exploring the ruins, we came across Zaglud Fatah, chief of staff for the 3rd Division of the Egyptian army. He was, in a relaxed way, hunting down the enemy. He had a couple of soldiers with him, walking ahead. Their approach to the job at hand was both efficient and casual. When they arrived at the shell of a building, they would jog right to the side of it and fire half a dozen rounds at its various formal and informal openings, then holler for whoever was in there to come out. Nobody seemed too concerned about the idea that any Iraqi might actually choose to shoot rather than surrender. "We took the town with few fighting, few fighting," said the chief of staff. "All we are doing is collecting prisoners. Many, many prisoners." The assault, he said, had begun four hours earlier, at 10:00 A.M., and had involved the entire division, under the command of General Yahed Alwan. There had been no serious resistance. They had spent most of the day receiving, herding, and sending rearward surrendered Iraqis.

As he was speaking, his men were busy announcing their arrival at another building, and the echo of their shots was still bouncing off the rubble when a group of Iraqi soldiers appeared out of it, walking nervously forward and yelling their desire that no one shoot them. One had a scrap of ribbed white undershirt attached to a stick, and he waved this energetically. The enlisted men prodded them into line behind us, and we moved on,

past the large buildings and into a shell-shocked copse of eucalyptus trees, where we found an abandoned Iraqi armored troop
carrier, stripped of its guns and with two flat tires. Here we
caught up with General Alwan, who was making his own tour
of the area. He had a swagger stick stuck up under one arm, and
he was swaggering. It was a nice swagger, not a strut but more
of a stroll, with just the slightest shoulder roll, a studied display
of modesty in victory.

We continued on, in a sort of parade, led by the general and
his two adjutants—flanking him and, it seemed to me, imitating
his walk—and we were passing by a bunker when five Iraqi
soldiers burst up from the ground and came running straight at
us. The adjutants started, and brought their rifles up, but the
general merely nodded as if to say, Ah, more prisoners, and he
was right. The Iraqis were unarmed and their hands were high
above their heads. They were only running in their eagerness
to quit. The general motioned with his little stick, and the Iraqis
fell in behind him, and our little procession continued on, to just
south of the town, where the prisoners were being gathered in
a big rectangular yard behind a metal fence. There were still a
few who had not surrendered, hiding behind the berm that
guarded this end of the town. The Egyptians had fifteen armored personnel carriers lined up pointing their guns at that
berm, and they could have blown the Iraqis away, but they were
not really interested in hurting them, and were willing to wait
until the holdouts got around to the inevitable. "Why should we
hurt them?" one of the adjutants said. "They are Muslim as we
are, Arab as we are."

We peeled off the parade and stopped to talk to a group of
enlisted men and junior officers whooping it up, laughing and
chattering and hugging each other. It must be an amazing feeling, the soldier's delight in discovering that he is going to end
the day's battle a victor instead of a corpse. Major Muhammad
Usri, leader of one of the platoons that had led the assault, said
he and his troops had taken four hundred prisoners since 10:00

A.M. I asked him if any of his men had distinguished themselves by any particular heroics, and he said no, everybody had played the same part. An enlisted man standing next to him interrupted. He was dressed à la Rambo, a red bandanna around his head and bandoliers of machine-gun rounds crisscrossed on his chest. This was not true, he said. Major Usri, in fact, was a hero. He had been the very first man to enter Al Abraq. "The very first!" said the soldier. "He is a historic Egyptian conqueror! We have proved today Egyptians are men! Egyptians are men!"

While they were waiting for the next round of surrendering, Dan and I finished our tour of the town. We peered inside a barracks, where nothing much remained, and at the vegetable garden, which had been surprisingly unaffected. The neat little rows of plants were untouched, and seemed to be thriving. The palm and eucalyptus trees, though, had been badly treated. Quite a few of them had been split, as if by lightning, and all of them had been largely stripped of leaves.

We found what must have been the commanding officer's bunker. It was first-rate, built entirely below ground and reached by a flight of concrete stairs, which were protected by a double wall of big sandbags. The top of it was covered with sandbags piled ten feet high and with a ton of dirt on top of that. The hall from the entranceway to the main room was only four or five feet long, but it took a right-angle turn to the left and then another to the right, so that any shrapnel coming in from outside would imbed itself in solid packed dirt, instead of the commanding officer. The main room was ten feet wide by twenty feet long, with an eight-foot ceiling. The roof was made of corrugated tin stretched over thick steel pipes and four-by-fours.

The furnishings were about as good as they could have been, under the circumstances. The dirt walls had been covered with sheets of fake-wood particle board, and curtains had been put up at the turn of the hall. The floor was poured concrete. A fluorescent light hung from the ceiling, powered by several car batteries alongside one wall. In the rear was a single bed, with a real (although thin) mattress and an iron bedframe. Opposite the bed was a small wood table that had served as a desk. A chair was still drawn up at it, and a couple of stubbed-out cigarette butts remained in the ashtray. Four more chairs were lined up against a wall, and on another small table stood a tea service for eight. It was an inexpensive set, but made of real porcelain painted with small pink roses and yellow trim, and whoever had owned it had taken care of it. Three cups still stood in a neat row, respected and respectable, with not a chip on any one of them.

We left Al Abraq at around three in the afternoon and back-tracked southeast, to pick up the east-west highway to Kuwait City. It seemed clear, from the look of things, that the war was going to be over very soon, and we thought we should head directly to Kuwait City so as not to miss the liberation. As we were driving past the debris of Saddam's army we stopped to look at a T-62 tank, shot and abandoned. Its turret had been knocked off and the big gun was lying on the ground, pointed uselessly in the direction of Saudi Arabia. The fires that had raged through the interior were only recently out, and where the round had entered the tank, there was a small, brutal hole with edges melted like caramel, still glowing a faint red. All around, the Egyptians and the Saudi armies were moving again, wheeling north and east from the positions where they had stopped in the morning's engagements. There must have been tens of thousands of vehicles maneuvering at the same time on this stretch of desert. It made for a certain confusion. Driving down the narrow cleared path across a minefield, we met a tank coming the other way. I backed up very slowly, concentrating on not letting the tires veer even a little bit into the charred earth on either side.

We hit the highway to Kuwait City at about four in the

afternoon, and turned east, into tough going. In hopes of slowing the allied forces' advance, the Iraqis had set charges of dynamite across the road every quarter mile and blown a ragged culvert, with asphalt buckled up around it. For the first ten miles or so, we could still go forward fairly quickly, because bulldozers had filled up the ditches, but soon we passed the point of the extent of the repair work. Now we had to move slowly, driving along the road for a bit, then turning onto the sand and going across the desert to get around the dynamited section, and then turning back onto the road. The desert here was richly studded with the sharp-edged pieces of blown-up and burned Iraqi machines, and with unexploded ordnance of all sorts.

At a stretch where we were briefly back on the road, we saw, suddenly—they hadn't been there the second before—a group of soldiers walking abreast across the road. As we got closer, we could see that they were wearing dark-green uniforms. "I wonder if they are Iraqis," Dan said, in a voice determinedly casual. We drove forward slowly, nervously. When we got pretty close, we could see that they were Iraqis, and that one of them was waving a flag of surrender—it was a white T-shirt attached to a piece of bamboo—in big, broad sweeps. There were ten of them, and none of them had coats, and they were shivering in the encroaching evening cold. When we stopped, they approached the car with their hands high in the air. They had no rifles. It occurred to me as I noticed this that I hadn't seen a single Iraqi soldier carrying a rifle since the ground war began. "Where are your rifles?" I said, sort of as an ice-breaker, I guess.

One, who it turned out was the lieutenant in charge of this platoon, stepped forward. He spoke a little bit of English. "Buried them in ground." I found out later that a great many of the Iraqi defenders in the front lines had buried their rifles and handguns as soon as the ground war began, understanding that to surrender still carrying arms increased their chances of getting shot. There must be thousands of automatic rifles buried there, and over time the shifting sands will slowly uncover them, and let bloom a crop of strange fruit. The lieutenant said he and his men had been walking for two hours after leaving their trenches. They had never fought. "Many days bombed," he said. "Much air. Too much." At the onset of the ground war, other units on his stretch of the line had fled to Basra, but the lieutenant and his men had talked it over and decided they would rather surrender to Americans than go back to Iraq. "Afraid of Saddam," he said. "Not afraid of Americans. United States is good. United States of America is good."

Now, said the lieutenant, he and his men were very cold and hungry and they would appreciate it if we would take them prisoner. I am five feet six inches tall and bespectacled and running slightly to poundage. Dan is taller and doesn't wear glasses, but he is not an overwhelming figure either. I don't think either of us felt that we were the sort of man who takes other men prisoner. I was embarrassed thinking about it. We said no, we had to push on to Kuwait City, and we could not take them there. They begged us, but we said no again, and to assuage our feelings of wretchedness at leaving them, opened our bags and gave them food: bread and chocolate, some cheese and a big hunk of summer sausage, a sack of pistachio nuts, bottles of water and cardboard containers of orange juice. When I looked in the rearview mirror, they were all standing in the road, the wind whipping them, sucking on the little straws of the orange juice boxes.

Five miles or so on, we came to a tangle of barbed wire across the road, with the orange markings we had come to know indicated a minefield. The field stretched well beyond the road on each side into the desert. Ahead, the asphalt had been broken with explosions for as far as we could see. I wanted very much to get to Kuwait City that night, but it was almost dark, and I didn't have the heart to try for it. I was afraid I would miss the edge of the minefield in the dusk, or hit another one farther up the road, or drive over an American cluster bomb.

We turned around and drove back down the road. The Iraqis were only a little farther on than where we had left them, trudging miserably ahead, and it seemed impossible to pass them by a second time. We got all of them aboard—four in the backseat, one in the front between us, three in the far back, and two standing on the rear bumper and holding on to the roof—and drove slowly on. After a couple of miles, we came across a Saudi army unit heading north up one of the supply routes across the highway. I flagged down a truck in the column and waved the driver out. I was self-conscious about finding myself a taker of prisoners, and it made me adopt a stiffly formal tone. "We have Iraqi prisoners," I said. "Prisoners of war. They wish to surrender." The Saudis were part of a support unit, mostly gas tankers and their escorts, and I am sure they had not seen any of the enemy on the hoof before. They got overexcited. The driver grabbed up the rifle on the seat next to him, slammed a clip into it, and began waving it in the faces of the Iraqis and shouting. In a few seconds, twenty or thirty more soldiers had come rushing up, jamming clips into their unused rifles, swarming around the Iraqis in a fever. The entire convoy had stopped to take the prisoners.

At first, in their jumpiness, the Saudis treated the Iraqis very badly, and I thought they might kill them. With their rifle butts, they knocked the food and drink we had given them from their hands, and made them put their palms on their heads. They tore their pockets inside out and threw everything they found on the ground. They screamed and shouted and made as if, any moment, they were going to shoot. The Iraqis, stunned and terrified, sat down in the dirt, their hands on their heads still, and their faces to the wind, in a ragged little line. One man clutched his Koran to his chest for protection and rocked, moaning, back and forth on his haunches. Another cried for Allah, and wept, and clutched at his crotch and hair in little paroxysms of terror. I watched them weeping and begging for their lives, and I had to turn aside so they wouldn't see me crying too.

In truth, though, the Saudi soldiers meant no harm, and after a short while calmed themselves and remembered their manners. They passed out new containers of orange juice, and packages of Kraft processed cheese and crackers, and cookies and cigarettes. One of them knelt next to the sobbing man, patted his head, and kissed him on the cheeks. The Iraqis, seeing they were not going to die, calmed themselves too, and by the time we left, it was a peaceful scene. The Saudi lieutenant who had taken charge shook our hands good-bye. He was twenty-seven years old, First Lieutenant Saud Otabi, and his smooth and boyish face was beaming at the glory of the win.

BLOOD AND SHIT

EARLY THE NEXT MORNING, we drove out of Hafar al-Batin, up the highway, across the sand, through the front lines, and back onto the highway to Kuwait City. Overnight, a clearing crew had made a path through the minefield across the road. The highway was pockmarked with small cluster-bomb craters and littered with the outsized trash of an army in disastrous retreat—the charred hulks of tanks and jeeps and trucks—but through this ran a scant passage.

The skies darkened, and by the time we were within thirty miles of Kuwait City they had gone from slate to indigo and were verging on pitch. The great fires of the oil wells made red-and-yellow torches along the flat sand horizon. Fifteen miles out we passed a Saudi Arabian army column, three or four miles long, stopped by the side of the road to pray, thousands of men kneeling in the sand, their rifles by their sides, the wind whipping them. As we came up on the outskirts of the city, we hit the first American checkpoint, two Marines and a Humvee blocking the road. The older of the two moved forward to stop us, but the younger one noticed the tattered piece of tape hanging by scraps on the door. "Sir! Inverted V!" he said, snapped off a sharp salute, and waved us through.

A little farther on, we encountered the first sign of liberation, a pickup truck tearing down the road, a fat man at the wheel, a half-dozen kids in back. The fat man was honking and the kids were yelling and waving a big Kuwaiti flag. We followed the truck to the second checkpoint, a small bunch of Marines from the 2nd Marine Division, members of a tank-killing company of 230 troops. The Marines were eighteen, nineteen years old, except for the company commander, Captain Mike Ettore. He was thirty-four, from Newton, New Jersey, and he had enlisted in the Marines when he was seventeen, he said. Ettore and his men were as pumped up as college jocks after a big win. "You want to know the truth about the Iraqis?" was the first thing he said. "They were an inferior enemy. Pathetic."

Ettore's battalion was famous, in an unfortunate way, for its part in the American military ground action in the Middle East that preceded the Gulf War. In Beirut, on Oct. 23, 1983, a suicide bomber drove a truck full of dynamite into a Marine barracks and killed 241 servicemen of the 2nd Division. "Since then, they've called us a hard-luck battalion," Ettore said. "But this time we did it right. This time, this battalion, in a modest estimate, killed three hundred Iraqis."

On the first day of the ground war, the 24th, Captain Ettore's company didn't find anybody to fight. On the second day, it met an Iraqi tank company. "That was our first battle. It lasted less than an hour. Everybody did what they were supposed to do and it was over. We used the TOW missile. It worked just the way they said it would. You wouldn't believe how good it worked. The lieutenant was briefing the platoon. It was foggy. You couldn't see anything. And all of a sudden out of the mist comes this tank column. Iraqis. We were totally surprised. But in the next thirty minutes we had thirty-three dead tanks, all on their side, none on ours. We killed them with a combo of artillery, TOWs, heavy machine guns, and M1A1 tanks. They didn't even want to fight us. They had been fleeing from the 1st Marine Division to the east and had come on us by accident. I'm not kidding. We just banged away on them and kept banging 'em really hard, and we just picked 'em off. We got guys in this company who are seven for seven, eight for eight with the TOW. That's the truth.

"They didn't want to fight. And anyway, their reaction time is really bad. The first tank you hit stops everything for them. And they just sit there. And our guys are just banging tanks faster than hell. Our M1s are banging two, three a minute. So, these guys, they see this, they couldn't surrender fast enough. They just wanted out of the whole thing."

The company's second battle came that night. "We came across a bunch of them south of a place called Ice Cube and devastated 'em. Fifteen tanks, nine, ten BMP's. After we banged 'em the first time, they withdrew. We consolidated our lines and then took a break. For a half hour, there was nothing going on. We were just drinking coffee. Then we said, Wait a minute, if we're drinking coffee, so are they. They're getting rest time too. So we started up again and banged 'em with the artillery. Later, when they surrendered, they told us that's what really broke their backs. They said they had thought the first barrage was it. When it stopped, they figured that was it for the night. Then the second one started up. That did it. The second one sent 'em out of their tanks and into the holes. And the next morning, they just came out with their hands up. Just quit. And—this is the amazing thing—these guys were all top tankers, sent down specifically to launch a counterattack. But they couldn't do it.

Over the course of both battles, Ettore's company suffered only two casualties: "One in the butt, one in the arm, both shrapnel." Only one Iraqi tank even managed to get off a shot, and it missed. "The incredible thing is, within our company, only myself and four other people had ever even been in combat before. Here are young kids who are eighteen, nineteen years old, with no combat experience before, and they really did great. Of course, the Iraqis are so bad. We planned like they were going to fight to the death. But they didn't. Just an inferior enemy."

Coming into Kuwait City, we drove through a suburb of villas and apartment blocks in a stream of traffic that was a parade, every car a honking, cheering part of it. Occasionally a group of people would branch out of the general flow and eddy into a smaller celebration. A carload of people would just stop in the road and all the people in it would pile out, to dance and wave flags and yell, and then another group would join them, and so on, until a good-sized crowd was whooping it up. Mostly the jollity accrued around artifacts of the defeated: a burned-out Iraqi tank, or a howitzer or the like. Around an abandoned Iraqi antiaircraft gun there were perhaps a hundred people, men, women, and children, waving Kuwaiti flags and pictures of the emir, cheering and hollering and generally making noise. They made their loudest noises according to gender. The men expressed themselves by shooting their automatic rifles or pistols into the air, the women by ululating, which is the Arab female noise of public emotion—a wailing series of glottal stops somewhat like keening with the hiccups. It falls strangely on Western ears.

When we got out of the car and the crowd saw that we were American, they all rushed around to talk. They talked like people who had been shut up for a long time, in a chattering rush to get out everything they had to say. Between the fervor to speak and the limits of crossing languages, what came out was a sort of telegram of emotions. "Listen! Kuwait is happy! I am very happy. I am very, very, very happy," said the first man who came up. "Yes, I am very, very, very happy. America is very good. Bush! Bush! Bush! Bush!" Another man grabbed Dan's hand and held it up in the air, as you would the victor's of a prizefight, and led a chant that everybody took up at once: "Boosh! Boosh! Yah, Yah, Bush! Yah, yah, George! Yah, yah, Bush!" A third man interrupted this with another telegram, one of bad news. "Listen! Iraqi people killed the people. They killed the people." He introduced himself: Ibrahim al-Khadi, resident of Kuwait City. "Everything you hear is true," he said, with much urgency. "They kill the people. They rape women. They kill thousands of people. They take them to their families and shoot them. Anything you can imagine they do, they do."

The man next to him nodded his head in agreement. His name was Nasser Seleh, and he was a district attorney in Kuwait City. I asked him to run down, professionally, the crimes the Iraqis had committed during the occupation.

"Too many crimes to count," he said. "It was like a hysteria. There is nothing in history like this. You cannot count the crimes of Saddam Hussein. He burned the three biggest hotels in Kuwait. This is very clearly destruction of private property, arson, theft, vandalism. He destroyed the bridges, destroyed the streets. Destruction of public property, theft. Three days ago, before they leave, they went through the streets, and even into the mosques, and they took men, just men, in large numbers. Took them to Basra. This is kidnapping. Then, of course, they killed many people, which is murder, first degree or second. They killed people and threw their bodies near their houses. They killed people like you would kill a chicken. The tongue can't say what Saddam Hussein did to Kuwait in the past seven months."

Nasser Seleh chose his words carefully, and his small, meticulous voice was out of place against the backdrop of the parade going by. Just about every car would slow down as it passed us, and people would yell and scream and shoot pistols and rifles in the general direction over our heads, and then that car would drive on, and another one a few seconds later would do it again.

A middle-aged man with a round, smart face joined us. He was a newspaper man himself, he said, Abdullah al-Khatib, a writer for *Al Rai Alam*. He had a lot to say, as reporters do. "The Iraqis left at three A.M. yesterday, Tuesday. They destroyed everything before they left. The took cars with them, and ran in the night like thieves. They took anything of value they could carry. They took all the machines, even the presses out of the ground, from our newspaper and sent them to Baghdad.

Abdullah al-Khatib had witnessed an execution by Iraqi Mukhabarat agents perform an execution on their last working day in town. "It was two boys, seventeen and twenty years old. Some people in the last days had started waving Kuwait flags or pictures of the emir and they said these two boys were doing this, so they took them to a place and had them kneel down and then put a gun to their temples and shot them."

He offered to take us in his car to the place, if we would give him some gasoline, as he had none to spare for nonessential driving. We poured half a jerry can in his tank. He chattered as he drove along, tour guide to the occupation. "They were very big on torture. They would pull out fingernails and put electricity on people, sometimes on the neck and sometimes on the back. Sometimes they would make sex with the women. They would take the man and take his fingernails off and take the women to the head office and then put electricity on their skin and afterward make sex with them, and then kill them."

Near a traffic circle where people were cheering and dancing around a Saudi tank was an empty, ugly little dirt lot, a hardscrabble spot of dust and stone and weeds. We stopped next to a red-and-white *kaffiyeh* lying on the ground. It had been drenched in blood, which was now dried, so the cloth was stained a dull brown-red. Next to it was a big patch of rust in the dirt, and in front of that were two sets of scuff marks. "This is the place where they take the young men to shoot them. The day before yesterday at midnight. My house is across the street and I saw this. Here is where they made them kneel down, and here they put a gun to their heads and shot them. They shot the boys in the head, one with a pistol in the forehead and one with a pistol in the back of the head. They fell here."

He led us on to the al-Adathi prison, a government building about a block away that had been converted into a prison by the Iraqi Mukhabarat. We walked there amid the revelers, and stopped to admire a young man. He had draped a Kuwaiti flag around his shoulder like a cape, and was as heavily armed as an extra in a spaghetti Western. He had a knife tucked into one side of his belt and a pistol in the other, and in his right hand held a submachine gun, a new model from the Belgian company Fabrique Nationale, elegant in its softly shining black matte finish. He was a one-man parade, each step a strut, each movement a swagger, the whole a celebration of being young, male, free, and armed to the teeth. He was, he said, a hero of the resistance, Hamed al-Mutari, twenty-five years old.

"It was very easy for me," he said. "I fight at night in secret, at midnight and after. I killed twenty Iraqi with my knife and my pistol. We would make friends with an Iraqi soldier and invite him to my house for supper, like a friend, and after supper, we would kill them. After, we would dig in the ground and put them in, in a good way, according to Islam." Once, he said, the Iraqis caught him and beat him, but he did not tell them anything.

Abdullah al-Khatib did not believe him. "Twenty Iraqis!" he said as we walked on. "I do not think so."

At the entrance to the prison, in a lot filled with stolen and looted luxury cars, we came across a sort of pilgrim: Mubarak al-Wawan, thirty-two, brother of Ahmed al-Wawan, thirty. Ahmed al-Wawan had been captured by the Iraqis in the sweeps for hostages two days before and was now among the missing. He was probably in Basra or Baghdad, but he had been taken here when he was arrested, and his brother had come now in hope of finding some sort of clue. I think he was ready to give up when we arrived, but he offered to accompany us around.

Just inside the front doors, scattered on the linoleum floor, were a dozen or so ledger books. The books were big, old-fashioned ledgers, with neatly lined pages and hard covers. They had been filled with entries written in black ink by some careful, elegant hand. Each entry denoted the arrest and disposition of some unlucky soul.

We toured the Iraqi living quarters first. The floors were covered with a black, ground-in grime that was sticky underfoot, as if it were composed of something viscous and wet that had dried imperfectly. The pale-green walls were decorated with graffiti. "Fahd Is a Son of a Bitch" and "Hosni Mubarak Is a Son of a Bitch" were one on top of the other. Nearby: "Jabar and Fahd = No Good" and "Saddam Is the Crown of the Arabs." All of the walls were stained and dirty, and on some of them were brownish splotches and smears. In one room, where I stood for a minute transfixed by an ocher arc that had been splashed across four feet of wall, Mubarak al-Wawan drew my attention away to a fancy lady's pump—black and backless with gold metallic straps. "In this room, they bring the women and make them have sex. More than one man. On the floor. It is very dirty."

"Dirty" was the word. On Arabian Gulf Street, the boulevard by the sea that is the heart of Kuwait City, and that the Iraqis trashed, a post-liberation piece of graffiti read "Diarty Iraqis." Apart from the misspelling, it was an accurate sentiment. The men who took Kuwait City were a remarkably dirty bunch, even in their own living quarters. In the corners of their bedrooms in al-Adathi prison, and all along the hallways, were piles of trash and rotting garbage—half-eaten food, old bowls of rice, the effluvia of spilled bottles and cans. In places the mess came up as high as mid-calf, so that you had the choice of wading through it or attempting to tread lightly atop it, like Jesus walking on a landfill. Charred patches on the floor showed where the cooking fires had been, and the walls and ceilings were dark with soot. The beds of the occupiers were thin, hard pallets of a deep and gritty gray. The ammonia stink of urine—ripe, high, and sharp—perfumed the air, and piles of aging feces could be seen lurking in the trash heaps and dotting the floors here and there. I later learned it was this habit of their keepers that most amazed and disturbed the Kuwaitis. Public land in Arabia is often dirty and sometimes filthy, but the standards of cleanliness inside the home are fairly high. The Kuwaitis, being rich, are particularly fastidious. The idea that a man would defecate in his own bedroom astonished them. Over the next few weeks, I heard about it over and over: "You know"—a tone of whispered incredulity—"those pigs, those animals, they shit all over the place!" And it was true. If you picked one substance as a trademark of the Iraqi occupation of Kuwait—other than blood, I mean—it would be shit. With the exception of their trenches, they shat up every place they went into that I saw. It was as if they were marking their territory with spoor, so that everyone would know, seeing a room decorated with festering little piles, that Saddam's men had been there.

Moving along, we came to the furnace room, set up by the Iraqis, Abdullah al-Khatib said, as an interrogation and torture chamber. It was notably cleaner than the other rooms—"They have to clean it often because of the blood," said Abdullah—but smelled so awful that the bile rose in my throat as we crossed the threshold. There were many flies, and they were very fat. On one wall, a large electric fuse panel was open, and several wires attached to it dangled to the floor. "They used to put the guys here and put two wires on them so electricity would go into them," Abdullah said.

A bit down the hall was a medium-sized room, about twenty-five feet square. Here, said Abdullah, "they would keep most of the prisoners. Sometimes, two hundred men at one time stay in this room." The room was bare, except for small, torn hunks of polystyrene littering the floor. "For pillows," Abdullah said. "The men used those for pillows." Adjoining the room was a smaller, glassed-in room, obviously designed as a supervisor's office. "Now this is one thing that is very bad," Abdullah said, pointing to it. "Sometimes when they catched a person, they would put him in here first and torture him so that other people who wait in the big room can see it and this will make them talk. This is a very bad thing to do, I think."

All of the people who had been held here (more than five

hundred total, Abdullah guessed) had been released or, in the
cases of those held in the last days of the occupation, taken to
Iraq. We saw only one person there, and he was a visitor like
us, a very old man, with a white beard and ragged clothes. We
came across him loading up a big hundred-kilo sack of rice on
a wheelbarrow. We startled him, but when he saw that we were
not Iraqis, he grinned widely, if mostly toothlessly. Abdullah
asked him what he was doing, and he laughed when he answered. "The Iraqis take a sack of rice from me four months ago.
I return now to take my rice back."

Abdullah invited us to tea. He had a big house in a nice
suburban enclave called Andulus. We sat in a long, wide *dat*, the
traditional Arabian reception hall, spare but luxurious, with a
plush peach-colored carpet, and banks of pink sateen sofa-
benches ringing the walls, and small teak incidental tables between them. It was a room for talk. Talk is a matter of serious,
ritualized concern among the upper classes of Kuwait. In the
mornings, over breakfast and tea, one talks with other men of
the immediate family. Over lunch, and in the early to late
afternoon, one talks with members of the extended family and
close friends, who visit, or are visited. In the later afternoons
and evenings, one goes to the *diwaniya*. A *diwaniya* is an open
gathering of men (the women have ones of their own, but it is
the male gathering that decides things), and is Kuwait's principal vehicle of governance, the way by which the ruling families
reach consensus. When the al-Sabah family wishes to test an
idea, or to get a sense of what the people are saying, its various
princes circulate among the *diwaniyat* and listen to the talk. It
is not necessary to do more. Only the literate men of the ruling
class, defined by law as those whose families settled in Kuwait
before 1920, may vote, a group that constitutes only six to seven
percent of the population. All of these men may be found in one
or another *diwaniya*, most any night, talking.

To talk properly, one needs a big, comfortable room, such as
this one, with sofas or padded benches around the walls, and

with tables at convenient points for holding teacups and ashtrays, cigarettes and lighters, and worry beads. We took off our
shoes and sat down, and a son brought us the first cups of tea,
and by the time we had finished and he was bringing the second,
four or five other men had wandered in, and the talk got under-
way in earnest. Mostly, of course, it was about the Iraqis.

Saed Abd al-Razak, a broad, plump fellow who had just
walked in and was kissing and hugging his way down the line
of men, all bobbing up from their seats for the embrace and then
down again, said that the Iraqis were irreligious men. "They
stole a microphone from the mosque, and sometimes they drink
and they don't really care about *jihad* at all. We say to them,
what about the *jihad,* and it means nothing to them." He made
a little joke in response at Iraq's expense, a much safer form of
humor this week than last. *"Allahu Akbar,"* he said. Everybody
laughed at that.

"Really, it is true," he continued. "They had no regard for
God at all. They arrested my brother one time, and one thing
they said to him was: 'Can you tell us what is the comparison
between the Prophet Muhammad and Saddam Hussein?' They
were trying to make him choose, you see, between insulting
Saddam and blaspheming the Prophet. My brother was very
smart. He said, 'I am not a religious man. How can I know such
a thing?' "

Very smart, everyone nodded in agreement.

"Another time I heard about, an Iraqi officer said to an *imam*
he had taken into the police station, 'Listen, boy. There are
seven heavens above us and above that there is God and above
God there is Saddam Hussein.' Well, the *imam* almost had a
nervous breakdown when he heard that, and he isn't completely
well yet."

Everybody laughed again, and a son came in and poured us
all glasses of Tang Instant Breakfast drink from a metal pitcher.
The talk turned to occupation horror stories. Saed Abd al-
Razak told of a doctor, one Hisham al-Obeidan. "They arrested

him without any visible reasons and took him away from his family for six days. When they took him away, they asked him, 'Do you wish anything?' And he said, 'Let me kiss my children.' They let him do so. After six days, they called his wife and told her, 'Your husband will be returning to you today in time for lunch, so wait the meal for him.' So she did. And they brought him back to the house at lunchtime, and rang the doorbell, and when his wife answered it, with all the children around her to greet their father, they shot him with two bullets and killed him on the spot."

The talk went on and on and on, and more tea was poured, and more cigarettes were smoked, and a boy came in to light the kerosene lamps in the corners. We wanted to leave, to get back to our car and further explore the city before the light failed altogether, but it was hard to do so. There is a kind of narcotic in the talk of a *diwaniya*. It washes over you in soothing murmurs and ripples of vowels and soft consonants, and although it never seems to be going anywhere at all, it also seems as if it will go on forever.

Every so often, I would rouse myself enough to struggle to the surface and try. "Must be going. Really, must leave now . . . got to go."

"No, no, stay, you must stay for dinner, soon, soon. . . . More tea?"

We drove through gathering dusk in a gathering celebration. Everywhere, on every street corner and road, there was a party in progress. A truck pulled up by us at one corner, and three little girls in party frocks sang to us, in pretty piping voices. "Welcome, soldier. You are welcome. Welcome, soldier," over and over, until we drove away.

There was endless honking. I suppose there must have been ten thousand horns sounding at the same time at any moment. In the mix, some voices came through, rapid little staccato beeps, long-drawn-out honks, fancy air horns playing melodies. We created a scene wherever we went. In some places we couldn't move forward more than a few feet at a time because of the crowds around the car. A father lifted his little girl up so that she could see the Americans. She was wearing her Sunday-best dress. She said, "I love you." It was a great sweetness, and I am sure I will never experience anything like it again.

The city looked as if it had been worked over by a gang of teenage vandals, drunk on Saturday night. The buildings were stained with black rain. The downtown areas were almost destroyed, virtually every building burned, or shot full of holes, the streets and sidewalks torn up by tank treads, the storefronts smashed and looted. The luxury stores lining Al Jahar Street had been torched. Smash and grab and burn. On Arabian Gulf Street, the seaside corniche, the Kuwaiti National Parliament building was fire-gutted, windows shot out, sodden, smoke-stinking furniture thrown out on the white stone pavilion that ran its length. Nearby, the emir's palace had been used for casual target practice by bored gunners on the shore batteries across the street. Its gold-domed clock tower was mostly holes. The front walls were all holes too, and the inside courtyards and buildings had been thoroughly burned. The great hall, a huge central room with a high, arched cathedral-like ceiling, had burned so fiercely that the steel beams of its roof had collapsed and lay in a huge spaghetti twist on the floor. There was nothing atop except the black sky. Nearby, the Foreign Ministry had been used for gunnery practice too, and looked to be a total loss. Half the supports had been shot away, and the rubble was still burning.

A little farther up the road, we came to a hospital, the al-Amiri. A line of cars was waiting to get into the second-story parking lot, and we parked and walked up the ramp to see what the attraction was. The lot was full of people, and in one corner there stood the object of their interest, an undamaged Iraqi antiaircraft gun, its barrel still pointed toward the sea. The people were lined up in front of the gun. A small boy was sitting on its metal seat, pressing the trigger and making gun noises. His father stood smiling next to him. After a minute, the boy's turn was up, and the next in line, a middle-aged man in a *dishdasha* and burnoose, took his place. He eased himself into the seat and shyly, but with a wide grin, grasped the controls. His wife took his picture, and then it was the turn of the next in line.

A PARTY

T HAT NIGHT WE SLEPT IN A ROOM in the Kuwait International Hotel, the high-rise next to the American embassy on Arabian Gulf Street. It had been torched and gutted, like the other hotels, but somewhat less so, and many of the rooms were habitable. The press from Dhahran arrived late at night, in a convoy escorted by officers of the Joint Information Bureau, and the big dark lobby was soon filled with people, barely visible, each moving in his or her own little pool of light from a flashlight or candle. When I woke in the morning, I found that the breeze coming in from the broken window of our room had covered me with a fine layer of oily grit and soot.

We breakfasted in the front seat of the car, on chocolate and Pepsi, and checked our remaining supplies. We had six cans of Kraft cheese, twelve sodas, a box of tea biscuits and half a box of shortbread, eight bags of M&Ms, one bag of bread, seven wedges of Laughing Cow cheese, a hunk of salami, a dense square of sticky and furry dates, half a sack of pistachios, a full jar of peanut butter, a half-full box of Ritz crackers, two cans of sardines, four cans of tuna, three cans of the bean dish called *foul madama,* a jar of orange drink, nine packs of Marlboros, three chocolate bars, a bag of C batteries, a bag of AA batteries, two flashlights, four jerry cans of gasoline, two candles, a mostly full bottle of Louisiana hot sauce, and a can opener. We were rich.

As we were washing up, with Najiron water splashed in our hands, an old Duesenberg convertible drove slowly by. It was a beautiful car, long and lushly curved, painted a bright but creamy yellow, like good butter. The top was down, and four pretty young women were sitting on top of the backseat, waving Kuwaiti flags and hollering, "Go Kuwait." As the car went by, two photographers ran up and shouted it to a halt. "Wave some more, wave more!" they yelled. The girls waved their flags. The photographers took some pictures but were not satisfied. There was a conference with the driver. The car moved forward a few feet, so that it was more squarely in front of the American embassy. The photographers took more pictures. When we left, they were having another conference, and a third photographer had joined them, and was asking the girls to wave the flags some more, with feeling.

The day was heavy with sooty mist and threatening rain under the black sky, but the liberation party was still joyous. Little girls were scrubbed and combed and ribboned and ruffled, in party dresses as bright and shiny as Christmas candy. They wore glossy patent-leather shoes and white socks with lace tops. The older girls were dolled up too, but in a manner mildly naughty, not nice, in universal rich-girl style, a concoction of oversized T-shirts and undersized skirts, and black sunglasses, and skin and bracelets of polished, pampered gold. The older boys were dressed in the male equivalent of this: sweatshirts and tight jeans and black sunglasses and gold watches and—accessorizing for the occasion—guns. That week in Kuwait City was the time of boys with guns. It was Dublin after the Easter Uprising; suddenly everyone was a rebel. There were many sorts of guns: all-purpose Kalashnikovs and Armalite assault rifles, old bruisers of Tommy guns, stubby, short-snout Skorpions and Beretta submachine guns, Smith & Wesson and big Astra .357 revolvers, Colt .45s and Walther and Browning High-Power automatics. Soldiers, who worry about damaging or losing the things upon which their lives depend, tend to treat their firearms with a care that is almost persnickety, but the boys of Kuwait City handled theirs the way they had learned from the movies, with a studied nonchalance. They slung their rifles over their shoulders and dangled them by their sides as they sauntered along, and tucked their pistols in their belts the way the celluloid hard cases do. Here and there I saw guns that looked as if they had seen service, with their wood stocks colored by oil and sweat, and the blueing wearing off the steel, but most of the hardware around town looked as if it had spent the night before still chastely wrapped in oiled paper.

The party's nebulae had spun out and swirled all through the city, but its hot center was on the corniche, and the very heart was in the two-block stretch bordering the International Hotel and the American embassy. At the embassy gates, two teenage boys had stretched across the road and up in the air on poles a sort of finish tape for the war, a huge Iraqi flag. A long, long procession of cars, hundreds of them, passed slowly underneath. The cars were dressed up too, with bunting and flags and big glossy color photographs of the emir. One old Cadillac was strung from chrome to chrome with gold and silver Christmas-tree garlands and papered with twenty-three pictures of the emir's old and dissolute face, covering the hood, the doors, the trunk, the windows. As each car drove honkingly under the flag, the girls in sunglasses would cheer and wave their hands, and the boys with guns would swing up their rifles or pistols and shoot at it, and the sky above. The gunfire was almost constant and it would be that way for days. During the day, you could not see the bullets, but at night the tracers made red tic-tac-toes and crosshatches against the sky. The spent rounds fell and bounced on the sidewalk and bored through the occasional skull. By the end of the first week of the party, bullets from heaven had accounted for a reported six deaths. I know for sure of three, whose fresh graves I chanced upon at Sulaibikhat Cemetery. "Abdullah Jassim, Who Died for Kuwait," read the stone on the mound of a man hit on top of the head by a little hunk of copper from on high. By the embassy and the hotel, where the shooting was particularly heavy, the street became carpeted in ejected shells, which made sharp little cracks, like metal popcorn, when you drove over them.

The prime minister's palace, a mile down the road from the embassy, was shot full of big holes and here and there blown clean away. A young man stood guard. He was wearing a gray designer sweatsuit and a black-and-gold baseball cap with "Top Gun" written across the front. He held an unusually poor rifle, an ancient M-1 Garand whose barrel and breech were acned with deep rust. Stuck in his waistband, though, was a .38 Colt Special, sleek and black and gleaming. His name was Najib Bastaki and he was twenty-four years old, a graduate student at Temple University in Philadelphia, home on summer vacation when the Iraqis invaded.

I asked him if he had fought with the resistance.

"Yes. We used to be afraid of saying that, but nothing can stop us now."

What, in particular, had he done for the resistance? I was just looking for a way to begin a conversation, but I saw from his unhappy expression that the question struck his ears as an accusation. "Well, you see, the word 'resistance' does not mean I had to carry a gun and fight," he said, the note of defense as clear in his voice as if I had actually called him a coward. "Some people did that, but not many. Mostly, all we did was get food to homes, and money. So I, for instance, had the responsibility of distributing food to eight houses in my area. Also money. I personally gave away more than ten thousand U.S. dollars. We would go out at night and early in the morning and slip money under the doors of the people. No one would know who had donated the money or who had delivered it. That way there could be no shame."

A passing car stopped, and the driver poked his head out the window to holler a telegram: "George Bush! George Bush! George Bush! George Bush! George Bush! George Bush!

George Bush! George Bush! George Bush! George Bush! George Bush! George Bush!"

"Just because I did not shoot people, I was still a fighter of the resistance," the young man said.

"Yes, of course. I am sure it was very dangerous for you, distributing food."

"Yes. Very, very dangerous. If you got caught doing it, the Iraqis would kill you, or take you prisoner. This never happened to me, but I know of people that it did happen to. And once, myself, I got hit by an Iraqi soldier."

"Really?"

"Yes, in the eye. Can you see?" He put his face close to mine and pointed to his right eye, where there was a very faint mark that might have been the slightest of bruises.

"Yes, I can see it."

"I am afraid it is almost gone now." He was morose. "It was much better before. One girl kissed it."

I hunted for a compliment to make him feel better. "That is a very nice pistol."

"Yes, beautiful. Here, you may shoot it." He pulled it from his belt and snapped the safety catch off and handed it to me, handling it with ginger lust. I pointed it up, and, feeling awkward and silly (but wanting to shoot it, wanting to be able to think to myself that I too was the sort of fellow who went around shooting guns in the air in the spirit of liberation), pulled the trigger. The percussion made a surprisingly modest *pop!* and knocked my hand back a little.

The young man went on about his food distribution. He wanted to make sure I understood that he had done his part. "The main things were rice, sugar, and ghee. We divided the city up into blocks and each block has, say, ten houses, and we would take the sacks of rice and fifty kilograms of sugar and meet secretly at night at a point we picked out ahead of time and get the food and then take it to our areas. In each area we would have what we called a main store and each main store would hold the supplies for ten houses. After we got the food to the main store, the guys in that block would deliver to each house in the next nights."

I said that he had certainly done a lot.

"Yes. And it was very important. It changed this city, you know. There are no more hard feelings. It is like we are all one family, because we all did this together. Now we are brothers and sisters with one heart."

A car full of yelling, laughing kids drove by. They had fixed up a rough effigy in an Iraqi uniform with a ring through its nose and a sign, "Saddam," around its neck, and were dragging it from the rear bumper, the straw enemy bouncing along in the mud and water.

"It must have been difficult, though."

"Oh yes. The Iraqis were animals. Sometimes they would come to the houses and burn the Holy Book. Or they would come and say, 'If this is God's house, tell him to come out.' They were not human. A girl I know, she was fifteen years old, very pretty. Some Iraqi soldiers jumped over the wall and got into her house. There were four girls in the house. They took the one who was fifteen and took her away. Some friends of mine later saw her body. Where her breasts were, they had cut her. They cut off one breast and put it in a plastic bag. There were markings where they had put a very hot iron on her vagina. The body was left lying in the street, naked."

"Terrible. A terrible thing. It must have been horrible, the occupation."

He looked a touch surprised. "Horrible? Not to me. It was exciting."

The Iraqis had expected an attack by water, and had built the corniche, Arabian Gulf Street, into a formidable line of defense. They had turned the seafront apartments on the upper floors of the luxury high rises into elevated pillboxes by filling in the

windows with cinder blocks and sticking in heavy machine
guns. The surf was thick with obstacles to rip out the bottoms
of landing craft and slow the troops washing in: first a line of
iron rods in star clusters of sharp points, then a jumble of jagged
concrete blocks and rolls of concertina wire. Above that, on the
narrow beach itself, was a double line of trenches, pillboxes, and
bunkers. The trenches were laid out in a line that took periodic
right-hand turns, which would have allowed the defenders to
enfilade the attackers, had there been attackers. These were
beautifully made trenches, infinitely better than the ones at the
front, deep enough to protect the full body of a soldier, and
lined with double thicknesses of concrete, cinder block, or
stone. They had been well equipped, too; most of them still
contained full crates of rifle ammunition and rocket-propelled
grenades.

The second line, about twenty yards behind the first, was
even stronger, with a pillbox or bunker for every fifty yards of
trench. The first one we went into had cinder-block walls and
a roof made of four-by-fours and plywood under a triple layer
of sandbags. Most of the structure was below ground, so that the
top of the sandbags was only three feet above ground level.
Concrete steps, lined with sandbags, led down into a room well
furnished with curtains, pillows, and two mattresses and lit by
electricity from a wire hooked up to a streetlight.

In the center of the line of trenches was the fire-control
bunker, much more impressive than the others, a five-foot-tall
pentagon of poured-concrete-and-cinder-block walls, fourteen
inches thick, with small, square windows, two to a wall. Inside,
the walls were painted white and covered with charts. One,
drawn neatly in crayon, showed the section's defenses, noting
the underwater obstacles and mines. Another showed the section divided into fields of fire, with the trenches and pillboxes
and bunkers drawn in blue ink and the vector lines in green.
Some conscientious soul must have spent some time on it; it was
a neat and precise chart. A red telephone stood on one table,

and behind a red-and-white-striped curtain there was a hollowed-out space filled with crates of antitank grenades and machine-gun rounds.

Most of the bunkers and pillboxes were clean, the only clean Iraqi living quarters I ever saw in the city. There was one exception, in which we found a deep litter of trash and clothes. It was disturbing trash; a lot of the clothing belonged to women. There were several dresses and a brassiere and a pair of peach-colored nylon tap pants. A few feet away was a doll, with yellow hair and blue vacant eyes and a neat little plaid dress. There was also a very little girl's pair of underpants, white with a picture of a giraffe on them. The giraffe was holding a teacup, and underneath was written "A Giraffe's Party!" Nearby was an open, mostly full jar of petroleum jelly.

On the sidewalk along the beach, middle-aged men with large cameras moved slowly, with the purposeful, curiously workaday look of the determined tourist. Where the girls had their sunglasses and the boys their guns, the family men had their Nikons and Camcorders. We stopped to talk to a large man who was wearing slacks and a T-shirt he had made for the occasion. On the front he had written, "Worry No More. Coalition Forces Are Here," and on the back, "Free Kuwait and the Green Berets."

"Baser Aldarweesh, I am damned glad to meet you, welcome," he said. "It is a glorious day, is it not? I am just witnessing the most breathtaking thing. I am riding around with some guys from the U.S. Special Forces and we see a group of Iraqis in civilian clothes. I say, 'Hey, those guys are Iraqis,' and the Special Forces guys stop the car and run out, and goddam, they kicked those guys' ass."

He stopped for a moment to take a picture of two young men waving Kuwaiti flags and leading, amid much cheering, a donkey. The donkey had an Iraqi army officer's cap tied to his head and a sign around its neck identifying it as Saddam Hussein.

"Goddam, I don't mind telling you I am glad to see those

guys go," said Baser Aldarweesh, turning away from the street. "Those Iraqis, goddam, they were crazy. If they were just having a bad day, they would kill a bunch of guys."

Farther on, we came across two gentlemen, slim and very well dressed, in good-quality cotton sports shirts and pleated trousers and loafers. They were in their twenties, and had gleaming accents of gold about them, in the thin, sleek watches on their wrists and the fountain pens in their pockets. One of the men was named Ali al-Halfah. He was a certified public accountant and the son of a prosperous merchant. The other was Kalef Wazzal, and I don't recall his occupation. They were full of scorn for the Iraqis.

"The first day of the war, I saw in the street many soldiers," Ali al-Halfah said. "They were stopping any car they see, and they just drive the cars away. They just take it, there is nothing you can do."

Nothing?

"Oh my, no. They are very brutal. They will kill you if you resist. They take many people away and kill them. They say any reason they want to kill you. They say, 'You said Fuck Saddam Hussein.' You might say, 'No, I do not say Fuck Saddam Hussein.' They say, 'We have a witness who hears you say Fuck Saddam Hussein.' And then they take you away. They take many people away. In the last three days of the war, they come to the homes and if there are any young people there, they take them prisoners and send them to Iraq."

What did you do?

"Well, I hid in my house. My father is an old man, and when the soldiers came, he would go to the door and say, 'I am the only one here.' Once the soldiers searched the house, but they do not find me. The truth is, the Iraqi people are very stupid. They are great thieves but they are so stupid it is not hard to hide from them." He gestured with his wrist to show the fine gold bracelet-watch the Iraqis never got. "We hide many things. We hide our cars. Rich people, who have Ferraris and Porsches and Mercedes, in the first week after the invasion, they hire cranes and put their cars on the roofs of their houses. The stupid Iraqis never find them. One man I know put his Jaguar in his swimming pool, and filled the pool up with dirt and planted a garden on top. He dug it out yesterday, and except for some dirt, it is as good as new."

The next day, a warm and blue-skied day, I went out on Gulf Street and let the parade pick me up and swirl me along. A jeep drove by me with two big American flags flying from its antennas and, on the roof, a life-size cardboard statue of Marilyn Monroe, in the publicity still taken for *The Seven-Year Itch*, where she is standing wide-legged on a Manhattan subway grate and the updraft is billowing her white dress up to her shoulders and she is holding it down a little with one hand, but not so much or so well as to fully hide her panties. All the boys yelled and cheered as Marilyn made her way up the street.

Two young men had made a mini-parade out of themselves. One of them was wearing a tiger costume, of the sort used by university team mascots in America, and the other had an American flag and a snare drum, on which he beat enthusiastic, if ragged, time. They walked right down the middle of the street and made all the cars stop for them, or go around. They had taken as their victory chant a line from a Neil Diamond song, which they had slightly mangled, and were chanting over and over: "Can't you see! We're coming to America! Can't you see! We're coming to America!" I walked up the street behind them for a while, and as I was passing the American embassy, an old lady came up to me and held out a sprig of sage. "I must give you this," she said. "Because the Iraqis destroyed all my blooms."

In front of the American embassy, the crowd was bigger than the day before, perhaps a thousand and exceptionally noisy. Fresh graffiti had come up overnight on the embassy wall:

"Saddam—Pushed by Bush" and "We Love Yankee." A woman of perhaps fifty carried a hand-lettered poster in each hand. One was a photo of Saddam, and underneath it she had written, "Wanted Dead or Alive. The Butcher of Baghdad. $100,000,-000." On the other, she had drawn a big red heart and written inside it, "Well Done, USA." A helicopter flew low overhead, and she stopped and blew kisses at it, sending each smooch up with a fine sweep of her arm.

A man with a big, bristling white mustache, came up to me and stopped to make a small speech. "Good day. I am of Egypt. Egypt, Cairo, Hosni Mubarak good—very good. Same thing America. Saddam Hussein—" he grabbed his neck with his hands and pretended to be choking himself; he did this with such energy that he actually staggered back a step, and his face turned a deep red. When he took his hands away, I could see big pale finger marks outlined on the skin of his throat. He beamed. "Thank you. Good day."

A small, smiling child ran up. "Kill Saddam," she said. "Kill Saddam."

The demonstration loosely turned around two armored personnel carriers parked across the street a hundred yards down from the embassy. On top of the carriers were two young Kuwaiti soldiers, very proper in stiff, spotless uniforms, and holding themselves in the unnatural poses of men who know that their picture is being taken on a historic occasion. They were sitting half out of the carriers' top hatches, with their hands on their .50-caliber machine guns as if they were ready to leap into action. They sat very upright, with their stomachs sucked in, and their chests out, and their chins tilted in the general direction of the embassy roofline. The videotape crews were shooting them from three different angles, and young women climbed up to give the soldiers red flowers. The soldiers stuck them in the barrels of the machine guns, which I am sure made the young women and the cameramen happy.

Wandering along, I came on a group of teenyboppers, singing

and giggling. "What are you singing?" I asked. One of them answered for the group. "We are [giggle] singing 'We are [giggle] slaves to God' [giggle]. It is a holy song we sing at Ramadan [giggle]."

At this, they broke down completely and ran laughing away. Four more teenage girls, slightly older, approached. They were wearing sweaters festooned with pictures of the emir, George Bush, Margaret Thatcher (it was widely believed in Kuwait that it had been Mrs. Thatcher who gingered Mr. Bush into doing the necessary), and John Major. The photos had been cut from magazines and carefully framed in red and silver glitter. "Can you sign my autograph book, please?" said one of the girls. She handed me a little book much like the one my sister Kate once had. It had a pink vinyl cover with a flower design on it and a little locking clasp of the thinnest and cheapest metal, colored gold. Its pages were divided into three pastel sections, yellow and pink and blue. I glanced quickly through it. It was about half filled, mostly not with autographs, but with pictures of various movie and rock stars from teen fan magazines. Each page that had been filled had been folded over, along the diagonal, which I remember is the proper form; Kate always did that too. Write "To Maha," said the girl. I wanted to think of something profound, or at least clever, but I couldn't. I wrote, "To Maha, on a wonderful day." The entry on the page before mine was "To a lovely Kuwaiti girl—Capt. Donald Henry."

For most people, I think, the worst thing about the occupation had been the daily grind of hiding from pain, and not knowing when it would find you. The celebration of the week of liberation was all about not having to hide anymore. On the beach I met a man struggling to keep three small children in line. He had his hands full. Every time he managed to rope one in, the other two would squirm away from him and run off toward the land mines and barbed wire. He was a mechanical engineer, thirty-four years old, and the father of the three running about: six-year-old Abdullah, five-year-old Apeer, and a girl, two-year-old Hasha. His name was Bader al-Abaidan. When I asked him to tell me about the occupation, he said: "We have been in Kuwait living peacefully forever. Nothing like this has ever happened before. It is like jumping from zero to a thousand miles an hour. Suddenly, everything happens, and we stay because we are not believing this. We do not know what to do. Life changes. My kids like to go out every day. And we always do. It is beautiful here. We never carried any ID. We never had any police bothering us. Anywhere you want to go, you just go. Everything is free and open here. But when the Iraqis come I had to keep the children inside all day, to protect them. They do not understand this and it is very hard for them. They say, 'Why should we stay inside?' I say, 'There is shooting outside.' They do not understand. To them it is just exciting noise." On the day the Iraqis left town, he let the children out to play for the first time in three months.

Driving around the city, I found myself in an upper-class neighborhood where the houses ran to the size of small apartment buildings, big square structures of three and four stories, one for each wife of a rich man. In a dusty vacant lot, two women were standing and talking. I parked and walked up to them. One was in her forties, the other in her late teens. The older one was wearing a bathrobe, and her face was drawn and lined. The younger was wearing jeans and a sweatshirt. They talked about what they had gone through, and their main complaint was one that would have struck some people as frivolous, but it was not to them.

"Look at me," said the older woman, pulling at her bathrobe with her hands. "See how my body is. See how my face is. This is what the occupation has done to me. For months, we cannot go outside, we cannot put on lights, we cannot eat good food— and this is what it has done to us."

"It is true," said the young woman. "They wouldn't let us out. The soldiers would shout at us if we went out, vulgar things, and frighten us, so we had to stay in."

"Look at us," said the older woman. "Our clothes are filthy. Our hair is dirty. We are ugly. We used to be beautiful."

They were wealthy women, part of the ruling class of Kuwait. The older one was a lawyer, well known, I later found out, and married to a sheik. Her name was Fatima al-Shammira. The younger one was her niece, an eighteen-year-old college student named Latifa al-Eidan. They lived down the street. We walked over to their houses, and they showed me the proximate cause of their loss of beauty. It was a medium-size mansion directly across from theirs. Two months earlier, the Iraqi governor of Kuwait, Saddam's brother-in-law, the famous killer Ali Hassan Majid, had appropriated the house and moved in. His soldiers had taken the house next door and set up an observation post and antiaircraft gun on the roof. From there they could see the whole street, and even into the windows of the houses across the way. Their presence sent the women into seclusion. "You see, this is the window of my room, right across the street from the gun." Latifa pointed. "For two months, I cannot open the curtains, because when I do, I see the soldiers looking down at me and they laugh and say, 'You are beautiful. Come up and see me,' and this frightens me very much."

"We cannot go outside," said Fatima. "If we go out, the soldiers might take us and make us no good. They do this to women, the Iraqis. Everyone knows this."

A young man, Nayef al-Rashid, the nephew of the man who owned the houses taken over by the Iraqis, showed me around. The house where Ali Hassan had made his home was still in decent shape, but a guesthouse that had served as quarters for some of the soldiers was pretty well trashed. It had been an ostentatious little bijou of a building, with mirrored walls and thick green carpet and violet silk sofas and leather armchairs, and chandeliers in each of its three rooms, but it was a slum now. The chandeliers had been pulled down and lay on the floor. The carpet was black with mud and dirt. In the bathroom, all the mirrors were broken, and the sink had a jagged hole in it and the toilet was overflowing with shit. In the two bedrooms, the bureaus had been kicked apart. The garden, surprisingly, was untouched, its lines of orange trees and date palms still flourishing, the hibiscus in bloom and fragrant. In a wire pen were a whole flock of geese, ducks, pigeons, and hens.

I was leaving, walking to my car, when Fatima and Latifa came running up. They had something they wanted me to see. It was very important, they said. Each of them handed me a photograph. Fatima's picture showed her seated at her desk, in a black leather chair, resting her hands on the desktop and smiling broadly. She wore a black lace dress that showed glimpses of her shoulders, and chest, and long black gloves. Over her gloves she was wearing two gold diamond rings and a gold wristwatch; around her neck, she wore a large, ornate gold necklace. Gold earrings dangled from her ears. She was wearing a lot of makeup; her lips were lacquered in Chinese-restaurant red and her eyes were rimmed in thick black mascara. She must have been twenty pounds heavier in the picture than she was now; the lines of her face were soft curves instead of sharp etchings. Latifa's photograph was her college identification card. She was pretty and sweet in a flowered dress, with her hair permed and a smile that was a dazzler, even with the braces on her teeth.

"So now," said Fatima, "you can see. We were beautiful. And look at us now."

"Yes," said Latifa. "Look at me now. Look at my hair." She

held out a handful of her hair, which was tousled and knotted in a rather pretty way, actually.

"You are both beautiful in the pictures," I said, feeling awkward and stupid. "But you are still beautiful." They thanked me, but they thought I was lying. "You keep the pictures," Fatima said. "The pictures are when we were beautiful."

TORMENTS OF
THE FLESH

T HE HALL AT KUWAIT UNIVERSITY'S SCHOOL OF MUSIC and
drama was a place of conspicuous civilization, a big cantilevered room with blue cloth seats trimmed in gold. The walls
were paneled in some rich wood, and a deep, broad stage
surmounted the orchestra pit. The first discordant signs of bar-
barism were feathers and bones. The building was of modern
design, with an exterior ramp that led several stories up to a
broad concrete platform, which in turn led to the doors that
opened into the top tier of the auditorium. The Iraqis had used
the platform as a pen for chickens and sheep, and what the
beasts had left behind made a rotting, malodorous mess underfoot.

Inside the hall a British television crew was videotaping the
statement of twenty-nine-year-old Abdullah Jasman, Kuwaiti
citizen, University of Pittsburgh graduate, and victim of a torture session in this unlikely setting. The crew had set their
camera up on the balcony, and Jasman stood a few feet away,
facing it. When I walked in, the producer in charge motioned
with his finger to his lips for me to be quiet. I stopped, and the
place was still and silent except for the man standing in front of
the camera, talking and crying. He was a square-built black
man, with strong, homely features; not the face of one for public
weeping. But this sort of thing no longer surprised me. In

normal life, you hardly ever see grown men cry; in war, it is a commonplace. Between the beginning of things and the end, I must have seen twenty men cry, not counting myself.

Near where the camera stood, there lay a broken rubber-handled truncheon. In a corner was a pile of academic robes, trimmed in azure and gold, sodden and reeking of wet rot and urine. Here and there the tile floor was spotted with drops of dried blood, little trails that went nowhere in particular.

"One day on the highway the Iraqis stopped us," the black man began.

"Could you just come forward a bit, Abdullah?" said the producer. "Need to get you in frame properly."

He moved forward a step. The producer said, "Now, that's a good chap. Where were we, hmm?"

"I was with a group of people. They covered our eyes and roped our hands and put us in a line and walked us up here." A door cracked suddenly shut, and he jumped in a rabbity little hop.

"Oh, sorry, Abdullah," the producer said. He gestured to his Ministry of Information guide. "You there, keep that door shut." Turning back to the black man: "Now then."

"They hang us upside down. Naked, no clothes; we are not allowed to sleep or eat. They try to get us drunk, but we do not. So they started torturing us. The three days passed like years. [He was crying hard now.] Human beings can't resist. You hear people screaming next to you and then you think you are going to be next. You can't resist. What are you going to do? [Now, racking sobs] You can't sleep. You don't know, if you sleep, if you will ever wake again. . . . All the people screaming, begging, screaming."

The producer interrupted him, to prompt him toward the thing that made for television. "Abdullah, could you tell us what happened to you in particular, here in this theater?" he said.

The victim pointed to the stage, on which stood a big section of steel set scaffolding. "On this stage, you can see the metal frame. They put both legs on that and they open them wide and they put a sort of wood on you that comes from one knee to another and they spread you open all the way. When you are open wide, it hurts you. It hurts you bad. They raped one of my friends here. They raped him. They were laughing. They said, 'This is what your president did to you.' I heard later he was dead."

He drifted back into hideous reverie. "You sat in these chairs, waiting to be tortured. You can't see anything. You can hear the voices loud and screaming. . . . They wanted to know where is my brother. I didn't tell them; I didn't know. . . . My family gave them five thousand Kuwait dinars and videos and a TV. . . . They let me go. . . ."

The producer gave him another little push. "And what did they do to you besides putting you on the rack, Abdullah?"

He pulled up his pants legs and showed the camera his calves, mottled with ugly deep black burn wounds. "They put electricity on you with batteries. They would put wires on your legs and your feet in water, so your whole body is electricity. They would put you with the electricity in the water twenty seconds, thirty seconds, and you would go unconscious and they would throw water on you and revive you and then do it again."

As he was finishing, he offered an observation on the nature of torture. "Torture not only hurts at the time. It will hurt all your life. You get up at night and you think that you are in a torture room, not in bed. You are in a safe place, and you think that you are not safe. It is like a fingerprint for the rest of your life." He shivered when he said this, as if fevered.

The producer thanked him, and motioned for the cameraman to turn off the machine. "Well," he said, "I must say, your story is really something." The black man stood silent, with one trouser leg hiked up to the knee and tear trails streaking the dust on his face.

All over Kuwait City after the Iraqis left, people talked of murder and torture and disfigurement and rape. Over the seven months of the occupation, they had become involuntary experts in these things. Familiarity had not bred contempt—pain and death command respect—but morbid fascination. They could not get over with what eagerness and thoroughness the Iraqis had hurt them. It was something almost beyond comprehension, something vastly out of the run of their experiences. They were an unusually insulated, unusually pampered people. For more than two hundred years, they had lived in a stable oligarchy, peacefully prospering since their beginnings in 1752, when Sabah bin Jaber became the first emir of the small seacoast town that had grown up around a fort (*kut,* in Arabic, from which comes Kuwait) built by the bedouin chieftain who then held sway over northeastern Arabia. The town of Kuwait, set on a firm coastal beach in the Bay of Kuwait, enjoyed two local rarities, sweet water and a good protected harbor, and was geographically well placed to trade between the interior of Arabia, the eastern coast of Africa, and the western coasts of India and Indonesia. It quickly became the dominant entrepôt of the region, with a large fleet of *dhows, boums* and *baghlahs,* trading in, wrote a British observer, "Bengal piece goods, Coromandel chintzes, Madras long-cloth, cotton yarn and various cotton manufactures of Malabar, Broach, Cambay, Surat and Gujurat; English woolen goods; silks, Arabian coffee; sugar and sugar candy; spices, condiments and perfumes; indigo; drugs; chinaware; and metals." It became as well the leader in the Gulf pearl trade, and by the turn of the twentieth century it supported a fleet of more than eight hundred diving *dhows.*

In 1938, the Kuwait Oil Company (one half Gulf Oil and one half Anglo-Iranian Oil, now British Petroleum) tapped the Burgan oil field twenty-five miles south of Kuwait City, the second-largest field in the world. Interrupted by the Second World

War, drilling began in earnest in 1946, and by August 1990, Kuwait had 950 wells pumping out 1.5 million barrels of oil a day, with proven reserves of 94 billion barrels, enough to last at those production levels for more than 130 years. The oil money converted Kuwait from a country of slowly accumulating wealth to one of super-riches; by 1990, the little city-state had a per capita income of $14,700, up there with Abu Dhabi, the United States, and Liechtenstein. The unemployment rate was zero; the inflation rate was about 3 percent. There was so much money, and so few Kuwaitis, that for most people work was something other people did. Of the two million people who lived in Kuwait, 60 percent were non-Kuwaitis, guest workers and their families. Foreign workers made up 70 percent of the labor force. Palestinians managed the government agencies and the businesses, Indians ran the hotels, Filipinas served as maids (and sometimes as forced mistresses), Egyptians built the roads and houses and glass towers of the new downtown, Sudanese and Senegalese and Algerians swept the streets and picked up the trash. Eighty percent of the nation's 3,200 physicians were foreigners, 90 percent of the ten thousand nurses. Except for the topmost level of deal-cutting and decision-making, foreigners did everything that needed to be done in Kuwait.

In return, Kuwait gave its guest workers a standard of living that was well beyond anything most of them could enjoy at home, with one of the most comprehensive social welfare programs in the world. Medical treatment was free, for everybody, and of sufficient quality to produce a death rate of only 2.4 per thousand, with a life expectancy for men of seventy-one years, for women, seventy-five. The public school system was well funded and free through the secondary level. University and technical schools maintained high standards and low tuition and were open to non-Kuwaitis. Seventy-four percent of the population above fifteen was literate.

A tiny, interconnected group of well-satisfied men ran everything. Only 6 to 7 percent of Kuwaiti citizens had the right to vote: literate adult males who had lived in Kuwait before 1920 and their literate adult male descendants. Of this group, only half, or 3.5 percent of the total population of citizens, had voted in the last election. The 1962 constitution gave all real power to the emir, Sheikh Jaber a-Ahmed al-Sabah, who was chosen by members of his family; other important government positions were filled by Sabahs or by men the Sabahs chose from the small, shallow pool of the oligarchy. There had been some experiments in participatory democracy, but they had not set well with the ruling class; in 1986, the emir had dissolved the young National Assembly and announced he would henceforth rule by decree.

In two hundred years, the Kuwaitis had never fought to protect their wealth, preferring to deal with predators through shifting treaty arrangements and allegiances, and through generous payments of protection money. Since 1973, when Iraq made a tentative land grab turned back by British pressure, Kuwait had given its big, belligerent neighbor a great deal of money, including $12 billion in loans for the war with Iran. In 1990, Kuwait's armed forces amounted to a little more than twenty thousand troops, about one-fiftieth the size of the Iraqi armed forces.

You could see the difference between Iraq and Kuwait simply by the way the young men of each nation carried themselves. Young Iraqi men, in their black vinyl jackets and pegged trousers, moved like Marseilles toughs, with hips rolling in subtle insolence and shoulders squared in puffed-up counterpoise above. The young Kuwaiti men walked tough too, but there was something distinctly off-note about it; it seemed an imitation, the swagger of a rich kid forced to walk home through the bad part of town because the chauffeur forgot to pick him up at school. To a country like this, a people like this, the nature of the Iraqi visitation was an astonishment and a bewilderment and a shock.

*   *   *

After I left the theater, I drove to a gas station in a middle-class residential neighborhood. Gas had been largely unavailable since December 2, when the Iraqis forbade its sale to Kuwaitis, but here and there stations were getting their pumps working again, and word of where there was gas circulated around the city every day. There must have been three hundred people and a long line of cars waiting on a crew of four or five men who were working with portable pumps and generators to get the gasoline up from the underground tanks. I put my cans in line and went into the little office of the gas station to escape the heat. There was a man behind the desk who looked in charge. He said that, actually, it wasn't his gas station, but he knew his way around pumps and engines, so his neighbors had made him boss. He was a tall, skinny man, with features that were all crags and hollows. He handed me his card, which identified him, in fancy script, as Basim Eid Abhool, Assistant Electrical Engineer, Kuwait International Airport. When I gave it back to him, I noticed his fingernails, or rather the lack of them. They had been removed, and what was left was just the barest baby beginnings of new nails, little strips of cuticle as soft and fragile as the shells of the smallest shrimp. "Ah, you notice my fingers?" the man said. "Iraqis, of course."

He told his story in a matter-of-fact way, leaning his forearms on the desk, and with his hands folded so that his fingernails were tucked away. A group of men gathered around while he talked, but they were quiet, so that all you could hear was his voice and the buzzing of flies. I sat in a hard little yellow plastic chair and wrote down what he said. He spoke slowly, so it was easy to get it all verbatim.

"It was on January 19. They arrested me outside, while I was walking. They took me to a prison. They say, 'Are you in army?' I say, 'Yes, but not anymore. Now I work at airport and am an assistant engineer.' They put me in a small room and they say, 'Exactly what do you do in the army?'

"I say, 'When I am in army, I am a writer, not a soldier, and now I am not in army anyway.'

"They say, 'You have friends, cousins, in army?' I say, 'I don't know.' They say, 'Do you know that your president, Sheikh Jaber, he is no good?'

"I say, 'I don't know.'

"They say, 'Do you know what your president do to your people?'

"I say, 'I don't know. What do he do to my people?'

"They say, 'He marry two hundred women and he take all your money.'

"I say, 'I do not know that. Thank you for telling me.'

"They say, 'The Iraqi people have come to give freedom to people of Kuwait.'

"Then a man comes in who has no uniform. He says, 'Put him in jail.' I stay in jail until Thursday. All the time, behind me in the other room, I hear screaming, 'No, no, please, no, I don't do anything, please.' I listen. I am afraid. On the second day, they come back and they say, 'Put your hands on the table.' I put my hands on the table and they take a stick and hit my hands. They say, 'Can you feel?' I say, 'Yes.' They say, 'Good.' Then two guys take my hands and hold them and they tell me to close my eyes and they take pliers and one by one pull out all my fingers [fingernails]. Then they put them in salt water. And go away.

"You know, the first day and the second day and the third, I feel terrible. But after that I cannot feel it. My hands, my arms, my head, all feels numb. On the third day, Thursday, they take me back to the room. They take my fingers and where the nails were, they take pliers and crush. It is too much. Much too much. I faint. When I wake up, they say, 'You have Kuwait money?' I say, 'No.'" They put me back in jail.

"On the fourth day, they say, 'Don't tell anybody what we do here. If you tell anybody, we will kill you.' And they let me go.

I go home. My family is all gone out of Kuwait, but my friends say, 'What happen to your fingers?' I say, 'It was an electrical accident at work.' Two weeks later, I see the Iraqis who did this to me at supermarket. They are shopping. One of them says hello to me and he says, 'How are your fingers? Are they good?' I say, 'No, they are not good.' He says, 'Come back to the police station and we will make them good.' And then they laugh.

"But now—*hamdililah*—I am good again."

A thin man, squatting on the floor, picking his teeth with a bit of wood, spoke up. His name was Wael Yusef al-Moutawa, twenty-three years old, an employee of the Kuwait National Petroleum Company. He said: "One day the Iraqi soldiers arrest me. I was carrying a gun because I was a resistance fighter. A Kalashnikov. They beat me, and after that, they take a rope and tie my hands behind my back and tie the rope on the ceiling and pull me up by my hands tied behind my back. They kept me hanging there. The first hour was not so bad, but then it got very bad.

"My father and mother came and they brought two thousand dinars to free me. They took the money and said to my parents, 'Soon, he will get out.'

"The next day, an Iraqi man comes to me and he says, 'You love Mr. Jaber? Okay, you watch this. This is what Mr. Jaber does to your people.' He brings in a girl twenty years old, maybe. I am staying on the wall tied up. I try not to see. The soldiers pull my head and say, 'You must see.' One soldier holds the girl hard and the other fucks her. She tries to stop them. She says, 'I am a virgin.' She says to the soldiers, 'You are a Muslim. You must be polite to me. You must be a good man. You cannot do this to me. I am a Muslim. I am your sister.'

"He says, 'I am not a Muslim.'

"She says, 'You do not believe in God?'

"He says, 'You have a God? Where is your God? There is no God. Who is Muhammad? An old man.'

"Then they rape her and I watch and I can see the blood

going out. They put her on the floor of the room and do it. And then they take her out, like a sheep. It was very shameful."

He thought about it for a minute and then he said, "I think there are no Muslims in Iraq. Not at all. Really, they are all crazy."

A smiling middle-aged man with a grocer's figure interrupted to disagree slightly. He introduced himself as Ali Zamoon, general manager of the Kuwait National Real Estate Company. He had been educated in America and had married an American woman. He had an American sort of theory. The Iraqis were not precisely crazy, but were brainwashed, a nation of Manchurian Candidates.

"One time I was stopped by some Iraqi soldiers while I was driving my car. They asked me why I had not changed my license plates from Kuwaiti plates to Iraqi. I said I forgot to do it, or something. But they could not get over it. They could not understand how I could have failed to change the plates after Saddam had told me to do so. They said, 'How can you disobey an order from Saddam?' This made me think about it, and I realized that there was something wrong with these people. Everything they did and thought was all about Saddam. It was Saddam! Saddam! Saddam! all the time. They were like robots. They would follow this man anywhere, doing whatever, because they could not imagine disobeying him. They could not see any point to disobeying an order, even if they knew it was wrong. One day I had a talk with an Iraqi officer I had come to know a little. I asked him, 'If they tell you from Baghdad to kill me, would you kill me?' And he said, 'Yes.' I said, 'Why?' He said, 'Because if they ask me to kill you and I say no, they will kill me and then kill you anyway.'"

The men who had dealt most directly and most often with the horror—the emergency-room doctors and morgue-keepers and ambulance drivers—had tried to make sense out of it by quantifying and classifying its various permutations.

At Mubarak Hospital, the fourth-largest in the city, Dr. Abdullah Behbehani, a small man with that perpetually harried air that you often see in doctors, sat with his hands neatly folded at his desk. He had occupied his mind—perhaps saved his mind—by charting the plague of murder and torture and rape in the same methodical way he would plot a plague of cholera or influenza. He spoke in a small, dry voice.

"All told, we saw approximately four hundred executions at this hospital, and from the beginning I kept careful track of the trends of atrocities. In the beginning, in August, they didn't practice any atrocities against the civilians. They were just interested in invading the country and destroying the army and annexing Kuwait. . . .

"However, it was clear from the beginning that they were very quick to kill. I give you an example. On August 3, the day after the invasion, the Iraqis came here to supervise the evacuation of Iraqi soldiers wounded in the first day of the invasion. We had taken in some of them and treated them, the same as we would a Kuwaiti. As the evacuation was going on, my anesthesiologist, a Kuwaiti lady doctor, was standing next to me and she said, 'God curse the devil,' which is a well-known saying in our culture. An Iraqi officer heard her say this and he said, 'You mean the devil with the beard?'—which was of course a reference to our emir. And she said, 'No I mean you Iraqis, because we were sitting here in peace and you invaded us.' So the officer immediately called over some army men and he told them to hold her and said, 'I will execute you on the spot.' He pulled out his pistol and pointed it at her.

"I had to beg him to spare her. I said, 'Look, we were invaded just now. We were Kuwaitis when we went to sleep last night and now we are Iraqis. You must give us some time to accept this.' After my begging, he said he would forgive her and let her live.

"This was the way it was always. You could not say anything, even a word, of rejection. The only punishment the Iraqis know is to kill. No trials. No prison terms. Just kill.

"When we, the civilians, started to resist and show that we did not like being annexed, the first thing we did was demonstrate peacefully—women, young men, and children. We would raise the Kuwaiti flag and pictures of the emir in demonstrations; we did this to show the Iraqis we did not accept annexation and we wanted our government back and we wanted them out. They immediately opened fire on the demonstrators. I personally had to amputate the leg of a thirty-five-year-old Kuwaiti female because of her bullet wounds. I saw young children killed. The Iraqi soldiers did not try to end the demonstration peacefully or anything like that. They just immediately opened fire against the demonstrators, many of whom were women. This was one week after the invasion.

"The atrocities began soon after that, in reaction to the Kuwaiti people refusing to go along with the annexation. They did this by refusing to go to work, refusing to open their shops, refusing to change their IDs, refusing to do anything except sit in their houses. Soon we began expressing our opinions on walls. Either by putting flags on them or by writing signs of rejection and refusal and signs saying that we wanted our government back. The Iraqis started shooting anyone they saw participating in this. They would shoot them immediately, on the spot. No trial. My sister witnessed two children shot dead in this fashion.

"The most serious atrocities began in the next phase, when the Kuwaiti resistance started trying to carry arms and kill Iraqis. The Iraqis responded with great force. They sent in a new governor, Ali Hassan Majid, and he brought in execution squads from Iraq. The execution squads were not regular soldiers, and they were very brutal. They began executing young men on a systematic basis. We started to see a lot of men between the ages of seventeen and thirty-two brought in here, not as patients to care for, but as bodies to bury. They were brought in in groups of five to ten. This happened almost every day for two to three months; every day we would see another group of bodies. In the beginning, the executions were straightforward—bullets in the head, bullets in the chest. At first they were killed in front of their houses. They would take the young man out of the house and blindfold him, and stand him up in front of the house and then shoot him in the head or the chest in front of his family. This method accomplished two things. One, it meant that they didn't have to deal with the body; they just left it for the family. Two, it contributed to the atmosphere of fear. These executions began in late August and lasted throughout September and October.

"In late September, there started something more severe. We started getting mutilated and tortured bodies. These were bodies that had not simply been shot, but had had their eyeballs taken out, their heads smashed, their bones broken. It was very painful for us as doctors to see this. We could not imagine how anyone who thinks of himself as a human being could do this to another human being. The injuries were very bad. You would see heads completely unvaulted, that is, with the top of the skull sawed off or cut off with an ax and no brain left in the skull pan. Or you would see multiple fractures, legs that had been broken four or five times. Or you would see severe burns on the face and body. Or fingernails that had been extracted.

"When the mutilations began, the Iraqis stopped bringing in the bodies of those killed. They started dumping them in the streets and then calling us and saying, 'There are bodies in such and such a street,' or 'near such and such a police station. Come get them.' And we would send out an ambulance and pick them up.

"We didn't know what these people had done to be killed in this manner. There were old people among those killed, at least fifty of them.

"Then, in November, worse atrocities began, involving women. We started getting numerous women brought in who had been raped and tortured. Rapes became very common after the first few months of the invasion. They would kidnap women, detain them, rape them, and then either kill them or let them go. I personally was on call when three cases of rape came in. I treated all three women. One, I recall, was a young woman who had been raped by three soldiers. They came into her home and hit her husband and smashed his face and broke his ribs with their rifle butts. Then they assaulted her sexually. I was very careful in documenting this by direct examination of her. The awful thing was that she had her period at the time, so they took her from behind—anally—the bastards. The poor woman. What made it even worse was that when the soldiers first came in and attacked her husband, he actually was able at one point to get his hands on a gun and he was going to try to shoot the soldiers, but his wife and his mother told him it was not necessary and got him to give the gun back to the soldiers. You see, they thought the soldiers were just there to beat them and question them, but after the soldiers got the gun back, then they raped the wife.

"I knew one particular woman. The top of her head was gone and bullets were in her chest when they brought her in. She had been picked up and detained for a month and a half. I knew her well. I think she was involved in a lot of resistance activity, principally in sending messages to the government in exile. She was less than twenty-four years old. She was married and had two children. Her name was Asrar al-Kabany. We knew she had been kidnapped right in front of her door, when she was taking out the garbage. She was—my God—she was completely mutilated! They dumped her on the street and the ambulance brought her in here and I saw her—"

As he was talking, the doctor had lost, bit by bit, the voice of the scientific observer, and now he was suddenly overwhelmed. He put his face in his hands and wept, and it was a minute or two before he could recover himself sufficiently to speak. "There was no brain inside her skull. Why should you take the brain out, for God's sake? I am sorry. I get emotional whenever I speak of this." The tears streamed from his eyes, really heavy crying, although silent; the sobs shook his shoulders.

At Al-Sabah Hospital—a big, crowded, dirty place, the hallways lined with various sitting and lying specimens of the hurt, the sick, and the lame—a surgeon named Ali Nassar al-Serafi invited me into a small office, where we sat in the dark and drank sweet coffee.

"From the very beginning, the Iraqis brought bodies in here. Most of the people were killed by a single bullet shot to the head. They brought them in here not to treat but to dispose of. They forced us to write fake death certificates for some of them, saying they had died in car accidents or something. Some people, before they killed them, they removed their eyes. In other cases, there was physical evidence that people had been mistreated by electricity or by cigarettes, or had been beaten badly. We saw people with multiple fractures of the hands or legs. The fractures appeared to have been caused by blows with heavy objects. Sometimes they would bring in people whom they had mistreated, and ask us to make them better, so they could take them away again for more. This happened seven or eight times to me.

"One man they brought in had massive bruising all over his chest and shoulders from beatings. I said, 'What happened to you?' He said, 'A metal door fell on me.' He was really very sick. I knew they had mishandled him and hurt him and that he was obliged to lie about it. I wanted to help this man. He was my countryman and he was begging me to admit him to the hospital for just two or three days, so he could get a rest from his suffering. But the Iraqis wanted me to examine him and make sure he could survive more beating so they could take him away again. I had to have a legal excuse to admit him, so I asked him if he had vomited or had lost consciousness and he said he had. I was able to tell the Iraqis he had suffered a concussion and must be admitted for several days. The policemen let me admit him.

"Later, two Iraqi security men came to see me. They said, 'We are investigating a case and we need this man back to continue our investigation.' I told them he was in need of admission for twenty-four, forty-eight hours. They said, 'Give him medicine and we will take him back with us.' I said, 'There is a danger if you do that that he will lose consciousness because of bleeding in the brain and die on you.' So they let me keep him for two days.

"On examination, I found he had been beaten with great severity. When I opened his shirt, I thought at first a tank had rolled over his chest. He had been beaten so hard that I found the symbol of the Iraqi army from belt buckles imprinted on his skin. He was conscious, but very, very sick. He got a little better over the two days, not much, and then the security men came and took him away and I never saw him again.

"They got someone in the information office to give them some death certificates, which they filled out however they wanted, and then forced me to sign. They liked to say the people had died by automobile accident, and when I protested that it was clear from the bullet wounds that they had died by gunshot, they thought of something clever. After they were finished with an interrogation of a person, they would take him outside and hit him with a car, and run over him. Then they would bring him here and say he had died from being hit by an automobile, and that was certainly true.

"We are still not sure of the total number of dead brought here. There were so many we lost track, and just now we are still doing autopsies to determine the cause of death for people we have in the morgue. There were a lot of people who were buried without autopsies, and without identification. We would just label them 'Unknown.' "

We walked out in the cool dusk air, around back of the hospital to the charnel house, a good, modern morgue, surrounded by a large courtyard, with white speckled tile floors and walls so that the blood and fluids of putrefaction could be easily washed away. The longest wall, opposite the door, was at least forty feet long and was lined from floor almost to ceiling with refrigerated drawers of stainless steel, twenty-two of them. The whole room was refrigerated, actually, which was a good thing, because the week's fighting had produced an overflow crowd. At least a dozen dead Iraqi soldiers were lying bloated and twisted in the peculiar positions of death, all entwined together on the floor, with blankets here and there cursorily covering them. Most of them had no shoes on, and their feet, puffed up from the gases, swelled out of their pants legs. Their skin was yellow-green. Even with the refrigeration, the stink of half-rotted flesh and formaldehyde was something awful. I lit a cigarette, and the smell was much worse mixed with hot smoke.

The morgue boss came in with us. He was also the hospital's chief ambulance driver, and he said he had picked up more bodies from more street corners in the last seven months than he could even guess at. There were times, he said, when the entire morgue and the entire courtyard would be filled with bodies. He was an old man named Subi Younis, shabby in dress and rough in manner, and very much at home among the dead. He talked slowly—I don't think he was very smart—and spent a lot of time thinking over each question I asked. He spoke in Arabic, and the doctor translated.

"Well, I would say we had more than four hundred bodies here during the occupation, and probably as many as seven hundred. They were all civilians. Some of them were Kuwaitis and some of them were foreigners. They would bring them in bunches. Just dump them here. Many times, the whole yard was covered with bodies. We buried a lot of people in mass graves. Maybe thirty, forty people in each grave, up at the Sulaibikhat Cemetery."

He pulled open drawers at random and slid each metal pan out halfway on the runners, so that the bodies were exposed under the bright white lights, and I looked at them, and wrote down the particulars in a child's compostion book I had bought in Hafar al-Batin, the paper cover of which was decorated in gay blue and red and purple flowers.

The corpse in drawer 16 was of a handsome man in his thirties. He had a full black beard, which was stiff with dried, caked blood. His formerly white shirt was blood-dyed a rusty brown, and blood had coagulated in purplish gobs, like horrible raisins, at his nostrils and ears and mouth. He had been shot twice, execution-style, in the chest and head. He had been brought in on February 19, and he was labeled "Unknown."

As we stood looking at him, two men came in. They were middle-aged, both of them, fat around the middle and dressed in clean, pressed clothes. They seemed quite out of place, but they were in the right spot; they had come to look, they said, for a cousin who had disappeared the week before. Since drawer 16 was already open, Mr. Younis said they might as well start with that one, and the men peered over my shoulder and looked down. "No, that is not who I want," said one. "No, it is not," said the other. "But the funny thing is, I know him. I can't remember the name, but I know the face. He lived in the neighborhood." He shrugged. "What can you do?"

Mr. Younis sighed. "So many killed, in all areas of the city. Why, I remember we had forty-five bodies one day. In one massacre. Came in from the police morgue in a truck."

His assistant interrupted him. "That is nothing," he said. "On

August 3, you remember, the day after the invasion, we take in eighty people on one day."

"Oh yes, that is true. I had forgotten," Mr. Younis said.

The corpse in drawer 3 had its yellowed hands tied behind its back with a strip of white rag. It was naked and it had belonged to a young man. When he was alive, he had been beaten from the soles of the feet to the crown of the head, and every inch of his skin was covered with purple-and-black bruises. His shoulders and chest were crosshatched with the marks of an additional beating from some sort of stick, or rod, or whip. His legs were striped with deep black bruises six inches or more long. Such torture would most likely have been sufficient to kill him, but he had probably died from one particular, terrible blow to the head. The whole right side of his skull was caved in, like the way a pumpkin gets several weeks after Halloween, rotting and gently folding in on itself.

The man in drawer 12 had been burned to death with some flammable liquid. His body, found in a suburban street on October 9, was shrunken and slightly mummified and curled fetus-like. The hands were claws, and what remained of the head was still barely recognizable as a head, but a head that seemed to have been slathered in some brown, viscous liquid—molasses, maybe—and then baked. The features had disappeared in the process, and the body was also labeled "Unknown."

The corpse in drawer 4 was hardly damaged at all, just one round little hole in the neck where the bullet had gone in and a messier, bigger place on the other side, where it had gone out again. "No, no, that is not him either," said the man looking for his cousin.

Corpse 17 was another fire victim. This one had been burned so badly it no longer looked like a body at all. It looked like something you might find on the beach on an early-morning walk, in the smoldering remains of a driftwood fire. It was only about four feet long and had no legs or arms; it was just a husk with something round stuck on one end that presumably had been a head. November 3; Unknown.

Corpses 18 and 19 had names. They belonged to the brothers Abbas. On January 20, the Abbases had gotten excited by reports of the war and had led a small, bloody insurrection against a police substation in their suburban neighborhood. The rebellion had failed and the bodies of the Abbas men had arrived at the morgue with those of five of their neighbors, rounded up and killed for the sake of good measure and collective reprisal. All of the dead had been shot in the head, and the eyeballs of the elder of the Abbas brothers had been removed. The sockets were bloody holes. "We believe the eyeballs were plucked out with fingers while he was alive," Dr. al-Serafi said, with a sad little shake of his head.

There were more in other drawers, but Mr. Younis said I had seen enough, and I didn't argue the point. We all went outside and I offered around my cigarettes and we all smoked in the cooling dusk breeze.

"You cannot imagine how it was," the morgue assistant said, after the silence. "It was easy to die. I remember, in my neighborhood, someone one day put up a poster of the emir on the supermarket window. The police saw it and soon the security men came around and they said to the manager of the supermarket, 'Who did this?' He said he did not know, which was true; he did not. So the security men took him outside right then and there and made all the people in the store and in the street gather around, and the one in charge said, 'We are going to have a demonstration today. The demonstration is called How to Kill a Supermarket Manager.' And then he pointed his pistol at him and shot him in the head."

"It is true," said Dr. al-Serafi. "No one can believe what we have seen. No one can believe that such things happen in the twentieth century. It is beyond human thinking. I could never have imagined this before, and I still do not believe it now. But I know it is true because I have lived with it every day for seven months." Many people in Kuwait City, he said, never fully grasped the horrors of what was going on, because they were not exposed to the daily evidence that those in the medical community saw, and because they did not want to believe what they heard. "I would tell people outside the hospital what I was seeing, and they would say, 'You are exaggerating.' And I would say, 'No, I am saying less than it is. I am only telling you I have seen today a man shot in the head and his eyes removed. I am not telling you about the man I have seen who is burned alive.' "

The Iraqis I had met in Baghdad had seemed to me to be generous, likable people—this had been true even of most of the bureaucrats. I had a hard time reconciling my memory of them with the overwhelming evidence of how the Iraqis had behaved in Kuwait. At first, thinking about it, I speculated that the horror inflicted on the Kuwaitis had been largely a professional job, conducted by the torturers and executioners of the Iraqi security forces, for practical reasons. There was some truth in this. The Iraqis did have what you could fairly call a rationale for conducting a campaign of terror—that is, to subjugate a hostile, numerically overwhelming population. When the Kuwaitis resisted, the Iraqis employed the methods they had found effective, over the past twenty-five years, in quelling dissent at home: arbitrary arrest and detention, widespread torture, frequent murders and public executions.

But the evidence was overwhelming that while the worst torture and the greatest number of executions and rapes had been committed by the security forces, there had also been many instances in which ordinary soldiers and officers had committed these acts, and for no evidently logical reason. A lot of people I talked to held to the view that the Iraqis were simply, fundamentally evil. I heard this again and again: the Iraqis were not normal, they liked inflicting pain, they liked brutality and destruction, they liked killing people. The subscribers to this belief pointed to history, which they said showed the Iraqis were a bloodthirsty people, even by local standards.

It was true that the Iraqis had an exceptionally violent past. The Assyrians, sweeping out from Nineveh, in what is now north-central Iraq, to conquer everything from northern Saudi Arabia to Turkey, had set a standard of behavior remembered three thousand years later. "I built a pillar over against the city gate, and I flayed all the chief men," wrote the Assyrian king Assurnasirpal II, recalling one victorious campaign. "And I covered the pillar with their skins; some I walled up within the pillar, some I impaled upon the pillar on stakes . . . and I cut off the limbs of the officers. . . . From some, I cut off their hands and their fingers, and from others I cut off their noses, their ears . . . of many I put out their eyes. . . . Their young men and maidens I burned in the fire."

Throughout Iraq's history, violence had served as the principal means of exercising political will and effecting policy. In his book *Republic of Fear*, the Iraqi political scientist Samir al-Khalil (a pseudonym) compares Saddam Hussein's reign with that of al-Hadjadj ibn Yusef al-Thaqafi, the governor of Iraq in the late seventh and early eighth centuries. Al-Hadjadj brought order to Iraq, then a chaotic, independent-minded province of the Damascus-based Umayyad dynasty, and established a bureaucracy that laid the foundations for the great Abbasid dynasty. Al-Hadjadj's inaugural speech, al-Khalil says, is known to every Iraqi schoolchild, and is regarded as a truthful depiction of the exercise of political power in Iraq:

"I see heads before me that are ripe and ready for the plucking and I am the one to pluck them, and I see blood glistening between the turbans and the beards. By God, O people of Iraq, people of discord and dissembling and evil character . . . For a long time you have lain in the lairs of error, and have made a rule of transgression. By God, I shall strip you like bark, I shall truss you like a bundle of twigs, I shall beat you like stray camels. . . ."

"The special problem of Baathi violence," writes al-Khalil, "begins with the realization that hundreds and thousands of perfectly ordinary people are implicated in it. Even Saddam Hussein's torturers and elite police units who do the dirtiest work are by and large normal. There are too many of them for it to be otherwise. From being a means to an end, violence has turned into an end in itself, into the way in which all politics (finally no politics) is experienced by the public in Iraq."

Corrupt regimes corrupt those who live under them, and in their own particular way of corruption. A regime corrupted by a lust for money creates a society sickened by greed and self-ishness. A regime corrupted by a lust for violence creates a society sickened by an appetite for the true sins of the flesh, the violation and desecration and destruction of it. The young men who came from Iraq to Kuwait—some of them, by no means all—found they had the appetite to do to the Kuwaitis the terrible things that the Mukhabarat did back home. And there was no one to stop them. Indeed, the masters of the evil, the professional sadists of the security forces, were among them, doing the worst of it; Ali Hassan Majid, the governor of the new nineteenth province, was known, by previous exploits among the Kurds, for his approval of the harshest measures. An astonishing and terrible thing: to be nineteen years old, a country boy, to find yourself in the richest place you had ever seen, a city filled with weak and trembling people, and to realize that you had within you terrible desires—to hurt these people, to rape a pretty girl and then throw her in the trash, to stomp a man's face under your boots—and that you had, as it were, permission to do so. It must have been blackly exciting at first, and then sickening, and by the end a descent into Conradian self-horror. All the physical signs of the occupation—the filth, the destruction, the garbage and shit even in the Iraqis' own

quarters—spoke of men sinking deeper and deeper into rotten-
ness. No wonder they had fled in the night. They must have
been ashamed to think they would be caught in the place of
their sins; they must have yearned to run with their backs to the
awfulness, to get home to Iraq and never admit to a soul what
they had done.

THE ROADS HOME

THERE ARE TWO PAVED ROADS heading north to Iraq from Kuwait City. The first begins within the city as Jahra Road, angles northwest to the city of Jahra, and then goes on some fifty miles to the town of Safwan, which straddles the Iraq-Kuwaiti border. From there the road makes its way to Basra, Iraq's second-largest city and major port. On the Kuwait side of the border, the road is a big, modern highway, six flat asphalt lanes with a divider in the middle and fluorescent lights along the sides. When the Iraqi occupation troops left Kuwait City late on the night of Monday, February 25, and in the early-morning hours of February 26, most of them took this road. The second road loosely follows the coastline of the Persian Gulf to run from Jahra to the Iraqi industrial city of Umm Qasr, and it is a much more modest thing, two scant lanes of battered old blacktop cutting through flats of rock and dirt and sand. A smaller number of Iraqis tried to make their escape on this road.

On both roads, the retreating Iraqis were intercepted by American warplanes, and later by armored units on the ground, and pinned under heavy fire. The battle was almost wholly one-sided. It began with attacks on both roads by waves of A-10 and A-6E bombers flying off aircraft carriers in the northeastern Persian Gulf and from bases in eastern Saudi Arabia. On the main highway, the Iraqi convoy was more than a thousand vehicles long—tanks, trucks, jeeps, cars, buses, ambulances, fire engines, police cruisers—all heavily laden with weapons and loot, moving slowly forward in a bumper-to-bumper traffic jam that stretched for miles. A similar but smaller convoy moved up the secondary road.

The attacking pilots afterward compared the experience to a turkey shoot, and to bombing the road to Daytona Beach at spring break. In the first wave, the American planes bombed the front and the tail of the Iraqi convoy on the main road, so that it could move neither forward nor backward. The desert offered no cover, and many of the vehicles the Iraqis had stolen were not capable of desert driving anyway. The pilots from the American carrier USS *Ranger* had so many targets to choose from that they extended their raids into daylight hours and had their loaders rack up whatever bombs or missiles were closest at hand rather than wait for the ship's elevators to bring up the designated ordnance. With each launch, the ship's sound system played Rossini's *William Tell* Overture. A variety of bombs and missiles were used, but the chief weapon was the MK20 MOD O Rockeye five-hundred-pound antitank cluster bomb. This bomb is a long pod of sheet steel that opens when it falls, to release 247 MK118 antitank fragmentation bombs, steel bomblets stuffed with a high explosive. When these blow up just above the ground, they send clouds of heavy little razor shards whickering through the air at four thousand feet per second. The fragments can penetrate six inches of steel armor. Additionally, the A-10 Warthog planes are equipped with the most lethal Gatling gun in the world, the General Electric 30-millimeter Avenger, with seven rotating barrels that fire 30-millimeter armor-piercing incendiary or high-explosive incendiary rounds at rates of, respectively, 2,100 and 4,200 rounds per minute. The Avenger is designed to expend 1,350 rounds in ten two-second bursts of 135 rounds apiece, and a single burst is enough to destroy a tank.

The bombing continued through the morning of February

26, despite an announcement by Saddam Hussein that he was withdrawing his forces from Kuwait. On the afternoon of the 26th, and on the 27th, American ground forces moved to cut the road to Basra in four places, blocking what was left of the Iraqi retreat. The principal cut was made by the Army's Tiger Brigade, which occupied a high ground called Mutlaa Ridge. The Tiger Brigade traversed the Basra road with forty-five M1A1 tanks and met little serious resistance. The air attacks had already reduced both Iraqi convoys to burning ruins, and the Americans found themselves occupied mostly with accepting prisoners, cleaning up the carnage, and burying the dead. The precise number of Iraqis killed on both roads is unclear, but it is smaller than one might expect, certainly under a thousand, and probably only several hundred. Oddly, the relatively low casualty rate was probably due to the very savagery of the attack; so fierce were the bombings that most of the Iraqis who survived the first waves gave no thought to fighting back, but ran away into the desert.

In the days and weeks after the war ended, these two roads became places of curious importance.

The Gulf War was an experience disconnected from itself, conducted with such speed and at such distances and with so few witnesses that it was, even for many of the people involved, an abstraction. It was difficult for the Americans, who had done their killing almost entirely from afar, to feel a connection with those they killed, or with the act of killing. It was difficult for the Kuwaitis, coming out of seven months of hiding, to believe that their powerful tormentors had really been killed. The roads north filled these vacuums. They were, for miles and miles, rich with the physical realities of war, glutted with the evidence of slaughter and victory. They became the great circuit board of the Gulf War, where the disconnectedness stopped.

*   *   *

By March 4, when I first went up the main highway from
Kuwait City, some of the wreckage had been pushed to the
sides, just enough so that you could thread a car through, taking
care to avoid the bomb craters, but most of it remained—
roasted, bombed, burned, crashed, blown up, shot to pieces,
tangled together in one long, incredible mess. In the first two
miles out of Kuwait City, I counted four tanks, thirty-four cars,
and twenty-seven supply/troop trucks. After that, though, the
going became so thick I couldn't keep track or write fast enough
to record all the cars, trucks, jeeps, etc. that had been pushed
farther off the road onto the sand. Much of the debris was in any
case unidentifiable, since many vehicles had met their ends in
burning, disfiguring pileups. In the stretch leading up to Mutlaa
Ridge, I stopped to look at some great, twisted pile of black
metal skeletons and entrails, and I couldn't tell if it represented
two cars and a truck, or two trucks and a car, or three cars and
an armored personnel carrier, or what.

The contents of the wrecked vehicles were spread out in a
dirty, smoking, occasionally bloody spume that stretched for
miles and miles—blankets, pots, pans, gas cans, children's toys,
tires, bottles, clothes, suitcases, hats, shaving brushes, razors,
televisions, books, a sack of onions, a carton of baby milk, an air
conditioner, radios, helmets—like a garbage slick riding the
water of an ocean dumping ground. The scavengers had descended on the road and begun looting the looters of Kuwait
City before the bodies even began to rot. They had been working the slick for days, and a lot of the best stuff—the jewels,
televisions, money—had been taken by the time I got there. But
there were still prizes to be gleaned, and all up and down the
road the gatherers were picking and wading through the offal
for the plums.

The bedouin, who were the first and most determined of the
hunter-gatherers, traveled in twos and threes, in aged pickup
trucks that stopped at each crash-cluster. They first carried off
everything of any obvious value—blankets, radios, suitcases,

etc. Then they turned their attention to the real source of wealth, the vehicle itself. While one man siphoned the gas, the other two would work at getting the thing up on jacks and stones, so the wheels could be removed. If the headlights seemed intact, they would take those—a headlight, hooked up to a car battery, makes a good lamp for a tent. The radio, the front windshield and its wipers, the seats if there was not a dead man on them; all these would go. There was much to be had in the engine compartment: battery, spark plugs, distributor, carburetor, air filter, oil filter, starter. Most of the time the actual body of the vehicle was too ruined to be of any use, but when they came across one that was not so badly destroyed, the bedouin took the side panels, hood, and trunk lid. These would be wired together to form fences or windbreaks, melted and hammered into useful items for the home.

The scavengers worked among tourists. From the city limits on, the roadway was full of Kuwaiti gentlemen come out to confront the enemy. It was like a pub crawl: a corpse crawl—drive a bit, stop the car, drink in the sight of the dead man, drive on to the next. Music blared from car speakers, and there was much honking and waving of flags. A group of teenagers had strung a clothesline of torn and dirty Iraqi uniforms between an eviscerated armored personnel carrier and a crashed car. They danced around it as if it were a Maypole.

For several miles I followed two plump and prosperous middle-aged men up the road. They stopped their Mercedes-Benz whenever they saw a crowd of more than a few people, which signified there was a body at hand. They carried a Sony Camcorder, and they followed the same ritual at every body. The first one we came across was in a Toyota, half blown apart from machine-gun bullets or shrapnel. The driver, swollen and wedged in place by the crush of his seat up against the wheel, sprawled out the door with his upper torso hanging upside down. There was a small crowd around him, about five people. A green wool army blanket had been loosely pulled over his face and head. One man approached and pulled the blanket back. The dead man's face was green. Not mildly green, like seawater, but a strong rich green, with some yellow in it, the color of a not completely ripe lime. Around the edges of things that stuck out—fingers and nose and such—the flesh was a yellow-purple-black. His head was swollen hugely, as if encephalitis had done him in instead of shrapnel, and his chest was crushed. The blood that had gushed out of him was dried all over his torso and neck and chin. Decomposition was melting him away. Wherever gravity tugged at his flesh, it drooped and sagged alarmingly, like wax warmed by a candle. An eyeball was missing and flies buzzed about the socket.

The man who had pulled the blanket back looked at this for a long moment, and then he leaned forward and spit in the face, and turned and walked away. One by one, the others in the crowd did the same. The men I was following were the last to participate. While the younger of the two videotaped the scene, the older man approached the body. He leaned forward and pursed his lips and cleared his throat to summon up courage and phlegm, and carefully, prissily, hawked a gob into the dead man's face. He stood back to survey his work, and that of his fellows. Spittle and snot flecked the face. His own shot had hit the remaining eye, and covered it like a cataract. He pulled the blanket back over the head, and his friend gave him a thumbs-up to indicate he had recorded it all.

Several hundred yards up the road, we found a Dodge K car with another crowd gathered around. The car was as full of holes as a doily. Pieces and shreds of decaying flesh were stuck all over the dashboard. On the seat lay two fingers and half of a third, all still connected by a webbing of skin. They were swollen little sausages of black, red, and yellow, with torn and fluttery remnants of what had been the juncture with the hand. A brain lay on the hump between the two front seats. It was still mostly intact and holding its shape, a black, puddingly mass. The body that the brain had once directed had been thrown, or pulled, from the car, and now lay in the dirt next to it, covered by a blanket. A hand protruded from underneath, and I saw that it was the one to which the fingers had belonged. As I looked down at it, I realized that another finger was lying next to my feet, a dusty yellow ragged-edged worm. A young man standing next to me saw me looking at it, and I guess my face showed my revulsion, because he bent, picked up the edge of the blanket, and kicked the finger under it; it sent up a puff of dust as it scudded along in the dry dirt, into the wet, hot darkness. I did not want to see any more, and I turned to go. The two plump men had already done their work here, and were back in their Mercedes, heading off to spit on the next of the waiting dead.

The desert on both sides of the road to Basra was thickly settled with the camps of American troops, their Humvees and trucks and half-tracks parked in circles around their tents, like wagon trains bristling with guns and antennas. Wandering late one afternoon with Bob Drogin, a *Los Angeles Times* reporter, I came to the camp of Captain Douglas Morrison, commander of the 1st Squadron, 4th Cavalry. He was thirty-one years old, a career officer, and as he stood in the mud by his Humvee, he seemed to me the *beau ideal* of the New Army. He was moderately tall, moderately handsome, and perfectly clean. He wore a pressed one-piece uniform that tucked neatly into shined boots, and he was slim and fit and trim of line.

He spoke in the voice of the New Army too, a crisp assured mix of techno-idolatrous jargon, euphemism, and boyish boasting, the voice of Tom Clancy and collateral damage and kicking ass. In the hundred hours of the ground war, Captain Morrison's squadron of troops, tanks, and armored personnel carriers had destroyed seventy Iraqi tanks and more than a hundred armored vehicles. It had suffered not a single casualty.

"The fight was very one-sided," Captain Morrison said. "They were totally surprised. They didn't expect to see us.

Because our main battle tank guns have a longer range than theirs, they didn't have much of a chance to react. One or two of their T-55s tried to return fire, and there was some small-arms fire, but not much. We took twenty-five hundred prisoners." What Captain Morrison had seen had upset him a little. "It was obvious from the EPWs [enemy prisoners of war] that we took that the Iraqis had suffered from a lack of medical care, food, water. Some of them were dehydrated. They hadn't eaten in days. Some of them were kids, thirteen, fourteen, fifteen years old. Some were old men, fifty, sixty. That bothered me. Sure it did. And it bothered me when I picked up four or five dead Iraqi soldiers on the road over there. It's something you remember. I'll never forget what I saw on that road, ever."

As we were leaving, Bob asked him about the coastal road, of which he had heard rumors. "Oh, that's really something," the captain said. "Nothing but carnage, just five to seven miles of bombed-out vehicles. Nothing but shit strewn everywhere."

The sun was setting, pink and purple, as we went back across the desert. There were several turns on the paths the army's bulldozers had scraped, and I must have taken a wrong one, because we found ourselves at a place where the road cut through high ground, forming the bottom of a funnel that collected rainwater, with dirt embankments on both sides holding it in. A lake of brown water forty or fifty feet long lapped at the embankments. I didn't get more than ten feet or so into it when the car stopped, stuck as solidly as if it had been planted. When I opened the door, the brown water swirled and eddied in, rising to a third of the way up the seats. I put the keys in my pocket and stood on the seat and jumped to the bank and scrabbled a hold in the mud and dirt so that I could stand up. Bob made the jump too, and we walked back in the direction of Captain Morrison's camp. We hadn't gone very far when we met a supply truck coming from that direction. The soldier driving said he would get us out and motioned for us to get into the back of the truck. It stank astonishingly back there, a rich, foul smell as thick as fog. The driver looked over his shoulder at us as he started forward, and saw us holding our hands over our mouths and noses, and made a gracious apology, like a host who has just remembered something he should have mentioned earlier. "Sorry about the smell," he said. "Pretty ripe, huh? Been hauling dead Iraqis all day."

He pulled into the water, the truck not even straining, and stopped in front of the Nissan, and maneuvered, backing up, so that the two were in line. Then he lighted a cigarette and looked at me and gestured toward his front bumper. "There's a chain up there."

The water was icy and came up to my waist. I hated getting into it; it smelled bad, like the truck. I found the chain wrapped around two big steel uprights welded to the front bumper. It was a long, immensely heavy thing, and I half-carried, half-dragged it through the water and muck back to the Nissan, and set out to hook things together. I had to hunker down until the water was up to my shoulders to find the hook underneath where the chain could be attached, and the stench rose up in my nose, gagging me. Once I got things hooked up, it was easy. The truck yanked the car free with no more to-do than a waiter pulling a cork out of a bottle. When we got to the other side, the driver came around and we unhooked the chain and threw it in the truck. We traded him some chocolate for a pack of cigarettes, and smoked. I was shivering so hard I couldn't light mine, and he did it for me. "Stinks in that water, don't it?" he said.

It does, I said.

"Same thing as in the truck. Dead Iraqis. Them's graveyards either side of that water. Couple hundred fresh bodies in there. That's where we been burying 'em. Smell gets into the water." That was the longest speech he had made, but still, I thought, a model of informative brevity.

*   *   *

The next morning we drove up the coastal road, and came presently upon the beginning of the destruction, the holes. An air attack makes a variety of holes in a road, from the five-hundred-pound craters large enough to swallow a car to the fist-sized chunks torn out by 30-millimeter bullets. The holes, and the intact blacktop around them, were littered with military junk—grenades and shells and machine-gun ammunition. The melting heat of the burning vehicles had cooked and exploded a lot of the ammunition, but much was still intact, full cases of American-made Mark 2 hand grenades (these are the old-fashioned pineapple kind), antitank rockets, howitzer shells as long as a leg, and hundreds of the little yellow beer cans that were unexploded cluster bomblets. You could not safely drive through this mess, so we parked and walked. Several hundred yards on, we arrived at a tank with its turret blown clean off, and near that was the burned-out hulk of a self-propelled 155-millimeter howitzer. The howitzer must have taken a direct hit from a big bomb, judging from the shape it was in. A self-propelled howitzer is a cannon mounted on an armored chassis, all heavy steel and the size of a railroad car. There was nothing left of this one but pieces. It didn't look like anything except a hundred yards of twisted, blown-up, burned, and blackened hunks of metal. The big gun lay on the ground on top of one of the larger piles of scrap. The treads were a hundred yards away, blown to component parts of gears and ball bearings. The ball bearings were big and chrome-shiny, and they looked like old-fashioned Christmas ornaments scattered in the sand. The huge gears were stuck in the sand too, grabbing at air.

Three antiaircraft guns mounted in pickup trucks, a supply truck, and a car, all of them shot half to pieces, had crashed into each other. The supply truck had collided so hard with the car that it had cut it in half. All around it, flung hundreds of feet away, were single-cot mattresses, skinny little gray things with blue ticking. The trash got more personal as we walked: bars of Hana soap, hard stale rounds of bread, shaving mugs and brushes, a busted-up VCR recorder, sacks of potatoes split open and lying about, a pair of children's shoes, helmets, tubes of toothpaste, a case of toilet paper.

We came across a wrecked half-track equipped with several ground-to-air missiles, but there hadn't been any effort made to fire the missiles at the attackers; they were still secured in their lock-down position. As near as I could see, nothing in the entire caravan had been fired; the attack, I suppose, had been a complete surprise. Amid the wholesale destruction, there were small signs that the attackers had had the time for even a little pinpoint shooting. One truck was untouched except for two neat bullet holes right through the driver's side of the front windshield.

After we had been walking maybe a quarter mile, everything became more or less charcoal. The fires must have been white-hot. Much of the machine-gun ammunition that had spilled out of crates and onto the tarmac had exploded; popped-off little copper slugs were so thick you scuffed through them, like leaves, as you walked. The interiors of all the cars and trucks were heat-stripped down to the metal, and the windshield glass had melted into gobs of silicon that had rehardened in blobs and drips on the black skeletons of dashboards.

I think the attack had come from the front of this long convoy, and the travelers in the rear must have had sufficient warning, as they watched those in front perish, to leap and run away, so the dead tended to be in the vanguard. The first four we saw had tried to run and had made it off the road and twenty or thirty feet into the sand when the shrapnel caught them and razored them full of killing holes. They lay together in a loose group, a light sheet of windblown sand drifting over them. The force of the explosions had denuded them in the moment of death. One man had one boot on one foot and one sock on the other and nothing else on at all. He was colored the yellow-black-green I was getting used to by now. The fellow next to him was a completely different hue. He had been bloated huge by gas and his skin had turned a Florida orange, so that his Tropicana belly puffed out like a balloon. The bomb blast had stripped him of his shoes, and about half of his shirt and trousers. It had blown off one of his legs at the groin and left a gaping hole, from which black stuff had oozed and hardened. The third man was intact and fully clothed except for both shoes and one sock, and, oddly enough, the other foot.

The fourth man was charred and green and lying on his back. Everything had been blown and burned off him, including most of himself. The blast had opened up his chest as thoroughly, although not of course as neatly, as a thoracic surgeon, and the crumbling, jagged ends of his ribs stuck up in the air. One arm had been ripped off and flung God knows where, but the other was utterly untouched and lay naturally by his side, with the palm up. The position of the hand made it a natural cup for collecting sand, and the man had gathered a neat little pile since he died. A dusting of fine granules clung like sugar on a doughnut to the bone ends that edged the black hole of his chest.

In the sand a few feet away, I found a small photograph of two somberly smiling young men in their twenties, standing in front of an improbable blue background. They had neatly trimmed haircuts and mustaches and looked like brothers. One had his arm around the shoulders of the other. There was no way to tell if one of the young men in the picture was one of the four on the ground.

The next grouping was about thirty yards farther on. There were six bodies in this bunch, one with both legs blown off, one faceup, another facedown, all of them colored, my notes remind me, in "vivid yellows and bright bile green and deep purple and red and black/like sunsets or black eyes." One poor soul had tried to make his escape in a Kawasaki front-loader, swiped I guess from some construction site in Kuwait City. He had been sitting up there in the open cab, chugging along at a few miles an hour, when the cluster bomb, or whatever it was, ripped him in half. The left upper side of him was hanging upside down from the yellow frame of the cab, but his whole right side and bottom half had been torn off. A leg, a black-and-red tattered mess of bone, flesh, and cloth, was ten feet away, half crooked at the knee, lying on the asphalt alone, as if it had tried to run away all by itself.

Near him was a man whose image remains among the most sharp-edged in my mind. The blast had removed all his clothes but had left no visible hurt on his flesh. He was lying on his back, naked in the sand, on a small upswell about thirty feet from the road. He was a handsome man, with a well-built, strong body and a good face. He wasn't much bloated. The explosion had positioned him in a classic manner. His left arm was draped gently across his chest, and his right arm was flung upward and out, as if he had just finished an exclamation. The gases of decay had, for some reason, singled out his penis and swollen it slightly so that it suggested the partial tumescence of recent arousal, and the breeze stirring his tufted pubic hair added to the illusion that this part of him was alive still. He looked like a nude study of a young athlete dozing after satisfying and spirited sex. The game was given away only by the flies in his eyes.

And so on, more and more. An oil truck, overturned, the driver nearby, another half-man, lying next to a torn and empty purple velvet jewel case. He was probably in his thirties, and he wore a colored bandanna tied around his forehead. His pockets were turned inside out. Looking back at the truck, I saw that the gas-tank cap was off. After this, I noticed the same was true all around me; the bedouin had already been up this road, probably the day after the attack, and had siphoned the pockets and the tanks, respectively, of the killed men and machines. But the road had not been picked over anything like the highway to Basra. There was plenty of stealable stuff left. Tons of ammunition, suitcases, helmets, clothes, blankets. An undamaged can of Soft & Gentle Hair Spray. A little tin box containing "30 Tablets Sexergine," a product from the laboratory of one Dr. K. G.

Herbrand, of Frankfurt, West Germany. An aluminum water pitcher, dented. A gray filing cabinet. A full sack of potatoes. A box of Crayola crayons. A dozen crates of dates, sticky and oozing under the sun. A typewriter. A cheap metal calendar souvenir from London, with Big Ben on it.

There were only a few other people on the road with us, all American or British soldiers, doing what we were, making the stations of the dead. We fell in with two older men; they were, it turned out, professionals at this sort of thing, both majors from the U.S. Army's Special Operations Command assigned to the unpleasant but interesting task of digging up dirt among the dead. One of them, a forty-three-year-old man named Jim Smith, was a specialist in Vietnam MIA cases, and the other, Bob Nugent, was an Arabist and linguist. There must be a euphemistic military title for their function this day, but really, they were simply lawyers' legmen, snooping about for the raw material that might one day make a brief in a war-crimes trial. They were especially interested in documents. Like the Nazis, the Baathi were meticulous record-keepers, and it was assumed that somewhere in their files would be the accounts of arrests and detentions and executions that could form the basis of a case. The four of us were together when we came to the most awful of all the *tableaux morts*.

By itself in the middle of the road was a medium-size flatbed truck that had been bombed and roasted. There were ten bodies in and about it, and all of them had been cooked to the point of carbonization, leaving shriveled, naked mummies; black, charcoaled husks with bared rictus grins and hands that had become claws. Their skin was stretched taut and shiny, heat-shrunk over their skulls. Two young soldiers were already standing there, looking at the scene with a kind of awe. One of them was taking a photograph of the driver, who had been caught behind the wheel in a fury of shrapnel. The bottom of his jaw was gone, so that his upper teeth gleamed by themselves in the charcoaled blackness of his face, above a gaping nothing that made it seem as if his mouth was still stretched wide in a scream. I am sure the soldiers had never seen anything like this, but, being young men, they were working very hard to act as if it were no big deal. They were like rubes at the county-fair freak show, determined not to let on that the sight of the geek biting the head off the live chicken was more than they really had bargained for.

"Waaal," drawled one of the young men, in the caricature of the Southern deputy sheriff, "them boys shore got themselves se-*vere*-ly fucked up."

"Yeah," said his buddy, doing Clint Eastwood. "Jes' wasn't their day, I guess."

They looked at it some more, and didn't say anything else for a while. The truly obscene has the power of the sacred to silence the vulgar. "Well," said the first of the young men, in a much quieter, less stagy voice. "Just remember, they started it."

They walked off, and I watched the two pros examine the wreck. They had adopted a pose, too, not one of nonchalant brutality, but one of just-the-facts objectivity, the universal stance of the cop and the coroner. "Say," said Bob Nugent, "this is interesting. Look right here, how this guy ended up blown against the cab." We all came over to look. Sure enough, one body had been thrown by the force of the explosion into the six or seven inches between the slats of the flatbed walls and the back of the truck cab. It was a small body, probably that of a teen, but there was no way it should have fit into that space. It was the sort of freak thing you see in the aftermath of a hurricane or tornado. The top of the skull was crushed like a shell, and through the ragged-edged holes you could see his brain, cooked hard and yellow.

We looked at the other bodies in the flatbed. The blasts had thrown them all into odd positions, which made it look as if they had been unexpectedly frozen in the middle of their desperate attempts to flee. One of them had his face down on the floorboards of the truck and his rear high up in the air, as if he were trying to burrow through to the ground. He couldn't have burrowed, though; his legs ended mid-thigh in fluttery ribbons of black. He was quite small, even taking into account the shrinking effect of his mummification. "I don't think he was more than thirteen or fourteen years old," said Bob Nugent. The corpse had been a pretty boy; you could see that even still in his cherubic face. The body next to him had been butterflied by the bomb, laid open from sternum to groin, and the fires had preserved him, so that his innards lay in their proper places, cooked into hard ebony coils and curves. Underneath the truck was the body of a soldier who must have been on foot when the attack started and who had dived under the stopped truck for cover. He had met his end in a position either fatalistic or prayerful, flat on his back, with his hands neatly folded at his chest.

Nugent took a camera from his pocket and focused on the scene on the truck, but then thought better of it. "Oh, I'm not gonna do this," he said, and shook his head and put the camera back. We walked on without talking about anything for a while. Months later, the sights of this road snuck up on me and gave me a period of depression and lassitude, but its immediate effect was quite different, and more troubling. Death close up and naked is a kind of pornography, and it induces the same kind of hot and shameful thrill.

Smith broke the silence. "Most of these guys were hit by cluster bombs, I guess. Then they got incinerated when the fires from that started cooking off the ammo, which made a super-fire."

"Yeah," said Nugent. "They must have come in low and over the desert and just whacked 'em bad."

We left the road and walked (carefully, with an eye for cluster bomblets) across the sand to look at a towed howitzer. It was undamaged, but no good. The Iraqis had exploded grenades in the breech, to spike the gun. "Well, I'm proud of them for that," said Smith. "They did one thing right. One futile last effort." On the ground next to the gun was a slide rule. Nugent picked it up and we all examined it. It was Russian-made, with Cyrillic lettering. Heat or shock had run a crack up the middle of its length, but it was a good rule, of wood and imitation ivory. It must have belonged to the howitzer's gunner, who would have used it to calculate range, as American gunners did forty years ago. Nugent and Smith could not get over this. "Incredible," said Nugent. "Imagine an army using slide rules up against an army using computers and AWACS. Incredible." Nearby was the body of a man missing his left shoulder and arm and half his head. On the ground next to him was a bright, shining bag of M&Ms, full and undamaged. A dog tag lay nearby, but I don't know that it belonged to him. It could have been thrown through the air from some other body. Nugent translated the fine, faint Arabic script punched onto the metal: Abas Mishal Daman. NCO. Islamic. Type O Positive.

"You know, I've been in the army twenty years and I've never seen anything like this," Nugent said. "Even in Vietnam, I didn't see anything like this."

I asked him what he thought of it all.

"Mixed emotions. As a soldier, you feel sorry for these guys. I mean, this is pathetic. This is an army that was wasted. It was mostly People's Army in KC. That's what all the indications are. Their equipment wasn't very good, and their boots weren't either. And the People's Army was always meant to be cannon fodder." He thought a bit more, and spoke again as we neared the next body. "But you have to remember, these guys did some terrible things back in Kuwait City. I guess I don't really feel as sorry for the fucks that were in Kuwait City as I did for the guys in the front lines, getting pounded day after day with the Republican Guard behind them and minefields in front of them."

It didn't seem as if this formulation was enough, though. He was looking for the big answer, and as we walked along, I listened to him grope for it. "I'm not a religious man. I'm really not. But when I contemplate all this, all the casualties we

inflicted, and I think of the size of the enemy that we faced—
four thousand tanks, two thousand APCs—and you look at our
casualties—practically nothing!—it's hard not to feel there was
some sort of divine intervention. . . . Lots of the troops are kinda
down 'cause they didn't get a chance to kill someone. But I think
it's wonderful, marvelous that casualties were so small. You
have to remember, we were expecting to take ten thousand
casualties the first week. . . ."

In the end, he settled for an obvious, if limited, truth. "Chiv-
alry," he said, "died a long time ago."

Driving back, we came across a few bodies we had missed
before and saw something I dreamed about later. A pack of lean
and sharp-fanged wild dogs, white and yellow curs, swarmed
and snarled around the corpse of one soldier. They had picked
his chest bare, and his ribs gleamed white in the sun. Because,
I guess, the skin had gotten so tough and leathery from ten days'
exposure, they had eaten the legs from the inside out, and the
epidermis lay in collapsed and hairy folds, like leg-shaped blankets, with feet attached. I watched them work over what was
left, which was not much. They skirted the stomach, which lay
in the sand to one side of the ribs, a distended black-and-yellow
ball. Nearby, a small flock of falcons wheeled over another
body. The dogs had been there first, and little remained except
the head. The birds were working on the more vulnerable parts
of that. The dead man's face was darkly yellow-green, except
where his eyeballs had been; there the sockets glistened red and
wet under the tearing, pecking beaks.

THE EMIR'S
NEW HOUSE

SIXTEEN DAYS after the Iraqis ran from the armies of the West, the emir of Kuwait, Sheikh Jaber al-Ahmed al-Sabah, returned from the Saudi Arabian resort town of Taif, where he had passed the occupation and liberation of his country. He came home to a dismal mess. Steaming, suppurating hills of garbage lined the streets of his city-state. Running water existed in only a few main lines and a couple of the big hotels. There was no electricity other than that supplied by generators, and there were very few generators. Food distribution had begun several days before, but was limited mostly to basics: rice, milk, sugar, cooking oil, and tomato paste. The beaches, the countryside, and various crannies of the city were still littered with unexploded Iraqi land mines, American cluster bomblets, and other objects suitable for the maiming and killing of curious children. The oil wells were infernos, the air was thick with soot. A great many weapons, from pistols to armored personnel carriers, had disappeared into private homes, garages, and warehouses. There was a good deal of shooting and beating going on around town, some of it organized for political reasons (mostly to scare off the emir's opponents), some of it revenge-taking against Palestinian collaborators or simply Palestinians, and some of it just for its own sake.

In the days before the emir's return, there had been mutterings of discontent, even among the rich, over his leisurely approach to liberation. Loyal subjects suggested he had not been able to return for fear of his safety in a city where the streets were filled with boys with guns and the air with falling bullets. A few days earlier, the minister of planning, Sulaiman al-Mutawa, had addressed this point. It wasn't true, he said; the emir's delay was entirely caused by the need "to find a suitable place for him to live in."

On the morning of his homecoming, I went to see if anything suitable had been found. The emir's old home, Dasman Palace, was located on the corniche across the road from two giant water towers built in 1977. The water towers were the most prominent symbols of new Kuwait. They were the architectural equivalent of escort-service girls, tarty and glitzy and overendowed, tall and skinny-legged up to a couple of giant globes, a design that made them seem tipsily top-heavy, as if they had been drinking pink champagne and were a little unsteady in their high heels. They were covered in some material, possibly eye shadow, of a bright, shimmering, unnatural blue. Across the street, the palace was a pleasing contrast, a nice old dame of a building, of modest wealth and good breeding. It was built between 1915 and 1930, when Kuwait City was still a seafaring town of mud-brick buildings and dirt streets, before the old clay wall that encircled the town had been bulldozed, and the old *suqs* replaced with department stores, and the *dhows* gave way to cigarette boats. It was a large building, but not a boastful one, a comfortable home of yellow brick, rising with few frills in a square arrangement around a smallish courtyard.

At the front gate, a particularly young hero of the resistance slouched in a broken desk chair, his back against a tree, his feet up on a cinder block, a picture of somnolent insolence. He waved me through with a sharp little wave of his weapon, a gesture that would have been more impressive had he been armed with something better than the broken wooden stock of a shotgun. I drove up the long dirt road, under the double row of eucalyptus trees, weaving the car through a collection of junk that included, inexplicably, many single shoes.

The courtyard had been a lush place once, but now it was all dust and decrepitude, dead plants and stumps of machine-gunned trees, with charcoaled hulks of furniture littered about, a broken table here, a sodden sofa there, an easy chair in the dry fountain. In the emir's own living quarters, the floor plan went like this: heap of burned mattresses, ripped-up photo portrait of the emir, pile of shit, broken woman's high-heeled shoe, box of unused .50-caliber ammo, burned sofa, pile of shit, mess of mildewy clothes, burned carpet, debris of cooking fire, pile of shit, etc. One room, used as a henhouse, was inches deep in feathers and guano.

I wondered if the palace's keepers were leaving it this way on purpose, so that the emir might see how the barbarians sacked his home, but I ran into the caretaker walking aimlessly through the muck, and he said this was not so. "No, no, it is just a matter of organization, nothing else," he said. "We must organize ourselves before we clean it up. It will be cleaned up in a week perhaps. Or two."

The emir's new, temporary, home was a place out in the suburbs called Bayan Palace. It was built in 1987 to hold the Fifth Islamic Summit Conference, and it resembled an unusually opulent community-college campus somewhere in Florida, a collection of boxy concrete buildings grouped around lawns and gardens, with rows of palm trees and fountains in between. There was a big building that looked like the community college's conference center and in fact it was a conference center. The other buildings looked like residential halls—short, square, flat-roofed, and thoroughly beige—and in fact they were residential halls (for visiting state delegations), six groups of them, each containing three halls clustered around a garden.

There was commotion around the group named after Bubi-

---

yan Island, and I stopped there and walked inside Bubiyan Two. Near the door was a table, and at the table was a short man, smoking a pipe and studying a stack of blueprints. His business card declared him to be Wayne Urbine P.E., Chief, Air Force & Special Projects, Savannah District, U.S. Army Corps of Engineers. The job of fixing up a suitable place for the emir to live had fallen, it turned out, to the American army. Mr. Urbine was proud to show off the stuff of his labor.

I couldn't blame him. Bubiyan Two was a marvel of men in motion, the only scene of intense reconstruction work I had seen in Kuwait. On the door to every room was stuck a little yellow Post-It note, listing the details within left to be attended to ("Remove valance . . . replace molding on bathroom door . . . new faucets in sink . . ."). Workers rushed from room to room, from pillar to Post-It, and as they finished each chore, one of Mr. Urbine's undersupervisors would put a check on the yellow note.

"There's between seventy-five and one hundred and twenty workers here, depending on the day," Mr. Urbine said, as we walked along the hall. "The contract for this job was let on March 3, and it says Bubiyan will be rehabilitated completely tomorrow afternoon. It will be finished on time."

Mr. Urbine had not seen the inside of Bubiyan until after the contract was signed, which made it an interesting challenge. "It's hard to define what the hell you're going to walk into until you walk in, and then you can definitize it," he said, chattering on the cheery way of a man at work in a job he knows well. "Basically what we did was we went room by room and made a complete checklist of all the things that had to be done. To replace some of the missing stuff that the Iraqis had taken, we've confiscated what was left in the other buildings and brought it over here, as needed. Lots of the silk walls and silk furniture had to be replaced. The Iraqis stole the silk for their wives to make dresses. Also they really liked the big satin bolsters and pillows on the easy chairs, so they stripped a lot of them, left feathers all over the place. They sort of half-stripped the chandeliers. Strange. No pattern to it. You'd go into one room and half the rounds would be missing, go into another and there would be still a brilliant, whole chandelier.

"Oh, there was a lot missing, here and there, odd things. All the marble newell posts. And the little glass soap bowls in the bathrooms. All the gold shower heads. Well, I can understand the gold shower heads, anybody's going to take those. But why the soap dishes? You know what I mean? I mean, they're nothing special. Just regular glass soap dishes. Can't figure why they took 'em. They also liked the washing machines. Took all of them. They left the dishwashers. I guess they didn't need them, because"—he laughed—"they weren't too sanitary in their eating habits, you know.

"There's one thing I'll tell you, you wouldn't believe. I've got to tell you. When we came in here there was, I'm not kidding, shit all over the place." He laughed again. "There's nothing in the Corps' job description about cleaning up shit, but maybe there will be after this. We'll have to add it."

Inside, Bubiyan Two was nothing like a community college. The whole palace complex, Mr. Urbine said, had cost $600 million to build, and it was easy to believe this. The architect's principal idea seemed to have been "Say it with marble." The hallways and staircases were marble, the bathtubs and sinks were marble, even the trash cans were marble. As we walked up a glorious stone stairway, Mr. Urbine stopped and stroked the wall. "Look at this. This marble is the finest in the world, from the quarries in Carrara, Italy, and every one of these pieces has been cut in what they call a matchbox cut. That's a cut where each piece matches the one next to it just right. Only a master stonecutter can do it." And it was true, each sheet of stone matched its neighbor as precisely as in a jigsaw puzzle, in creamy slabs of white, beige, pink, blue, and black, with rich Roqueforty veins running from panel to panel in perfectly synchronized streaks. The look was so buttery-rich it seemed you could have scooped out a little spoonful of wall and spread it on a piece of bread, had their been any bread in the emir's city.

On the second floor, a dozen workmen were busy attending to the needs of a bedroom suite. "Each floor has two suites consisting of five to six bedrooms, a head-of-state room, a reception room, and of course a sitting room," Mr. Urbine said. "You know, Kuwaitis like to sit a lot."

The suites were all the same. The bedrooms were done up with yards and yards of silk moire covering the walls—lingerie on plaster. The furniture echoed the theme, with chairs and sofas as pleasingly plump as harem girls sheathed in satins and sateens. "These silk wall coverings are the kind of stuff you can't get except in probably three stores in New York," Mr. Urbine said, running a light hand over the fabric, making the silk give out a soft, dry whisper. The walls of the conference rooms were paneled in wood of a color somewhere between Marilyn Monroe and Faye Dunaway, inlaid with strips of brass set in geometric patterns. The big table in the middle was also of the simple blond-wood design, but the incidental tables and chairs were faux Chippendale and Louis XV, pieces of rococo fakery in sugar-frosting white and baby blue and gilt. Large, fine crystal chandeliers hung overhead, three to a suite. The kitchens were as sleek and shining as laboratories, and just as filled with gadgets. The bathrooms were tricked out in marble, the floors, walls, sinks and tubs in stone of a pink, blue, or black. The faucets, taps, shower heads, and drains were all gold-plated, and so were the toilet handles.

It had been hard work, re-silking the walls and rounding out the chandeliers and hunting down all the little pieces of gold needed to make a bathroom fit for a king. "We all worked several all-nighters, and a lot of workers individually work all night regularly," Mr. Urbine said. "Generally, we are putting in a minimum of twelve-hour days." The labor was divided up by race and class. Supervising the job were three Corps men and a team of Kuwaiti architects and engineers. A Saudi contractor was providing the labor for the million-dollar job; Filipinos, Indians, and Palestinians did the actual labor, with the Filipinos handling most of the skilled work and the Palestinians doing most of the grunt chores. On top of everyone was the royal family.

"We get plenty of attention," Mr. Urbine said, puffing on his pipe as we left Bubiyan Two. "It's really a constant circus. The cousin of the crown prince is here all the time. She's an architect, and she's sort of overseeing the job for the crown prince. She's a real pistol. Matter of fact, she carries a pistol, tucked into her belt like Annie Oakley. Has a bodyguard too. The crown prince also comes by. He came by last weekend to check it out, sat down in the chairs and looked at the wallpaper and everything. Made a few comments about the wallpaper, didn't seem to like it. But he said the chandeliers looked good."

So, all in all, he was pleased? I asked.

"Overall, he's very delighted with the way it's coming. The cousin is a little more particular, if you know what I mean. It's kind of like having your wife on the job. Move this here, move that over there. *You* know."

We were making our way through a wonderfully diverse collection of trash: a littering of pills and vials from the clinic, a mound of white linen cloths, gold-plated ice buckets, sterling silver forks and knives, silver-plated dishes and trays. Mr. Urbine picked up a napkin the size of a small tablecloth. "Irish linen. We're using these things to clean diesel engines. My wife would kill me."

Stacked near the door was a great pile of new sofas, chairs, desks, and mattresses—modern stuff, still wrapped in plastic. "The Kuwaitis had already gone ahead before the end of the war, before we got here, and ordered furniture, not knowing what would be left," Mr. Urbine said. "It was top priority getting it all up here from Dhahran. Why, we got this stuff in here even before the Red Cross convoy."

He stopped by a large, dry fountain. "Each building has its own fountain. We won't turn 'em on, though. We're not going to waste water on fountains when people can't even find water to drink."

This was a surprise. I had not guessed Mr. Urbine harbored, as the Jesuits used to say, Doubts. In the doctrine of the U.S. Army Corps of Engineers, to question the morality of the job at hand—be it paving a swamp or reluxing a palace—is a Doubt of a large and serious nature, akin to postulating the fallibility of God.

I asked Mr. Urbine if he was bothered by the nature of the job.

"Well, I kind of question it," he said, speaking slowly and carefully, picking his way through heresy and blasphemy to an unwelcome revelation. "It's sort of a values question. You go out there and you see thousands of people waiting in line to make a phone call and you come in here and see all this opulence, and there's still someone complaining because there aren't enough damn gold fixtures. You know what I mean? Values."

In the Palestinian neighborhood of Hawaliya, two men were pushing a car past a smoldering garbage hill the size of a bungalow. The car looked as if it had been parked on a Manhattan street overnight; the door locks and ignition were popped, and where the radio had been was just a jagged hole with wire entrails dangling out. "Kuwaiti soldiers do this," said one of the men. "At a checkpoint. Because I am a Jordanian. They laugh at me and say, 'You bastard, you walk from now on.' I go to police station and complain. Police say they will do nothing. What can I do?"

Down the street, a long line of people waited for a garden hose that had somehow been tapped into a city main. Each person had his jerry can, or garbage can, or tin bucket. "After the liberation, we hoped that things would get better, but things stay the same," said a man holding an empty ghee can. "The face only changes."

A few blocks on, at a Sultan supermarket, where a government food distribution center had been set up, was another long line, about five hundred people, mostly women in black. Young men with guns blocked and guarded the door and were letting in only a few shoppers at a time. There wasn't much inside anyway. In the front of the store was a bathtub full of brown rice; you could buy several scoops in a paper sack. Along the walls were stacks of cans of tomato paste and powdered milk. In the rear was a row of metal bins, empty except for one that had a few inches of sugar left. The store manager, one of those round and oleaginous men who appear the same at thirty as at fifty and whose heart thrills to the sight of a shrewdly calculated markup, showed me around. "You don't seem to have much to offer," I said.

"Why, the people have everything already," he lied with bland abandon. "If you go to their homes, you will see. They have everything. Fresh fruit, fresh vegetables, they have it all in their homes."

"Where do they get it?"

"Not here. Elsewhere."

When I left the store, a group of men rushed around me, full of agitation and annoyance.

"He does not tell the truth. He is Kuwaiti man. To hear the truth, you must speak with other men. We come here at four o' clock in the morning and wait seven, eight hours, just to get the little things, rice, milk, ghee. No meat. No fruit. No vegetables. The Kuwaiti man says we have food in our homes. From where? From where would we get this food? For seven months we have had nothing. They only give us a little bit of things because we are Palestinians."

What do you think of the emir's return? I asked. Do you think that will improve things?

A shrug of resigned dismissal, and a little joke: "I hope he brings food."

The International Hotel had become Kuwait City's media center. Satellite dishes and generators surrounded it, the sofas in the lobby were filled with people balancing computers on their laps, press officers and public-relations officials roamed the halls. By the end of the first week the rooms that had been free were renting for a hundred dollars a night. I moved out of mine and joined a colony of squatters who had moved into the cabanas by the swimming pool. The pool was half filled with black water and trash, but life among the cabanas was pleasant, in a low-key way, like camping out but less taxing. The squatters were mostly newspaper reporters and so were all on the same schedule. In the evenings, after we filed our stories, we would make dinner from a common stock of canned food piled on a table with a kerosene stove, and sit by the black lagoon of the pool and talk. In the mornings we would have coffee together. When the wind blew from the sea, the sky was a pale, clear blue (otherwise, it was black from the burning oil fields), and it was nice to sit and write in the sun.

The Kuwaiti Ministry of Information had its office set up in the lobby by the end of the third day of the liberation, and by the fourth day, the Washington public-relations firm the Kuwaitis had hired had set up shop too, in a room down the hall from the Joint Information Bureau office. I went in there once. It looked just exactly like the office of a Washington public-relations firm, with desks and AT&T telephones (three of them, satellite jobs). The man in charge wore around his neck a laminated press credential that announced, in big block letters, THE LIBERATION OF KUWAIT CITY.

Every day the Ministry of Information and the flacks from Washington covered the walls of the lobby with media advisories.

"Media Advisory: Human Shield. There will be a press conference for three German, one Italian, one Russian, all LADIES who stayed in Kuwait during the Iraqi occupation. They will be speaking about their experience during this period."

"Media Advisory: All Media People Are Requested to Submit their visit program a day ahead to the Information Press Desk, PRIOR TO THE VISIT, so that we can organize the tour properly."

"Media Advisory: The Kuwait Government and the U.S. Army Corps of Engineers are conducting tours of DAMAGE ASSESSMENT OPERATIONS in various locations throughout Kuwait City. If interested, please contact Jim Parker, Plaza Hotel, Room 1614."

My favorite Media Advisory: "If Tortured Families Are Desired, Please Contact the Kuwaiti Information Press Office."

Amira Marafie was a small, energetic man, full of plucking motions and jumpy little starts, and, oddly enough, it was his main function in life to sit. As head of one of Kuwait's twenty-five richest families, he spent almost all his time in a chair, listening, occasionally talking, and worrying. He lived with his large family in a big (but not very fancy) house, in a neighborhood where more than 150 Marafies lived. In the mornings he put on a white *dishdasha* and went outside and sat in his garden, in an old armchair around which were grouped other old and diverse chairs and sofas and tables. Various of his children brought him tea and breakfast, and pretty soon other male Marafies began dropping by to see him about this or that piece of business, or just to say hello. He sat all day, sometimes holding forth at large, sometimes holding small conversations with his unshaved cheek close to his visitor's ear. At noon the children brought out platters and steam trays of rice and meat and vegetables and bread. In the afternoon they brought out thermos jugs of Turkish coffee. In the evening the men got in their cars and drove to the Marafie *diwaniya* hall, where they sat on red velvet sofas on blue-and-gold Persian carpets and had more tea and coffee and cigarettes and talk. Afterward they came back to the courtyard and the children brought out dinner.

Amira was good at his job. He had seen the Iraqis coming, and a few days before they arrived, he had laid in a supply of T-bone steaks and pâté and frozen shrimp that lasted through the occupation. Nothing unbearable had happened to a single Marafie in the long seven months, and this was thanks to Amira too. Knowing that a wise man plays to his strengths, he had not wasted time fighting the invaders but, rather, had purchased them. He had set up a system of bribery (he ran hotels and department stores, and knew the importance of system), with each Iraqi receiving so much, according to rank—a car for a very important officer, a television set for a slightly lesser one, a cassette player for the next, and so on, down to transistor radios and cold medicine and aspirin for the soldiers at the neighborhood checkpoint. When the occupation started, Amira Marafie had nine hundred television sets in stock. By the time the Iraqis left, he was down to eighty. Everything was insured; the Marafies had not lost money. But it was money that Amira was worried about.

Where was it all? Sitting *en diwaniya* early one evening the week of the emir's return, Amira gestured out the open front door to the garden full of fresh, deep holes. A couple of servants were still digging, although there was hardly any daylight left. "I had five hundred thousand Kuwaiti dinars on hand when the Iraqis came. I took in another nine hundred thousand in Iraqi dinars on the black market. We had to hide the money, of course. Mostly we buried it in the garden here and at the house. We would bury between forty thousand and fifty thousand dinars per night, between two and three in the morning; the more dangerous it got, the more we would bury. It was complicated. First we would count the money in blocks of five thousand dinars and put a paper band around each block. Then we would wrap each block in a plastic wrap, like Saran Wrap, you know. Then we would put eight or ten blocks together and seal them with heat-shrink plastic; we used a machine I got from one of the department stores. Then we would put that in vacuum-sealed bags, then that into plastic trash bags. Then bury. I kept track of the money on my Apple computer, recorded where each bag was and how much it contained. We have been digging it up now for two weeks, and we have found all of it except for twenty-five thousand which is missing. There was fifty thousand missing, but yesterday my Indian manager handed me a bag with twenty-five thousand in it. He said he had found it in the grandfather clock in the dining room. He found it by accident; I don't even know how it got in there."

But what was stirring the soul of Amira Marafie, and that of other men of money all around the city, was a more fundamental matter. The men who had stayed in Kuwait when the emir and his ministers fled had gotten used to running things, indeed had come to decide they were better at running things than the Sabahs were. They looked at the faltering, bumbling pace of the reconstruction, at the returning royals lolling about doing nothing at all, and they were appalled. "We are completely disappointed," Amira fumed. "We are *extremely* disappointed. For seven months we suffer and now we get nothing. Not one loaf of bread. We need milk, we need electricity, we need food, and what does the government do? Nothing. We say give it to us. We'll do it. We had a fantastic organization during the occupation. While our lives were in danger, we established a very complex, very effective organization. Not one family went hungry. Now there are trucks of food in Kuwait rotting because the government doesn't know how to distribute anything."

"The Sabah family said they would be ready to go as soon as Iraq left Kuwait," said Nader Marafie, Amira's brother. He moistened his lips with a little sip of tea. "We expected them to take two or three days to get things ready, not three or four weeks. We were told trucks of food were waiting to roll in. They were not. We were told the police force would be ready to come back right away. It was not. This is not good."

Why, I asked Nader, did not the Marafies continue running things for themselves, as they had during the occupation? Why wait for the government to organize commerce? The Marafies could run their own convoys of trucks to Saudi Arabia, buy goods and bring them back, open for business.

"It is not easy," Nader sighed, settling back in the cushions and lighting another cigarette. "There is no official exchange rate yet, so how could we know what to charge people? Besides, it is not easy to get food. How can we get to Saudi Arabia? Where would we get trucks?"

I thought about the Al Sultan Saleem Restaurant, a Palestinian neighborhood joint. It had been open for a week now, serving bread, tea, *foul,* and occasional pieces of dubious meat. It accepted payment in Kuwaiti dinars, Iraqi dinars, U.S. dollars, and Saudi rials.

Nader continued: "The government must organize things to make it less difficult."

At just that point, there was a surprise. Through the open door walked two princes of the Sabah family. They moved with stately grace across the blue-and-gold-and-red Persian carpet and settled, amid an excited buzz, in the seats of honor on either side of Amira. Servants ran with glasses of tea and ice water, and fresh ashtrays. I thought for a moment that someone might say something to the royals about the balky pace of the reconstruction, or what the government must do, but no one did, and the conversation picked up its pleasant hum again, as the *diwaniya* settled into its fourth hour.

It was said there were some people in Kuwait City who were angry enough to do something about it. There was dark, whispering talk of revolution. It was arranged that I meet a young rebel. I was deposited on a street corner one afternoon, and a few minutes later a pert, white Mercedes-Benz convertible slid silently up beside me. The man at the wheel was in his early twenties, a handsome, slim gentleman, clean-shaven and sweet-smelling. He wore Vuarnet sunglasses and a UCLA sweatshirt. He drove fast, recklessly, sending the car around corners with a flamboyant screeching of tires. The house he took me to was his parents', but they had spent the occupation in London and had not yet returned. It was a lovely home, modern and spacious and filled with light. We talked in a room that was a young man's vision of the high life, a furry sea of white shag carpeting and fat white leather sofas and a bar in the corner that was a glittering, glassy cornucopia of bottles—Stolichnaya and John-nie Walker and Jim Beam and Gilbey's. An elaborate music system was arrayed along one wall, and a pool table stood in the center, under a fake Tiffany lamp. We sat down on the sofas, and as the rebel offered me a Marlboro, two young women came in. They wore tight hip-hugging slacks and rainbow makeup and had bouffant hairdos. They posed at playing pool as we talked, leaning forward to stick their bottoms in the air with each shot, and pouting in exaggerated concentration.

"The people are angry," the rebel said. "They all see clearly now the problem with the government. They see that the government is run by incompetent people. Before February 27, we had this city running good. We got all the basic things we needed to live. But then the government comes back and there is no water, no electricity, scarce food. And the government people are fighting among themselves and do nothing. All they distribute is gratification for their egos. All is chaos. The people see this. They see that the resistance ran things efficiently for seven months and now these guys come back and want credit for that, and do nothing to improve things. The people see this and they are angry." He stopped so we could watch one of the young women sashay across the room to put on a new CD. "The government brought in trucks of milk and bread after the liberation, but they are fighting too much to distribute it. So the trucks just sit there and now the milk is spoiled and the bread has fungus on it. The people know this."

What, I said, are the people going to do?

It was a wrong, or at least impolite, question. The rebel fell silent for a minute, and when he spoke again, he was unhappy. "Well, you know, Kuwaitis don't like violence," he finally said. "They like to talk. They can speak and speak and speak. But they don't like to get into confrontations with the military or the police. So it is difficult." We watched the young women play at pool some more, and soon I left. Walking out to the car, I noticed the trash pile by the side of the house. It was composed entirely of liquor bottles, hundreds of them.

It was up in the no-man's-land at the border between Iraq and Kuwait, in and around the little town of Safwan, that you could really see things falling apart, the well-wrought war collapsing into the misbegotten peace. Safwan had been a decent-sized border city of about twenty thousand people, with a *suq*, a truckers' hotel, and a few modest restaurants. It had been bombed and shelled and shot up so thoroughly during the war that it was hardly there anymore. The very few buildings left standing were battered and full of holes; the dirt streets were cratered and littered with the trash of the retreat; the date palms and tomato patches had been pounded into the ground. Most of the people had fled. Those that remained were all refugees of one sort or another. Safwan was the point of confluence for the human signs of the emerging bad end: Shiite families in over-crowded, overloaded taxis fleeing the Republican Guard's rampage through Basra and Najaf and Karbala; beaten, battered Palestinians dumped on the line by the enforcers of the new religion of Kuwait-for-Kuwaitis; the flotsam of half a dozen countries, unwanted by either side. I drove up there, past the junkyard on the Basra road, three times, and every time it was worse.

Near the border at about the spot where someone had stuck a painted wooden sign—"Farewell"—was an impromptu camp, the stopping place for those people returning from Iraq whom the Kuwaitis did not want back. Every day, they came straggling and limping down the road, and every day the Kuwaiti soldiers on patrol shunted them off to the side. The castoffs were a mixed crew—Palestinians, Egyptians, Sudanese, Moroccans, bedouin—bound together by the common thread of being unwanted. They scavenged among the wreckage and rigged up lean-tos from the side panels of cars, beds from backseats. At night they made paltry fires from scraps of wood and trash. The fires were dangerous, because the ground was thick with unexploded ammunition that in the heat of the flames would pop off, sending little copperheads whizzing away in unpredictable and lethal directions. But it was bitterly cold at night, so people took their chances.

There was no established system of proper medical care, but sometimes American medics set up roadside clinics. At the remains of what had been a gas station but was now an underbrush of broken cinder block and plaster, I watched them treat a group who had just wandered in from Basra. They had arranged their clinic on the rear deck of an armored personnel carrier converted to a field ambulance. On one side of the machine someone had pasted a Bart Simpson sticker. "Don't have a cow, man," Bart said. When I walked up, they were working on a young girl, probably four years old, pretty, with chestnut hair in ringlets and curls. She was filthy, her skin black with grime, her blue dress nearly black, her bare feet encrusted in dirt. She had been burned by something, and the burn had not been treated, and had become a pus-wet wound on her left calf. It took two people to hold her in place; she was wild-eyed with fear. The chief medic sat on the edge of the deck. He had a farmer's tan and a farmer's forearms and hands too, thick and strong and freckled, with light-reddish-brown hair that was gold in the sunlight. Three soldiers were serving as nurses, and he kept up a chatter of instructions to them while he cleaned the girl. "Hey, Chris, gimme some more of those Q-Tip swabs. And got a tongue depressor? I need a tongue depressor. No? Well, just gimme those Q-Tips then." I asked him his name. He said, shortly, Sergeant Theron Williams. He wasn't being unfriendly, just busy. He swabbed the wound with a soft Q-Tip he held in one thick, dirty hand as he steadied the girl's leg with the other. He was brisk and efficient and a little rough in his movements, like a mother changing the diaper of her third child.

The chief nurse was Christopher Mickey, from Iowa, stationed at Fort Riley, Kansas, a private first class. "Lots of wounded here," he said. "We sent three pregnant women outa here yesterday by medevac. Yeah, these guys are *all* beat up." He gestured to take in the crowd around the medic track. There were nine or ten people waiting in line, all with obvious burn wounds or cuts, and another twenty or thirty sitting in the dirt nearby.

Sergeant Williams finished cleaning the girl, put an anti-bacterial salve on her wound, and covered it with clean white bandages. "We are seeing a lot of burns, some shrapnel. Lots of kids got blisters on their feet and cuts from walking on glass." He motioned forward the next person in line, a young woman in an incongruous dress. It was ankle-length, and of deep-blue velvet, a ballroom dress, trimmed with lace that had been white, but was now brown. She had wrapped a piece of green rag around her throat, like a choker, and secured it by bringing it up under her chin and tying it in a bow on top of her head. Private Mickey cut it off her, carefully, with round-edged scissors. When he pulled it away, I saw that it was soaked with pus. Underneath there was a raw burn patch in the hollow of her throat. She stood very straight, with her hands clasped in front, as the wound was swabbed. The medic wrapped a new bandage white and tight like a silk stock around her throat and then, slowly and carefully, so as not to inspire fear, brought his hands up to her shoulders and touched them to indicate that she should pull down her dress a little, so he might see. She lowered the top a few inches. Her shoulders and upper chest were covered with angry little red patches, as if firedrops had rained on her. "I ain't never seen so many burns in all my life, man," Williams said.

I left him to his work, and went over to where a large family was hunkered down in the dirt. The head of the family was a leathery man who looked to be a laborer or a farmer, middle-aged and stocky. He said that he was Egyptian and that his name was Muhammad Iman. He wore a gray robe with an old tweed suit coat on top. In the lapel were stuck five straight pins, arranged in a neat vertical line. Some Americans had given the family some packaged army rations, but not enough for every-one to get a full meal, so they had divvied everything up. The father had gotten a portion of chicken stew and a tiny bottle of Tabasco sauce. From time to time as we talked he looked at the Tabasco bottle; I don't think he understood its purpose.

"We came here from Basra," Mr. Iman said. "We walked and got some rides in cars. Too much fighting in Basra, so we leave. Too many people dead in street. Maybe there are ten dead in any street in Basra you walk in. Egyptians, Palestinians, Iraqis, Iranians. Women too." He ate while he talked, shoveling the food in with steady dispatch, and he had to open his mouth wide to accommodate both duties. I noticed that he had purple gums. "Any man go in the street who is an Egypt man, they kill him. The Iraqi people are very mad at Egypt men now because Egypt fights against them in the war. I must take my family from our home so they do not find us, and we sleep the night in the street." He held up a soggy gray blanket. "We get wet."

He had only just come across the border that morning. I don't think he knew yet that the Kuwaitis would not let him any further into the country. I didn't tell him. I gave him a cigarette, which he lighted with greedy pleasure, and which prompted everyone around me to clamor for the same. I gave out a pack in a few minutes, and everyone lit up together and puffed and talked away. "I am from Rumaila," an old woman said. She was barefoot and had a dirty pink towel tied around her head. "Some people in family is dead. From missiles. Americans shoot two missiles from airplane. This before six days ago. No, not from airplane. From same as that." She pointed to the medic's APC. "The missiles hit bus. Sixteen people in bus. All my family. I am in car with bus. Three in bus is dead and thirteen is hurt. A car comes and takes them away to hospital, and Americans say we come here. So we come."

The worst off of all the people at the border were the deportees dumped there by the Kuwaiti troops: Palestinians, Algerians, Sudanese, and Moroccans caught by Kuwaiti revenge-takers, tossed in jail for beating and questioning, then dumped here. I talked one day to the remnants of a group of twenty-five who had arrived the afternoon before. They had made a shelter out of a junked green station wagon by the side of the road, just over the line in Iraq. Two of them were sitting in the sprung and sagging backseat, as if they were waiting for their driver to show up and take them somewhere. I asked them why they were still here. The older of the two spat on the floor of the car. "Where we go? Where I go? I have no documents. If I go up the road, the Americans say, 'Where you think you go? Where are your passport, your identification papers?' I have none. The Kuwaitis stole everything, my passport, everything. Did I say my watch? My watch."

He was a hungry, dirty man, barefoot, with dried blood caked along one side of his head at the hairline. He looked at his feet when he talked. "They tortured me. They arrested me from my home and took me on a bus with a lot of other men to Fawaniya and then they started the torture. They beat me in the head with a pistol." He said his name was Abdel Khadir Boukhatan, thirty-one years old, an Algerian who had been living in Kuwait for a year and working as a taxi driver. "They arrest me because Algeria was with Iraq in the war. There were one hundred and nine men in the jail, all in one big cell in a special building in Fawaniya. The torture is with electricity, with cable. They put electric wires on the body. They keep us fifteen days, and then they put us on bus and bring us here and throw us out. We have one fellow, a Moroccan, who was beat in the head and fainted. He is maybe dead. The Americans took him away."

His carmate, a young Palestinian, said, "They beat me with cables and sticks." He held out his wrists to show the red marks where the ropes had dug into him, and pulled up his sleeves to show the mottled gray of healing cigarette burns. "Every day, they would come and torture and beat us. We were blindfolded all the time except to eat. They tied my arms behind my back. They beat me with a pipe and with a cane and with rifle butts, and burned me with cigars. Why? Because they said we were with Saddam Hussein. Yesterday they take us all and bring us here. We have no money, no papers, no passports, no food, nothing. Look—even no shoes." His feet were shod in cheap plastic slippers. "I have nowhere to go. My mother, sister, brother, aunt—all were born in Kuwait. Where should I go? This car. I live in this car now."

A Kuwaiti military policeman, on duty with the Americans at the border, stood a few feet away during these recitations and listened. You could see from his bearing, and the polished neatness of his uniform, that he was a professional soldier, not one of the young rebels of the resistance. He wore dark sunglasses, and as he listened to the Algerian and the Palestinian his face showed nothing. Afterward, I asked him what he thought of their stories. He made a face of elaborate disdain. "Algerians, Palestinians, Yemeni, Sudanese, all the same. Eh. Probably they are looting, or collaborating. They are people like that. You open the hand to give them everything, they bite the hand. And they continue to bite until you make the hand into a fist and strike them."

The Algerian was listening to this, and it made him angry. "No, I do nothing wrong in Kuwait. If I do anything wrong in Kuwait in the war, why I stay there? I would go away. Nothing, I did nothing." The Kuwaiti officer shrugged and walked off.

There was an American field headquarters across the road, three or four big tents and various vehicles parked around them, guarded by military policemen with M-16 rifles. The MPs were under orders to stop nonmilitary personnel from stepping onto the headquarters turf, but after a few minutes, Colonel Robert Westholm, who was the only officer designated to talk to the press, saw me standing and waving and walked over from his tent. He was a tall, heavy man, with maybe fifteen or twenty pounds of fat on him, and his uniform was clean and beautifully ironed. I asked him about the Kuwaitis dumping their beaten deportees on the border, and about all the hungry people around Safwan.

"That is Kuwaiti business at the border," he said. "What they are doing in terms of letting people in and throwing people out, that is their business.

"I'm a military man," he said. "Food, care, for these people, that's not my problem. That's a Kuwaiti government problem or an Iraqi government problem, depending on which side of the line they're on. We've provided humanitarian assistance on an emergency basis, but we're not in the business of humanitarian assistance and can't do it full-time. Besides, people are not really hungry here, I don't think. Not starving certainly."

The colonel may in fact have been a heartless man, but it was true that there wasn't really much he could do. Nobody had given anybody any orders to deal with the problems that peace had brought to Safwan, which were, writ small, the problems of the whole looming postwar mess. There was no system for getting anything done, only vast confusion. The most basic questions were unresolved. Who was in charge here? Whose land was this? Who was making the rules? You could wander in and out of shifting realities and surrealities.

One day, I drove past the American border checkpoint without noticing it (the afternoon was warm and I was dreamily lost in the sun on my face and the breeze coming through the broken window), and kept on driving, past Iraqi army bunkers and abandoned vegetable farms. I stopped at one to see if I could find some tomatoes to buy (the tomatoes were supposed to be very good around here), but I found only an old lady alone with her mule, both of them with their bones poking up against their skin. I gave her half my remaining bread—four loaves—and two chocolate bars, some orange drink, and half a dozen cans of tuna. She grabbed the bread and tore a big piece out of it with her teeth and sat down on the ground to eat.

Driving on, I went another ten miles or so, and came to a checkpoint. I wasn't surprised to see the soldiers were Arabs. Most of the checkpoints were manned by Kuwaiti or Saudi or Egyptian soldiers, part of the American effort to keep a low profile. The soldiers at the checkpoints were supposed to stop each car and examine identification papers, but they usually waved through anyone with a pink face. I slowed down a little and waved, expecting to get a wave back, but the soldiers, seven or eight of them, stepped into the road and pointed their rifles at the windshield, so I stopped. One, an officer, spoke to me in English. "Get out of the car," he said, and I did. "Where are you going?" he said. No place in particular, I said. "What are you doing here?" he said. Nothing much, I said.

To my mild surprise, the other soldiers began searching the car. They made a pile on the ground: maps, notebooks, batteries, cigarettes. I didn't really mind. I still wasn't paying any attention, and I vaguely thought I had just run into an unusually thorough patrol. I looked at the officer and noticed that his uniform was familiar. Probably Egyptian, I thought.

"Are you Egyptian army?" I asked, as politely as a befuddled tourist.

He gave me a look. "No," he said. "Iraqi."

I laughed at that. No, really, I said. No kidding. What are you really?

"Really," he said, slowly, incredulously. "We are *really* Iraqi army. This is Iraq." I looked at him seriously for the first time and saw that his brass belt buckle bore the Germanic eagle that is the symbol of the Iraqi army. I looked around. The others had made a neat pile by the side of the road of my food and maps and blankets and the rest. My Sony shortwave radio was on top of the pile. "Why did you come here? Why are you in Iraq? You are a spy?" the officer said.

No, no, no. Just stupid. Not paying attention. Big mistake.

"You write bad things about Iraq?"

No, no. I only write bad things about Kuwait.

"Ah. Sabah is a pig. He marries many girls. You write this?"

Oh yes. Many times.

He nodded with satisfaction. "Okay, you go now. Go back to Kuwait."

Turning to leave, I thought of my radio. It was new, and had cost $137, and suddenly, with the kind of madness that sometimes comes in moments like these, I thought that I couldn't afford to lose it.

Give me back my radio, I said.

"What?" Incredulous, and I don't blame him.

I want my radio. It's mine. I paid for it.

"No, I keep radio," the officer said. "And I take this too." He leaned forward and grabbed up the three notebooks that were sitting on the front seat. "Now, you go," he said.

The notebooks represented three days' work. I begged for them back. "Please, please, please," I said. He held them up in the air and smiled and shook his head. "Okay," I said, "I won't go then. Give them back or I won't go back to Kuwait." I folded my arms and leaned against the car.

"You go," he said.

Not without my notebooks.

"Go." He made shooing motions with his hands at me. I shook my head.

"Okay." He gave back one notebook.

"Please, please, please," I said. He handed over the second one and held the third up in the air, grinning. I wondered if I was supposed to jump for it. "Please. Then I go. I promise. And you can keep the radio. It's a gift." He tired of me abruptly and tossed the last notebook at me. "Okay, go."

As I wheeled the car around, the Iraqis waved cheerful good-byes. "Good America! Good Mr. Boosh!" yelled one.

I had driven about halfway back to the border and was just calming down when three men jumped out from some dunes by the side of the road and hailed the car to a stop. They were Iraqi soldiers too, although just barely. Their uniforms were nearly black with dirt, and only one of the three wore shoes. They crowded around the car. "Hello, mister," said the one with shoes. "Food, mister, food." I told him I had no food because his colleagues up the road had taken it all. He apologized. I must have some of his food. His name was Khalid, he said, and he was the platoon commander here.

I followed him up a path through a line of sand berms and a shallow trench. We passed by two supply trucks filled with dark-green crates of .50-caliber machine-gun rounds and with piles of shiny metal canisters. "Chemical. To make fire on people," Khalid said, pointing to the canisters. "We never use." Just beyond was a little adobe hut that must once have belonged to a poor farmer. Khalid ushered me in grandly; he was, astonishingly, house-proud. He shared the hovel with the other two soldiers, and their thin gray pallets were crowded together on the concrete floor. The room smelled earthy and damp and of animals, like a cellar in an old house where an old dog sleeps. On the walls by the bed were a few color photographs, torn from magazines, of heavily made-up girls. Just face shots, no skin; Arab pinups are as chaste as, and rather like, high school graduation pictures. In one corner were a shallow tin bowl of tomatoes and a couple of cheap aluminum pots, one with cooked rice in it, the other with water. The Iraqi gestured to take it all in. "Beautiful, beautiful," he said.

We sat and drank a little water. He offered me a tomato, but I declined. He said he was tired of the war and that Saddam was no good. All the senior officers had gone days before, he said. He was only a lieutenant. He didn't know what to do. He knew the shooting had stopped, but he didn't know why. When I told him the war had been over for two weeks, he looked at me dubiously. It didn't matter anyway, he said; he could only surrender if his superior officers came back and told him to. "If Americans come, I fight," he said. I don't think he had any idea that an entire American army was sitting in the sand a few miles from him, and would have sent over a couple of armored personnel carriers to kill him except that he wasn't worth interrupting their volleyball games for. He wasn't really interested in fighting anyway. "Americans good people. George Bush good people," he said. "Very good." He walked me back past the trucks and the trench to my car. As I was leaving he asked me for cigarettes, and I had to tell him the other fellows had taken those too, which brought forth a wistful outcry. "I want cigarettes," he said. "I want beer. I want to go to Sheraton in Baghdad. I want to go to Meridien. I want to go to America."

The evening the emir came home, the usual parade of pouting girls and boys with guns was cruising past the hotel in the Ferraris and Porsches and Corvettes they had taken out of hiding. Older men sat on the sidewalk in lawn chairs. The gunfire competed now with music from car radios and boom boxes, and the racket was deafening. I walked around asking people what it meant to them to have the emir back; a stupid question, their bored glances said, it didn't mean a thing at all. He had come by jet, and a select group of dignitaries and diplomats and relatives had met him at the airport. He hadn't said a word, and the motorcade had taken him off to someplace secret.

A young man leaning against a BMW loosed off a clip into the air before he answered me, swinging the Kalashnikov casually and letting the bullets spray in a long, chattering buuu-uurp-uurp-uurp out over the water. "Of course, some people are happy the emir is home," he said. "Of course, I am myself. But the main thing is, we are just having a good time. It is a party every night! It is a wonderful time!" I asked him if he thought things had changed much in Kuwait in the last seven months. "Not so much," he said. "We always used to come out here and party before the Iraqis came too. Especially on Thursdays and Fridays we do this. The only difference is now we are on the sidewalk instead of the sand because of the mines." He thought for a moment. "Also, now we shoot guns."

Sometime that night I decided to leave Kuwait, and I was gone the next day. I made a deal to leave the Nissan behind with a free-lance photographer who needed a car. She was supposed to drive it back to Dhahran later, but she never did and eventually someone else had to. The car was in awful shape, mud-covered inside and out, the front windshield cracked from top to bottom and a sock sticking out where the gas cap had been. It still stank from its bath in the corpse-water.

I hitched a ride on a C-130 that took me to Dhahran, where I met Max, and we went together to Paris. The first night there I ate a three-tiered *fruits de mer* of Belon oysters, and *palourdes*, and *praires* and *violets*, the sweet, delicate clams from Brittany and Provence, and mussels, cockles, and tiny, coiled winkles, the meat teased out of the shells with a straight pin, and *crevettes roses,* the little sharp-beaked shrimps that boil up as pink as sunset, and hairy spider crabs and crawfish, with a pot of *aioli* for dipping things in. I drank a bottle of Puligny-Montrachet with it, a fat, luscious wine, dripping fresh from the silver ice bucket by the table.

THE CAMP OF
LOST CHILDREN

T HE MONTHS AFTER THE END OF THE WAR were full of sorrow
for thousands of people, but sadness has its gradations. The
most wretched thing I saw was a refugee camp, a relatively
small one, established by the Islamic Republic of Iran in the
province of Kurdistan. It was a camp of a specialized nature, the
place for those refugees who were minors, and whose parents
had died, or disappeared, somewhere in the wintry flight of a
million people across the mountains that make the wild, beautiful border between Iraq and Iran. I went there one day in
mid-April, arriving in late afternoon. The camp was about ten
miles outside the city of Saqqez, set in a broad valley of pastures
rolling in gentle swells and dips to a horizon of old, soft mountains.

The compound was enclosed by a cyclone fence, shiny and
new and topped with a spiral of concertina wire that glittered
in the rosy dying sun. There were no trees inside the fence, nor
any grass, just dirt and rock and mud and half a dozen big
buildings of corrugated tin. I parked at the gate, next to a
leftover roll of the concertina wire. A little girl, three or four
years old, wearing a raggedy gingham dress, was half perched,
half leaning on the roll. Concertina is the nastiest of all barbed
wires, studded with little blades, nearly as sharp as razors. I

stared at the child; it was unbelievable that she could press up against the roll without her legs running blood.

Walking through the gate, I became surrounded by a chattering rush of children, hundreds of them. Many were hardly dressed, wearing only tattered nightclothes and pajamas; some were barefoot; all were filthy. I went, carried along by the crowd around me, into the closest of the big shedlike buildings, a long, dark place with a concrete floor and plastic sheets over the open windows. The floor had been divided into pens, made of sheets of tin tied at the corners with twine. The pens filled the barn to the dim recesses of its corners, and people filled the pens. Some of the pens were as small as five feet by seven feet, others as large as twice that, depending on how many people lived within. Most had small kerosene burners for cooking, and in most the concrete floor was covered with old carpets or blankets.

At the first pen, I met a young woman named Najad Ali who was a pharmacist from Kirkuk, a large city in northern Iraq. She spoke English, and she explained the system of the place as we walked from one pen to another. "In this building is one hundred and sixty people. In the whole camp, five thousand. Everybody here is from a family that has lost a parent. It is about sixty percent children, the rest women, a few men. Each house"—she called the pens "houses"—"belongs to one family. In this house here," she said, stopping, "is five children, no mother, no father. In this house is four children, no father, but still have a mother. In this one is three girls, no father, no mother, but is an aunt with them."

She was herself living with a sister a few years younger. They had become separated from their parents during an Iraqi army helicopter attack on Kirkuk. "Honor to God, I believe they are still alive," she said.

We sat in a carpet in her pen, with a great crowd of people pressing around us and everyone talking at once, and she yelled in my ear further facts of her life. "We live as prisoners of war. We have been here ten days and they will not let us leave, even to go to Saqqez to buy food or take a shower. The food is not good, there is no healthy water, and there is no healthy toilets, no showers. The medicine we get is no good. It is expired. No doctors come here, only a nurse, and she does not have the medicine we need."

"No, we live worse than prisoners of war," a man broke in. "This place is not for humans living. Is a place for animals. Chickens and cows live here before us. Now we live like animals. We go to the bathroom on the ground. This is true—human beings going to the bathroom on the ground like animals."

This man—Barhram Abbus, a mechanical engineer from the Iraqi Kurdish city of Sulaimaniya—took up the job of guide from Najad Ali and walked me from barn to barn, introducing me to people and translating. We went to a big shed of three rooms, the first and smallest holding twenty-six people in three to five pens. In this building, the floors were not concrete but dirt. There was only one window, high up and covered with several layers of plastic, so the room was nearly as dark as night. Someone had hung a stopped clock on one of the walls. We paused to see five children, ages six to twelve, living in a pen by themselves. Mr. Abbus whispered in my ear: "Mother and father both dead." The oldest boy, who was ten, spoke for the family. He said (translated Mr. Abbus in my ear): "My mother is from helicopter dead. My father too. I am running. When I see my father is dead I run and run. I run in the city and my uncle takes me. I am running and he running and we go to the mountains and we walk for much days and we come here."

The next pen, two little girls. In my ear: "Mother, father both dead, but they do not know, be careful what you say." The older girl, Ashti Khadur, age eight, barefoot, held a doll in her hand. I couldn't think of anything to say, so I said something stupid;

I asked her if she liked it here. "No," she said. "Is bad here because is too many people. Only little space. I want to go home. Is no place to play here."

In the second room, seventy people in five pens, an old lady was asleep on the floor. She was covered with a sheet of plastic, and water from the roof was leaking on the plastic, but she didn't move. An old man lying next to her plucked at my leg. "Mister. Mister. This place for animals. This place for animals." In the pen next door, there was a one-day-old baby, a boy, named Halow, said Mr. Abbus. He was swaddled in a pink blanket on a bed of carpets and horse blankets. His mother held the boy's face up so I could see him, and wept silently as she did so, the tears rolling in perfect unison down her round cheeks.

And onward, across a field of mud and shit and piss and garbage, past the overflowing portable toilets—there were four that I could see for the whole camp, and no showers at all—to a new building, very large, with five hundred people living inside. It was a very long shed, and I think it must have been the milking barn, because running the length of the floor were two deep trenches where the cows' tails would line up. The trenches had been mostly covered with sheets of metal, but were still open here and there, and I could see they were half filled with garbage and worse. The air had a thick, sickroom quality.

We stopped at a particular pen, or rather, no pen in particular. A woman lay on the floor, curled up on a piece of carpet, with a baby lying on its back next to her, both of them hollow-eyed. We lay down next to her to talk, all in a line; she whispering into the ear of Mr. Abbus, he whispering in turn into mine: "I am sick in stomach, twelve days sick. No doctor ever comes. All day I lie here. I cannot move." A tearing, retching cough interrupted her, and we waited for it to end, but she coughed on and on—terrible, liquid sounds. We got up and dusted ourselves and went on. Mr. Abbus shook his head.

The next pen we stopped at had no fire, no food. In one corner a boy lay unconscious, in the other a woman in the same condition. "You see the mother?" Mr. Abbus said, with a note of almost satisfaction in his voice. "You see the child? They have nothing to eat today, nothing to eat yesterday, nothing to eat before. Cannot move. Cannot eat from the sickness in the stomach. Cannot drink. They are going to die for sure soon."

I had arrived in Iran a few days earlier, on April 17, the day after the American government announced that it would station troops in northern Iraq to stop the Iraqi army from killing the Kurds. I spent a night in Teheran, and the next day went, with a Dutch Red Cross man and a Dutch television crew, to the city of Urmia, the capital of the province of Azerbaijan, in the mountainous northwest quadrant. That night, after a boiled chicken dinner in the lobby of the small hotel where the relief workers and the reporters stayed, I met an Austrian Red Cross official who was pink with choler. He had just driven forty-seven tons of relief supplies 2,400 miles across Yugoslavia and Bulgaria and Turkey, to this place, only to discover that the Iranians were not really interested in distributing salvation to the starving Kurds. "They want to help the Kurds, but not too much," he said, in angry revelation. "They don't want them to starve, and they want to get credit for not letting them starve, but they don't want them to get comfortable enough that they decide to settle here. Well, I guess that is no surprise. Nobody in the world likes the Kurds, you know."

This was true.

The problem with the Kurds is suggested in their faces. They don't look like anyone else around them. They are too light-skinned to be mistaken for the Arab people of Iraq, and they don't have the slightly feline cast of the Persian face. They have lived for several millennia in the mountains and river valleys that make up the border areas of northeastern Iran, northern Iraq, southern Turkey, northern Syria, and Azerbaijan, and they look more like the people of the wild west coast of Ireland than

those of the Middle East. They are beautiful, with auburn hair
and skin that somehow manages to be both olive and pink, and
eyes of either hazel or green. The men tend to have powerful
noses, often the kind of dramatic beak that starts out on a line
close to the horizontal and then breaks halfway along the length
to the nearly vertical. They are mostly short people, and often
remarkably strong; even Kurdish children can walk for many
miles in mountain territory.

Kurdish mythology offers two accounts of their origin, both
of which make the point that Kurds are not like anybody else
in the world. The first stems from a legendary episode in which
a creature named Zahhak usurped the throne of Persia. Zahhak
had growing from his shoulders two snakes, for whose sustenance he required every day the brains of two youths or maidens. A wily minister hit on the scheme of mixing a calf's brain
with each human brain and thus realized a net saving of one
youth or maiden per day. He had the survivors smuggled to the
mountains, and they founded the Kurdish race. The second
story has it that King Solomon, who held sway over the spirit
world, one day sent five hundred Divs, his spirit minions, flying
to Europe to bring back five hundred fair women for his harem.
When the Divs returned, they found Solomon had died in the
meantime, so they kept the women for themselves, and from
these unions the Kurds were born. Less fancifully, the Kurds say
they are descended from the Medes, an Indo-European people
who, perhaps as early as the twelfth century B.C., migrated south
and west from north of the central Persian plateau and by 612
B.C. had settled in and gained control over the Zagros Mountains region of northeastern Iraq and northwestern Iran.

Although the Kurds have, in the late twentieth century,
developed a shaky, rough sense of nationalism, the traditional
and true Kurdish loyalty is tribal, and Kurdish history is generally a story of the men of this tribe killing the men of that tribe,
and all of them together more or less united in the principle of

killing anyone from the outside who might try to lord it over them. Kurds make difficult neighbors.

The Kurds of Iraq, who number between three and four million people, have fought one or another of the governments of Baghdad off and on since 1943. For reasons of state, the governments of Iran, the Soviet Union, the United States, and Israel have at various times in recent years supported the Iraqi Kurds, and for reasons of state have betrayed them. The second-most-important betrayal occurred in 1975, when the American secretary of state Henry Kissinger and the shah of Iran decided to abandon military support of the *pesh merga* ("those who walk before death") guerrilla army of Mustafa al-Barzani, the head of the Kurdish Democratic Party and the most powerful tribal leader of Kurdish Iraq. The decline of Barzani's forces fractured the Kurdish opposition, leading to the rise of various rival groups, the most significant of which was the Patriotic Union of Kurdistan, headed by Jalal Talabani, tribal leader of an area in and around the city of Sulaimaniya, in southern Kurdish Iraq. Between 1975 and 1991—a period that included the Iran-Iraq war, in which Iraqi Kurds fought with the Iranians against Iraq—an estimated 180,000 Iraqi Kurds disappeared at the hands of Iraqi military and government forces, and more than four thousand Kurdish villages were destroyed, as part of a massive government program of forced resettlement.

The most important betrayal—most important because it stopped the clearest chance there ever was for the Kurds to get out from under the rule of the Baath—occurred at the end of the Gulf War, in late February and early March 1991, when the American government under the direction of President Bush turned away from the Kurdish uprising it had encouraged, allowing the helicopter gunships of the Iraqi army to strafe civilians in the cities of Kirkuk and Sulaimaniya, and spurring the flight of somewhere between one and three million people from their homes. It was the television pictures of that terrible exodus—the scenes of weeping mothers burying their dead by the side of the road, of thousands of men scrambling for loaves of bread thrown from trucks—that had brought me reluctantly back to a war I had thought was over and won.

At five in the morning of April 20, I went, with a volunteer Red Cross guide named Kasim and an unsmiling young man from the Office of Culture and Islamic Guidance, to visit the city and refugee camps of Sar Dasht, along the border with Iraq, a four-hour drive to the south. We went in two cars, both Iranian-made models called Peykans, styled, Kasim said, after the British Hillman; they reminded me of a Dodge Rambler, a car my father once owned, but were smaller and tinnier. The seats were covered with thick, matted pelts of some man-made fur.

We headed south, skirting the great salt lake of Urmia, through the foothills of the Zagros Mountains, a country of green valleys and brown sheep and beech trees that grow tall and bushy, with every branch and twig pointing to the sky. On the crest of almost every hill there was a small watchtower of medieval cast, with a crenellated top and narrow slits for windows in the stone, and with a couple of bundled-up young soldiers on the roof, hugging themselves and stamping their feet against the cold morning wind. The soldiers were there to watch over the local population, the Kurds; like the Iraqis and the Turks, the Iranians were forever busy at the endless, hopeless task of taming the mountain tribes. We drove through the relic of one dreamlike episode in that fight, the city of Mahabad, a large, busy farm town that was, briefly, the capital of the Kurdish Republic of Mahabad, a nation that lasted no longer than Brigadoon. It was established by a local tribe in January 1946 (the Kurds are masters at seizing moments in which power is shifting) with the support of the Soviet Union and defended by the army of Mustafa al-Barzani. But when the Soviets withdrew from Iran, the Kurds lost Mahabad, and the government controlled it now.

Indeed, the government controlled all of Kurdish Iran, the provinces of East and West Azerbaijan and Kurdistan, having won the last round of open warfare, which began with the Islamic Iranian revolution in 1979 (another moment seized) and ended in 1984 with 27,000 or so Kurds dead. But that control was as tentative as a classroom monitor's in a tough high school, and you could see this in the streets of Mahabad. The square at the town center was decorated with state-approved art: Saddam Hussein with a red nose like a cartoon drunk and Uncle Sam with a grotesque blue nose like a cartoon Jew, both on their knees with Iranian soldiers holding swords at their throats. But the people walking by Uncle Sam were in an ongoing state of sartorial rebellion. In Teheran—and even in Urmia—men and women dressed modestly in public, in the mandated postrevolutionary style, the men wearing slacks and suit coats or vinyl jackets, the women *chadors* and face masks or at least ankle-length overcoats and voluminous scarves. The men and women I saw now wore clothes of flamboyant independence. The basic male suit was a wonderful hybrid, a sort of zoot-suit bottom with a bolo top. The trousers were high-waisted, pleated, and voluminous through the thighs, tapering to slightly pegged cuffs. The close-fitting jacket was cut short at the waist and worn unbuttoned but tucked into a great colored sash, ten feet long, wound in overlapping layers to make a cummerbund. These suits were woven, at their traditional best, out of goats' wool, into a herringbone fabric that was so tightly meshed that it was nearly wrinkleproof and as tough as canvas; the weave gave a slight moiré effect to the cloth, which was dyed brown or wheat or blue. The women wore gypsy clothes, long, loose skirts of many semitranslucent layers, and blouses and several scarves, all of this in hues of pink and purple and red and blue, and decorated with tiny spangles of shiny metal.

*   *   *

There were ten refugee camps around Sar Dasht, comprising about five thousand tents. The two hundred tents of Camp Number Ten were spread out over the roughly terraced sides of a big hill. You could see at a glance that it was a bad place. Without the most rigorous attention, refugee camps become instant slums for the same reasons that slums are ordinarily, if more slowly, made: too many people in too small a space, with too little money and nothing to do. The poor are as different as the rich, not only from me and you, but from the way they were themselves before they were poor. In their better lives of just three weeks before, most of these people, I am sure, had lived with a reasonable attention to cleanliness (it is next to godliness in Islam too), but being very poor makes the trappings of decency seem like frivolous affectations. What is the point, when you think you might die of disease or hunger sometime soon, of carting the trash away from the tents or washing one's hands or scrubbing clothes?

The ground was a stew of mud and stagnant water and garbage. It is surprising how much garbage even people with hardly any food can make. The children played in the stew. I watched a little girl of five or six years, wearing a set of pajamas decorated with teddy bears and hearts, playing in a puddle, poking at the muddy water with a butcher's knife. "Terrible, isn't it?" said a voice at my shoulder. "Every day the children die, two, three a day."

The voice belonged to a man in his twenties, dressed in blue jeans and a brown vinyl jacket zipped up to his chin. He offered a quick tour of the camp, and we walked down a slippery mud slope, both of us sliding and nearly falling in our leather shoes. At the bottom of the hill was a small stream where a group of women and girls filled up pots and plastic buckets. They carried the buckets back up the long hill, sloshing and banging against their legs, with slow, difficult care. There were no men doing any water hauling. The women of Kurdistan do almost all the work of that kind.

Near the stream was a fresh grave, a small, ill-formed mound of red, hard-clumped dirt four feet long, with a large hunk of some sort of white, quartzlike rock at the head and a smaller one at the feet. It was a poor site, in the shadow of an unfinished, abandoned cement building—an army barracks, maybe—and without a scrap of green anywhere around.

"Dies yesterday. Four years old. The water from the stream is not good. Dirty. It makes the children sick."

We walked back up the hill to stop where a woman was squatting in the mud by a small fire, cooking. With her red hair and brown eyes, in her outfit of purple and pink, in that poor setting, she looked just like a tinker's wife, boiling up potatoes by some country road in west Ireland. Potatoes, though, would have strained her budget. She had only onions in the pot and a couple of tomatoes; she lifted up a spoonful to show us, and the stew was pink water gruel. My guide asked her a few questions, and she answered back in Kurdish, which he translated snippets of. "Is meal for twelve people," he said. "It is maybe"—he held out his hands to make a small bowl—"this much for twelve people. Not enough."

On the way out, I stopped to look into a white tent that stood by itself behind a rope fence, an oasis of sanitation and order. It was a clinic set up by a doctor from the French relief group Médecins Sans Frontières. The doctor was examining an infant girl, prodding and poking her. I asked him about the new grave. "Yes, I hear two children died yesterday," he said. "But I don't know for sure. They take them and bury them without telling me." He sounded exasperated at this. "It is very difficult. I am sure there are deaths every day, but I cannot keep track. There are no records, no organization. People come and go as they please and it is not possible to know when they come and go because there are no controls."

*   *   *

The border was an hour's drive from Camp Number Ten, at a natural crossing point, where mountains on both sides gave way to a high-valley pasture, a huge shallow saucer of long green grass, through which coursed the Kanchi River, swollen by rain and the spring melt. A dirt road ran alongside this, parallel to the border, which was marked by a tiny stone hut, and then, on the other side, ascended up a narrow pass between two nearly vertical mountain sides and curved off out of sight. Along the sides of the road and all over the pasture were tents, perhaps a couple thousand of them. Some of the tents were machine-made canvas jobs from the relief agencies, but most were cruder affairs, rigged up from tree branches and twine and heavy-duty clear plastic sheeting, or just from pieces of burlap or carpet or blankets. The scavenging for tent poles and firewood had stripped the hillsides bare, and there wasn't an intact tree anywhere in the valley. But it was still pretty to look at. Children splashed in the shallow water at the edge of the stream while their mothers washed clothes. Sitting in the green grass, pounding the laundry on the rocks, the women in their purples and pinks and blues made, from a distance, flowers of themselves.

The encampments crowded right up to the edge of the road and spilled into it, the men squatting and smoking, the women tending the fires, the sick and old lying on blankets or sheets of plastic, or sometimes simply in the dirt. The air smelled good here, much cleaner than in Camp Number Ten, a mixture of ozone and horse manure and grass and wood fires.

The road itself had become a kind of shopping strip set up by local Kurds, who trucked their wares in from nearby towns to sell at exorbitant prices. Every foot of it was taken up with commercial enterprises. A boy selling ladies' leather pumps, suitable for dancing, worked next to one selling hard-boiled eggs, several dozen arrayed in cardboard cartons, with one egg perched on end, on top, in a little holder hand-fashioned out of strips of metal cut from an old ghee can; in front was a small red saucer of salt, so you could peel your egg and salt it and eat it right there. Next to that was a small hill of burlap bags filled with pistachio nuts, and so on down the road to the border shed: crates of oranges and piles of plastic sandals, shiny new aluminum cooking pots and tent poles, boxes of sugar and tea and tomato paste, jerry cans of gasoline and cartons of Pepsi, huge plastic sacks of fresh apricots, trays of Winston cigarettes and Luv soap. Small boys walked down the road holding trays of pink-frosted cookies and spongy, sugary cakes. Older boys carried heavy wooden boxes of cooking gas in metal bottles. "Cakes, cakes, cakes!" yelled the small boys. "Benzene, benzene, benzene!" yelled the older boys. I ducked into a little wooden shed and found it was a restaurant, with a fire of coals in a metal box fanned to red-hot by an electric blower hooked up to a generator. I got a cup of tea and a couple of lamb *kebabs,* grilled while I waited, and ate lunch on a pile of Kurdish and Persian carpets rolled up in the corner.

Afterward, I sat in the sun and smoked a cigarette and watched the traffic go by. Along the edge of the river, drivers flicking beech branch switches moved along a train of fifteen donkeys, each with four big burlap bags of Thailand rice tied to its back. There was a nice economy to the operation; driving the train through the shallows of the river allowed the donkeys to drink without stopping the forward movement. Plodding along, the train moved past the border post into Iraq. The lone Iranian guard, sitting on a stool by his hut, paid them no mind. In the other direction came a different sort of supply train, a stream of men walking down the pass bent double with loads twice their size tied to their backs. One had four large carpets rolled up and tied together, and to his shoulders; another carried a six-foot-tall teak bookcase. Behind him a middle-aged man of perhaps five feet three inches and weighing maybe 130 or 140 pounds carried a a full-size General Electric refrigerator.

The most amazing sight was a man bent parallel to the

ground under the load of four large television sets, still in their factory boxes, held together by a carpet secured with a rope strapped around his middle. To steady the massive load, a second rope ran longitudinally around the boxes and passed from the rear over the top of it and down the front so that the carrier could clutch it in his right hand at his shoulder. He kept his left hand stretched out in front of him and slightly to one side for balance, and he moved forward with small, slow steps. He deposited his load at a spot in the road that served as an open-air major appliances shop, with refrigerators, stoves, and washing machines lined up in the dirt.

The man in charge of the business explained it to me. "Everything comes from Sulaimaniya, in Iraq," he said. "The people bring it by truck or car as close as they can get to this border that way, and then carry it the rest of the way, maybe ten, eleven, twelve kilometers. I buy from them, and sell to people who come here from Urmia and Saqqez, other Iranian cities, because they know they can get good prices here now; there is a lot of goods come in every day so the price is low. I sell a new refrigerator for seven hundred dinars, a stove for five hundred."

We wanted to stay at the border longer than we did. The Islamic Guide hustled us out. He was nervous and angry at us, and I couldn't figure out why. "We have stayed too long. We must go. This is very bad," he fussed and lectured all the way back up the road to the cars. Kasim, the Red Cross guide traveling with me, whispered why. "He is afraid. It is going to be dark soon, and we are going to be in Kurdish territory. He is afraid they will shoot at us. It is a very bad problem around here. The *pesh merga* sit in the hills and shoot at cars that are not from here."

By the time we got to Sar Dasht, the sun was already setting, and the Islamic Guide said we would have to spend the night there, in an army barracks, rather than chance the roads. It took an hour's argument to convince him otherwise, and he fidgeted in a nervous funk until we could see the lights of Urmia.

*   *   *

Every day for nine days I went to one place or another filled with masses of sick and half-starving people sitting in the mud. It all became very much of the same, which is the great problem with refugee stories, and with being a refugee. Death by malnutrition or disease is a process of dismal accrual, not dramatic change, and each day the people who are dying thus look more or less as they did the day before, which makes it hard to sustain interest in them; the world attention span for a given population of refugees is about a week at most.

On the ninth day, April 26, I went with Kasim to a group of camps near the town of Paveh, close to the border in the region of Bakhtiari. They were, I suppose, the most beautiful refugee camps in the world. There were four of them, each occupying its own side of a steep, green mountain. Wildflowers—scarlet poppies, tiny bluebells, yellow daisies—covered whole pastures, and tall firs with needles the color of deep seawater grew in thick forests. The footpaths of shepherds, no more than twelve inches wide, cut across the face of the mountains in faint scars against the green. The higher paths were a few thousand feet above the valley floor. From fissures in the shale, streams of cold, clear water poured out, tumbling down to a wide, slow emerald river. A rope footbridge crossed the river, and along its banks women were washing clothes in large, flat pans like paella pans, and children were wading and splashing.

More than twenty thousand people lived in and around the camps, in neat rows of white Red Cross tents strung like laundry flapping in the wind across the mountain sides, in rambles of green Iranian army tents, in plastic and tree-branch lean-tos along the road. I started at the first camp, and went, as the day passed, from tent to tent, camp to camp, swept along in a stream of complaint.

"My sister is very sick. Two times we take her to the doctor, but she does not get better. Her cough is very bad. . . ."

"My wife, she is very nervous, very nervous. Her behavior with the babies is changed. It is not good. When they talk, she does not listen anymore. She cannot. She is too nervous. . . ."

"I have no money. I have already spent all the money I have. In Sulaimaniya I have a large house, a car, everything a man could use. Now, I have nothing. I need money to buy oil and rice. . . ."

"The children are dirty all the time. This place is not clean. Look at my baby; she is covered with sores. . . ."

Somewhere along the way, I picked up a man named, for the purpose of this writing, Mozafar. He was a Kurd from Sulaimaniya, twenty-nine years old. He spoke Kurdish, Arabic, Persian, and English, and was a hustler. He made a proposal. He and I would cross into Iraq and work our way up through the Kurdish-held territory along the border to Zakho, on the Turkish border, a city now held by American troops. He would serve as translator and guide. In exchange, I would help him get past the American soldiers into Turkey. "I cannot return to Iraq, and I cannot stay here anymore. I hate it here," he said.

I hated it myself at that moment, and with no more thought than that, agreed. We went to his tent, he packed a small bag, and we drove up the dirt road to the mountaintop that marked the border. The road was packed with people moving in both directions, in every sort of vehicle—cars, taxis, big red Mack dump trucks, tractors. At the crossing there was only one Iranian soldier, and no Iraqis at all. I took my three bags from the trunk, and paid Kasim and the driver. When we walked past the border guard, he didn't even look up.

WHITE AND GREEN,
GREEN AND WHITE

M OZAFAR AND I walked side by side down the Iraqi slope
of the mountain, each holding one strap of the largest of
my three bags, a fat black duffel sack that swayed like a sedan
chair between us. The dirt road was steep and rutted, and we
had to walk slowly, leaning a little back, so as not to stumble.
Mozafar walked with a heavy limp, his right foot turning
sharply in at every step, and his right hip rolling awkwardly
forward to compensate. After about an hour, we arrived at level
land, the floor of a narrow, high valley through which cut a
stream. Vendors had set up shop along the road there, and I
stopped and bought a pair of Nike-knockoff sneakers; they were
flimsy, cheap things, worth maybe ten dollars, and they cost
seventy, an early and fair indication of the state of the economy
of Kurdistan.

Just past the piles of sneakers was the first *pesh merga* checkpoint, a young man of eighteen or nineteen, holding a Kalashnikov loosely at his side. He regarded us with no surprise—on
that road, at that time, the routine way of travel was on foot,
with bag in hand—and offered to take us to the headquarters of
the area commander. We walked on, through a landscape of
grass and jumbled rocks and curiously stunted trees, and as we
were crossing a stone bridge over the stream, I asked Mozafar
when we would arrive at one of the destroyed villages he had

spoken of. "Why, you are in one right now," he said. I looked around again at the skinny fields and the terraced hills, and suddenly the rocks and trees organized themselves into a coherent picture, like that trick drawing that changes from a wine goblet to two faces. I saw that I was looking at the ruin of a town and orchard. Those rocks were not scattered haphazardly about, they were set in the lines and squares of fences and foundations; those trees were planted in the rows of an orchard, and they were stunted because they were dead. "This was Terwella," Mozafar said. "Very old village, very nice. When the Iraqi army returned here after the war with Iran, they destroyed all with dynamite, poisoned the trees."

Across the bridge and around a bend, we met four more men with Kalashnikovs. They ushered us into a white Toyota Crown sedan, a clean, new car, marred only by two small bullet holes in the front windshield, on the driver's side. "Very nice, yes?" the driver said. He had to almost yell to make himself heard over the moaning whistle made by the air rushing through the holes. "Taken from Iraqi security offices in Kirkuk." The Mukhabarat, I later found out, favored Toyotas—Land Cruisers for country work and sedans in the city—and the *pesh merga* had liberated, it seemed, the entire fleet in their area. Over the next eight days hitching rides through Iraqi Kurdistan, I would pass from Toyota to Toyota, as if on an elaborate, endless test drive.

We stopped at a spur of land commanding the road and overlooking the valley, where there stood the remains of a stone house, three walls and half a roof. Behind this had been set up a large canvas tent, and in the tent sat six or seven men. This, Mozafar said in my ear, was the command post of Hussein Halifa Muhammad, the local military leader. He was sitting in the farthest corner, next to a pile of Kalashnikovs and RPG-7s, rocket-propelled grenade launchers that, with their wooden stocks and funnel-shaped muzzles, look like blunderbusses. He rose for a greeting as mannered as a benediction.

"Welcome to Kurdistan. We are honored that you are our guest. We thank Mr. Bush and America. You will stay and we will have tea." He did not offer his hand to shake; his arm ended in a stub of scarred flesh. After I had taken off my shoes and sat down, and we had started in on the first cup of tea, he began the conversation with an explanation of his terrible wound. "I lost it in Halabja," he said, waggling the stump lightly. Halabja was a city about forty miles from where we were; it was famous for a 1988 attack by the Iraqi army in which, it was said, Iraqi fighter planes had used nerve gas to kill large numbers of residents. "My home was destroyed and I got injured in the hand. They cut it off in the hospital. Also look—" He pulled up first his shirt and then his right trouser leg, to show a collection of mottled, shiny scars. (This would become familiar too. It seemed half the men in Kurdistan had been wounded somehow, and I would get used to having conversations punctuated by invitations to examine ruined flesh.)

The sun coming in the open front of the tent lent a drowsy warmth to the air, and a light breeze skittered sugar granules across a sheet of brown paper laid out on the floor in the corner. The paper had been made into a map, with pencil and crayon markings showing the positions of the Iraqi and Kurdish lines. The Kurds live in the northeast quadrant of the country, an area running from the plains of Kirkuk up through hills that rise to the rounded, green mountains of the Zagros chain along the border with Iran and finally to the higher, rougher peaks of the Taurus Mountains, where Iraq meets Turkey. Although the dominant population in the region is Kurdish, there are also large numbers of Turkoman and Assyrian people. The Turkomans, who came to this area from Central Asia a thousand years ago, number about two million, and live mostly in the provinces of Mosul, Arbil, Kirkuk, and Diyala. The Assyrians, a Semitic, Christian mountain people who claim descent from the ancient Assyrian Empire, live mostly near the northern border, in isolated stone villages thousands of years old.

The news reports I had read before coming here and the great masses of refugees in Iran, suggested that all these people had been forced to flee, and that Kurdish Iraq was held wholly by the Iraqi army, but I could see already that there was no Iraqi army anywhere about these parts, and the lines on the commander's map made clear the more complicated truth. What existed in Kurdish Iraq was a stalemate, a balance of power along topographical lines. The Iraqi army held the big cities of Kirkuk and Sulaimaniya and much of the area of the plains, which they could defend easily with lines of dug-in tanks. But as soon as the land began rising to the hills, the Kurds claimed it. From the Iranian and Turkish borders, Hussein Muhammad said, the *pesh merga* controlled the territory in a broad swath, anywhere from thirty to seventy miles wide, running from about twenty miles south of where we were to the city of Zakho at the Turkish border. The land was a wilderness of hills and bluffs and rocky mountains and high pastureland, half covered with forest, cut by few roads, isolated from mountain to mountain by deep ravines and heavily wooded valleys, the kind of ground that in itself could defeat an invading force.

There was something about the land, or in the people who lived on it, that gave rise to ferocious, tenacious fighting. The Assyrians, those fiercest of Biblical warriors, inspired a fear great enough to linger still, a couple of millennia later, in the romantic fancies of a young English lord:

> The Assyrian came down like the wolf on the fold,
> And his cohorts were gleaming in purple and gold;
> And the sheen of their spears was like stars on the sea,
> When the blue wave rolls nightly on deep Galilee.

The Kurds, who produced the greatest Arab warrior, Salah al-Din, have always fought among themselves and against the various outside forces who attempted to make them submit to any sort of governance. For centuries, while this land was under the weak control of the Ottoman Empire, the only real authority was tribal. The attempts of the central government of Baghdad to win it over began almost immediately with the formation of Iraq after the First World War—"We used to fight a little war with them every summer in Iraq," wrote Freya Stark—and have never stopped.

In the intensely nationalist, Arabist country that Iraq increasingly was from the 1930s on, successful military operations against the non-Iraqi, non-Arab people of the north became both a recognized means of political advancement and a tool for forging national unity. In the summer of 1933, Iraqi army general Bakr Sidqi organized a military and propaganda campaign against the Assyrians. He armed Kurdish tribes and instigated them to kill their Assyrian neighbors, and after this initial period of murder and looting, led a mechanized machine-gun unit of the Iraqi army into the Assyrian town of Sumayl to slaughter the male population, along with incidental women and children.

"This took some time," writes the historian R. S. Stafford. "Not that there was any hurry, for the troops had the whole day ahead of them. Their opponents were helpless and there was no chance of interference from any quarter whatsoever. Machine gunners set up their guns outside the windows of the houses in which the Assyrians had taken refuge, and having trained them on the terror-stricken wretches in the crowded rooms, fired among them until not a man was left standing in the shambles. In some instances, the bloodlust of the troops took a slightly more active form and men were dragged out and shot or bludgeoned to death and their bodies thrown on a pile of dead."

The Iraqi population was wildly enthusiastic about what the army had done. In Mosul, Stafford says, the people erected triumphal arches "decorated with melons stained with blood and with daggers stuck into them. This delicate representation of the slain Assyrians was in keeping with the prevailing sentiment." General Bakr Sidqi became a national hero, and three years later he led the Arab world's first modern military coup, against King Faisal.

Fighting between Baghdad and the people of the north has continued, with intermissions of varying duration, ever since. In 1943, Mustafa al-Barzani established an autonomous government in his family's area, around the town of Barzan. The Iraqi army defeated him and forced him to withdraw to Iran. The 1958 Iraqi revolution allowed him to return, and by 1961 he had built an army of 50,000 to 60,000 men. His *pesh merga* troops fought the Iraqi army for nine years, with the Iraqis able to hold, then as now, the cities, but unable to force the Kurds from the high ground. An estimated 50,000 people, mostly civilians, died.

In 1970, Baghdad offered autonomy to the Kurds, and a cease-fire was called to work out the details, but after four years of negotiations, the deal fell apart, and fighting began again. Barzani made the mistake of trying conventional warfare, and by 1975 his army had been driven to the border of Turkey. Supported by the Iranians and the CIA, the Kurds held out for a while. But the deal between Secretary of State Kissinger and the Shah of Iran to abandon the Kurds and normalize relations with Iraq destroyed Kurdish chances. Barzani and 600,000 other Kurds fled to Iran and elsewhere, and the Iraqis slaughtered thousands of those who remained behind, before a general amnesty was called.

It was at about this time that the Iraqi effort to conquer the north took on a clearly genocidal character, with the imposition of the first of a series of systematic campaigns to destroy—by TNT—the Kurdish mountain villages and deport the people of the villages to desert camps in southwestern Iraq. The goal was to remove all Kurds from the vast area comprising the provinces of Diyala, Kirkuk, and Mosul. Before this huge task was interrupted by the onset of the Iran-Iraq war in 1980, somewhere between 50,000 and 350,000 Kurds were forcibly deported from their destroyed homes.

Fighting was endemic throughout Kurdistan during the Iran-Iraq war, and complicated, with various Kurdish groups making shifting alliances with the Iranians against the Iraqis. When the Iranians sued for peace in 1988, the Iraqis immediately turned their attention to depopulating Kurdistan, launching a broad program called Operation Anfal, under the direction of the Office for the Organization of the North, headed by Ali Hassan Majid, Saddam Hussein's brother-in-law and the future governor of Iraq's nineteenth province (formerly the emirate of Kuwait). Operation Anfal forbade any humans or animals to go into any of the depopulated areas, which included most of the hill and mountain country of Kurdistan. The penalty for disobeying was death.

"My father was a fighter," Hussein Halifa Muhammad was saying to me. "He was in the Kurdish Democratic Party and he fought from 1961 to 1975. I have been fighting myself since 1980 to now. I am thirty-nine and I am not tired of fighting yet. My son is seventeen and he is a fighter too, and he will continue to fight after I am gone, if this needs be." He didn't sound at all bothered about this, or even much interested; it was as if he were saying, "My father was a farmer, I am a farmer, my son is a farmer." A black cricket jumped on a pile of clothes in the corner, and the pile stirred itself, becoming an old lady. She sat up and coughed and looked at us with rheumy and uninterested eyes, then sank down again, to go back to sleep.

"My mother," said the commander, and continued talking, pointing on the rough brown map to various places of bloody interest.

As he was talking, there came suddenly, and loudly, the heavy whup-whup of a helicopter flying overhead. I gave a nervous jump, but no one else flinched. "American, not Iraqi," said my host. "Now, here on the map I will show you exactly how we counterattacked in the famous battle of Laylan. . . ."

When, an hour later, he concluded the history, we had one last glass of tea, and he wrote, with his remaining hand, the safe-conduct pass that would take us through his territory and into the territory of the next leader. He wrote in a longhand so beautiful it was nearly calligraphy, on a lined page torn neatly out of a big red ledger. When he finished, he read it over carefully, signed his name, and sealed it with a stamp and pad he took from his pocket. This was to be the pattern for the next nine days, a slow meander from camp to camp, sit to sit, talk to talk, tea to tea. There was no way to hurry it along. Every ten miles or so brought us into the territory of another chief or subchief, and etiquette demanded that each leader receive us properly, without untoward rush. When, eventually, all of the hostly obligations had been met, a safe-conduct pass would be written and armed men and cars would be rounded up to take us to the camp of the leader next in line. The short drive from one camp to another could by itself take a few hours. All Kurdish military leaders are politicians, or all Kurdish politicians are military leaders, and they brake for handshakes.

That first night, we slept at the camp of Muhammad Hamas Saed, forty-three, a commander in Jalal Talabani's Patriotic Union of Kurdistan, with 1,250 men under his direction.

Two large canvas tents were set on a small plateau about a hundred yards from the top of a tall hill, or small mountain, with the long, fairly steep hillside descending below to arrive eventually at pastureland that rose up in turn to the next, lower hill. The land continued on like that, in pretty falls and rises into the distance, where the big Surwan River curved and twisted and doubled through the valley. When the angle of the sun was a little lower, the river would become rose gold, but now it was still sterling, shining whitely against the green. Beyond that were mountains taller than these, with snow on the peaks.

Saed's wife, Frozan, was young, like her husband, and the two of them looked like what you would think a mountain rebel leader and his wife should look like, almost to the point of exaggeration. The skin of his face was leathery and lined from outdoor life, and stretched tight over high, sharp bones. He had black hair swept back from his forehead in a widow's peak, black eyes, a black beard. He carried a rifle at all times, and a pistol tucked into the sash at his waist, and it was easy to imagine him shooting someone. She had the Arab-Celtic look, with hazel eyes and auburn hair, and wore sparkling purple pants cut in a voluminous style under a long pink skirt made of several layers of some thin, translucent material. Around her neck was a pink scarf, and at first she kept it drawn across her lower face as a shield against the eyes of strange men, but after a while she relaxed a bit and let us see her unveiled. They had been married for four years, had met in Iran; she was Iranian Kurdish. They had one child, a three-year-old girl named Danielle, who played on the blanket while we talked. It is the custom in the Middle East to dress up little girls like miniature ladies at party time, and Danielle was an improbable sight on a Kurdish mountainside. She wore a clean white dress of some frilly cloth, with Goldilocks bears dancing around the flared hem, and underneath that she wore white tights and red patent-leather shoes with red-and-white polka-dot bows on them. Her ears were pierced, and held dainty gold rings that matched her dainty gold necklace, a single thin ribbon of gold with a small gold heart dangling.

As the sun began to set and the first breezy beginnings of the cool night cut into the sunny air of the afternoon, Saed led me a short way down the hill from the camp, on a path in the grass through a small wood to a tiny clearing of overwhelming green. The grass was as thick as the pile of a carpet, giving way to a tangle of ivy and bushes of much darker green, with purple undertones, and this in turn gave way to trees of all sorts and sizes; willows and oaks and elms, saplings as delicate as ankles and barrel-waisted giants all mixed together, and dense with leaves, crowding and overlapping and piling on top of themselves. In the middle of the clearing was a pool of jade water, contained by stone walls covered with moss that was at bottom, tinged with the black of humus. Below the waterline, the stones were covered by a fine blue-green layer of algae. The only thing that wasn't green was the waterfall that made the pool; it was crystal and silver and frothily white-white, cascading forty feet down in a dozen streams, some no bigger than the freshet from a bathroom faucet, some as thick as fire-hose streams, twisting and braiding down from a mons of moss hanging off the bluff above.

I took off my clothes and my glasses and walked out on the stone wall that held the pool, the water overflowing its top rushing cold over my feet and splashing up my legs. When I got to the middle, I sat down, feeling the shock of the water slapping over my thighs and crotch, and the slippery stone underneath my butt. Saed had given me a bar of soap, and I splashed the sudsy water up over my chest and face, under my arms, scrubbing my hair, gritty and stiff with road dirt. Then I eased into the pool and went under, completely into the green, and let it wash over me.

As I was drying and dressing, I watched Saed. He had crossed on the wall to the other side and climbed a little way up the hill. He stood still for a moment and then brought his Kalashnikov up to his shoulder, aimed, and pulled the trigger. The water and the stone and the trees echoed back the bang of the shot over and over, and all the birds—I had not even noticed them, but the trees must have been full—skyrocketed up, shrieking and cawing. He shook his head in disgust; a miss, I guessed. He sat down and smoked a cigarette, patiently, and the birds returned, some of them at least, and settled back down on the branches. When it was quiet again, he stood up very slowly and moved off to the left, up a side hill, until he was twenty or thirty feet away from the pool. He made no noise I could hear. At a sapling, he stopped, and tucked the rifle into a V made by two thin branches. He spent a long time aiming, and I was able to find the target: on a branch perhaps sixty yards distant, a small blackbird. I kept my eyes on the bird, and when the rifle cracked, I watched it fall sudden and straight to the ground. Saed tramped through the brush and brought it back. He held it out to show to me: a small bird, no bigger than his hand, and beautiful, with silky blue-black feathers. It was untouched except for a neat, bloody furrow a quarter inch deep, a red-raw stripe across its tiny chest. If he had hit the bird squarely, the bullet would have blown it to pieces of feather and bone.

Back at the camp, Frozan had built up the fire into a hot, small flame and put on the grill a battered black pot full of rice and water. Saed sat on the blanket and prepared the bird. First, with an old gray metal pen knife, he cut off its head. Danielle sat at his side and watched him. He leaned over to her and handed her the bloody black head, holding her hands in his, to show her how she could move its bright-yellow beak open and shut. She giggled. "Juju. Juju," she said, making the beak move. Saed smiled down at her. "She says 'juju' all the time. It is a word she makes up. Everything is juju now. Birds are juju. Flowers are juju."

He plucked the bird with swift, almost automatic movements, beginning with the long tail feathers, which came off at only the slightest tug, and working his way over the back and then the chest, pulling off the outer feathers; they fluttered around in the air a little before falling to the blanket. He spent more time plucking the downy, blue-gray underfeathers and the minute pinfeathers from the legs. His thick fingers moved as light as a harpist's.

When he had finished plucking, he used his knife to clean the edges of the bullet wound, and cut the bird open from end to end, then raked out the cavity with his forefinger. He speared it on a stick, and Frozan put it on the fire.

The bird was divided up according to the dictates of custom

and manners; the females got none and the guest got most, a tiny pile of charred and stringy meat. We had white Thai rice too, and spring onions picked from the fields around us, and tea. After dinner, I took a big Hershey's milk chocolate bar from my shoulder bag and we all had a piece, eating it slowly to stretch out the luxury. Saed got out a little collection of rags and a bottle of oil and stripped and cleaned the weapons he carried every day, a Belgian 9-millimeter automatic pistol and the Kalashnikov, a Chinese model, with a folding metal stock and a banana-clip magazine. He had rigged up a crude speed-loading arrangement, a second clip strapped with heavy silver duct tape to the first. He cleaned the pistol well and quickly but lingered over the Kalashnikov. "It is my favorite," he said.

Mozafar and I slept on thick, soft pallets of padding and cotton tick blankets in a tent with a pile of guns and boxes of ammunition, and with two birds in a bamboo cage. They were songbirds, and in the morning they cooed us awake. I walked back down to the pool to wash up before breakfast and noticed something I had missed the day before. Tucked away behind a screen of ivy and tree roots was a small cave formed by erosion eating away the side of the bluff. It went back ten feet or so, and the rear recesses of it were dark shadows. In a corner were a small pile of blankets, a pillow, a couple of plastic bottles of water, and a box of ammunition. I guessed it was meant as a bolt hole, a place where Frozan and Danielle could be hidden in the event of a sudden reversal of field.

The next day we began in earnest the tour through the wasted countryside. In what had been the resort town of Biyara, there remained half of an old hotel, with the second floor mostly collapsed onto the first, resting with slight tipsiness on an uneven bed of broken concrete slab and shattered cinder-block walls. A young couple had made a home in what remained of a corner room. Explosives had blown away the side exterior wall altogether, and half of the front exterior wall, and half of the hallway wall. The side interior hall was more or less intact and served, with the remains of the other two walls, to hold up about two thirds of the ceiling. The man and his wife had piled up pieces of concrete and cinder block into rough walls three feet tall along the lines where the front and side exterior walls had been, leaving the rest open to the air and the view of the ruined village and the valley and the hills beyond.

Nothing in the room was square or plumb; the floor sloped alarmingly to the outside, and the walls leaned against each other. But the linoleum floor was swept and mopped, and where some tiles had been broken, pieces scavenged from other rooms had been fitted in. The man's rifle hung on a nail driven into the one intact wall, and his pistol hung in a leather holster next to it. In the most secure corner, that of the hallway wall and the interior side wall, a bed of several blankets was laid. Next to it was a metal folding table, and on the table was a little wood bowl with three eggs in it, and another of china, with four oranges, and a pitcher of milk.

"This village was a famous tourist spot, famous for beauty and richness," the man said. "Every year we take from this area more than four million dinars in sheep and fruit. We didn't need for anything, ever. But now look." He waved at the dynamited buildings, the gray ghosts of the dead plum trees up and down the sides of the hills, the rows of new white stones in the graveyard. "They destroy all. For nothing they destroy it, for only that it was a Kurdish town. They killed all, white and green."

This was a phrase I had heard several times the day before and not understood; I asked Mozafar, who was translating, what it meant. "White and green is everything. White is people, green is trees. Iraqis kill all, white and green, green and white," he said.

"I am here when the Iraqis come and destroy this place," the man said. He rolled up the sleeves of his shirt so that we could see the shiny burn tissue on his forearms and hands. "They use napalm. It was like liquid coming from the bombs, from the fighters. More than three hundred people from this town were killed, and one thousand went to the hospitals in Iran. They used gas too. Maybe cyanide. It smelled of almonds. Our eyes closed and our bodies burned and our skins turned red and purple. Every cell in the body for taking in air closed.

"The attack was on the 17th of March, 1988. The planes came in low from the Kirkuk direction. Six planes the first time and twelve the second time. They attacked from midnight to morning. We ran from our homes in the night and walked to Iran. The slow didn't make it. More than two hundred of the dead were children, more than fifty were women. We buried them in big graves, and later the *pesh merga* came and dig these up and make decent graves.

"In 1990, they come back with TNT and blew up all the houses so no one would return here and no one would remember this was a Kurdish place.

"I came back here from Iran in March this year, after the *pesh merga* freed this place. Before that it was impossible to come back. Since the day in 1988, all this was military zone, forbidden to enter. Now it is ours again. More than three thousand people are here, in this town and nearby. It is our land. We will build a new city."

We passed somewhere along the way from Patriotic Union of Kurdistan territory to that under the control of the Kurdistan Democratic Party, from Talabani's tribe to Barzani's, which meant a hand-off. Saed took us to a place near the former town of Ahmed Awa, off the road and up into the first line of foothills, where we found a camp of a hundred or so *pesh merga*. The men lived in tents and lean-tos and the remains of several large buildings. Eight or nine Iraqi army supply trucks and several gasoline tankers were parked in front, and two Iraqi army antiaircraft guns were pointed at the sky. We found the men in charge resting in the shadows of a line of old willow trees by the stream, passing the time between breakfast and lunch. Some of them were in their forties or fifties, and some were in their early twenties or even teens. Sitting by the water, I was placed between a father and son, and I was struck by the difference between the generations. The father carried only one weapon, a pistol tucked discreetly into his belly sash.

I asked him where his rifle was, and he gestured off to the side. "I do not like guns," he said. "When we are sure of a good life, we will put guns away and hate them forever."

His son was twenty-one years old. He was as heavy laden with weaponry as his father was light. He had scrounged from somewhere a set of Iraqi army fatigue pants, shirt, and web belt. A pistol hung in a leather officer's holster from the belt, and he wore a bandolier of bullets around his waist, with two more crisscrossed on his chest. His Kalashnikov was slung across his back. From various points on his torso hung six banana clips of rifle ammo and five grenades. He was a Christmas tree of munitions. He said: "I have been in the mountains for four years. Before, I was in the city. I do not like it there, because the government is hard on me. Here I like the life very much. I love the mountains. In the city I eat meat, and here only bread and water sometimes, but I prefer the life here. It is free and good, and I learn here to take life as it comes, with freedom, like Americans and Europeans. I will not leave here."

"Myself," said the father, "I would like very much to live in the city again. It is more comfortable, and I am too old for this, out here in the woods." He sighed. "But what can you do?"

After tea, the son took us in a jeep up the road that followed the course of the stream, through pastures of purple and blue wildflowers and red-as-wine poppies to a camp on a higher plateau, where headquarters was. We were ushered into a very large tent, big enough for twenty men, and presented to a man who looked, to my mild surprise, like George Bernard Shaw. He reclined like royalty, or perhaps like Shaw, on a deep pile of carpets and cushions, smoking a cigarette. He got up and led me through a beech woods to a clearing where there stood a tent and rough shed by a fat, fast stream. His wife was kneeling by the edge of the water, scrubbing clothes with a big bar of brown laundry soap. His three children, two girls and a boy, were playing in the grass. We sat on a grassy bank, with the sunlight coming through the doily of the leaves to dapple us, and the wife brought us cocoa in tiny, fine china cups on a silver tray.

"I was a rich man in Baghdad," said Shaw, leaning up against the tree, rolling a homemade dumdum bullet through his fingers. "I had a house that cost four hundred thousand dollars and a Mercedes and a Dodge Diplomat. I worked for a German company as an engineer. And I was an officer in the People's Army. I left all this to come here, and I am happy here. The water comes down from the top of the mountain, and soon the fruit will be ripe. It is a good life."

He called to his wife. She was up to her elbows in a metal bucket of suds, but she wiped off her arms and came over. "My wife had three women to wash the clothes and clean the house in Baghdad," said Shaw. "But ask her if she is more happy here or there."

I dutifully asked, and she sort of answered. "It is very easy for me really," she said. "Washing outside is fine. Cooking outside is fine. These things are not important, because we chose this life. No one makes us live this way. We want freedom, and if you want freedom, you must leave everything. You mustn't care about washing machines and ovens. You must care only about freedom." She went back to her scrubbing pail. It was an old ghee tin, fire-charred, so I guessed she also used it for cooking. Her stove and fireplace was three cinder blocks set on the ground.

It must have been practically a delirium of delight for the boy; he was living a ten-year-old's fantasy, camping in the forest with a band of desperadoes. He had dressed himself as much

like the big boys as he could. Around his waist, over his Teenage Mutant Ninja Turtles T-shirt, he wore a shortened Iraqi
army web belt, and from the belt hung a bayonet in a sheath.
The knife reached almost to his ankle and banged against him
whenever he moved, but you could see that he loved wearing
it. He couldn't stop touching it; every few seconds, his hand
would stray to it, and he would give the pommel a little caress,
or run his fingers down the stitching on the scabbard.

I asked him what he wanted to do when he grew up. He gave
me a look that just scarcely stopped short of being a full eye roll.
"A *pesh merga*," he said. "Because I am Kurdish and that is what
a Kurdish man does." He had a pretty, winsome face, and it was
impossible for me to imagine him killing anyone, but he had a
greater grasp of reality than I did. In just six years he would be
eligible to join his father's army.

When we left the camp in midafternoon to visit the front of the
Kurdish lines, we traveled in a well-armed convoy of five vehicles with Shaw leading in his red Toyota Crown—an especially
nice one, with plush velvety red seats, air-conditioning, and a
stereo cassette sound system on which played, over and over,
the collected hits of Tom Jones—with another sedan and a
pickup truck behind us. In all, we were fourteen men, with
sixteen Kalashnikovs, two sniper rifles with telescope sights,
eleven pistols, a rocket-propelled grenade launcher (RPG) with
a trunkload of ammunition, and a tripod-mounted .50-caliber
BKC machine gun in the back of the pickup truck. We drove
on little roads through a landscape of tall green grass and
thistles and poppies, interrupted at intervals by the wreckage of
a city.

These cities were new, part of the archipelago of places the
Iraqi government built to house the Kurds made homeless by
the first wave of demolitions of the old mountain villages. The
government said they were model cities, and that their purpose

was to acquaint the Kurds with the amenities of modern living, but the Kurds thought of them more correctly as glorified concentration camps, ugly, sterile sprawls of cinder-block houses, designed for population control. At any rate, they were gone now too, blown up in the later rounds of destruction. The ex-city of Sayed Sadeq was the largest of the ones we passed through that day. It had once held forty thousand people, and it stretched for a long distance along both sides of the road. You could see by the foundations and the street grid that there had been thousands of buildings here, but there was nothing left now that rose more than three or four feet above the ground. Everything had been pancaked by TNT, every building reduced to a flat, post-holocaust mess of broken gray concrete slab and rust-red spaghetti-tangled steel. "One thing you can say about Saddam," said Shaw, "he knows how to destroy things."

At a deserted and shot-up Iraqi army base, we picked up three more pickup trucks, two with heavy machine guns, and another eight men. Ten miles on, at a checkpoint consisting of two young men and a couple of rifles, we unloaded ourselves to walk the final quarter-mile, the reason being, as far as I could see, to make a proper entrance. That we did, proceeding up the road as a small but unusually well-armed procession, with Shaw imperious at the front, splendid as Salah al-Din, flanked by two men with big M-60 machine guns at port arms, and another forty men and guns bringing up the rear. The sun was shining down on us, and we kicked up a cloud of dust as we tramped.

The *pesh merga* front was surprisingly low-key. No trenches, no pillboxes, no tanks, no artillery, no watchtowers, barbed wire, or mines. Just six men and two machine guns on tripods in the road, with a tripod-mounted RPG off to the side behind a little wall of sandbags. The road kept unheedingly on, dipping down into a slight valley and meandering across more peaceful pastures to a town I could dimly make out in the distance. That, said Shaw, was Betsan Sar, about three miles away, and the Iraqi front lines were there. Through binoculars, I could just see a line of black beetles along a hill. These were dug-in tanks. There was a huddle of dots in the road that was the checkpoint. Traffic passed more or less freely between the points, with a wave-through on the Kurdish side and only a brief stop by the army. A small flock of black mountain sheep, with curly horns and witchy white-and-black eyes, moved slowly and stupidly by. "As you can see, this is a pretty relaxed situation," said Shaw. "The fact is, the Iraqi army is more afraid of us than we are afraid of them."

That was an exaggeration, of course. The Iraqi army could have sent the *pesh merga* running deep into the ravines and mountains if allowed by America to use its helicopters and fighters, but the fact that Shaw could say that with a straight face was telling. The place where we were standing, the land we were traveling through, had been under army control for nearly a generation, and the reclamation of it was an extraordinary thing to the Kurds. They owned their own land again, and they luxuriated in that.

Heading back down the road after we left the front, we stopped for an impromptu picnic. At this time of year, there grows wild and prolific in the fields of Kurdistan a plant called *rawah*, a long thick green stem with a red tip. It might be a sort of rhubarb, but I'm not sure. These plants are in fruit for only a couple of weeks, and to pick them fresh and eat them raw on the spot is one of the great treats of spring. With their rifles on their backs, the men picked bunches of the weeds, brought them back, and peeled the hairy outer fibers off, and we all sat in the grass and ate the wet, raw stalks. They had a taste that was part wood and part celery and part fresh green beans, and they were as tart as alum, so astringent they puckered the mouth. Afterward we shot with pistols at fish and frogs in the stream but missed them all, not that anyone cared.

*   *   *

Nowhere was the sense of recovery and new freedom more evident, or more poignant, than in Halabja. We arrived there in the late afternoon, about an hour before sunset. The city is set at the foot of a curved range of small mountains, near the bank of the Surwan River, among fields once plowed and planted but now reverted to wild, and awash in the reds and blues and purples of flowers. As we got closer, Shaw, who had been quiet for a while, spoke. "Two hundred thousand people lived here," he said. "Now look what you see, and when you see it, say to yourself, 'This is the face of Saddam Hussein.'"

I was prepared by Terwella and Hormel and Sayed Sadeq and all the other large and little scenes of sacking we had seen, but Halabja shocked me. It was the sheer scope of destruction, the magnitude of effort that had gone into destroying it. A city of 200,000 people is big enough that even an army of men with TNT can't make it nothing at all, but the destroyers of Halabja had done as good a job as anyone could.

The city was laid out in a grid of small streets lined with stone and concrete houses, with a main shopping street running from a square in the center of town, and I would guess 80 percent of it had been leveled. The little one-room shops lining the main street were open, roofless shells, and most of the houses on the side streets were at least half blown away. There were variations in the overall theme of demolition. Some buildings had been dynamited on the cheap, with charges placed only at two corners, to blow out one wall and part of two others and to bring down half the roof. Others had been more thoroughly exploded, with charges at the base of all four corners, and of these, nothing remained but the cracked, crumpled roof slab resting on top of a few feet of rubble and, in some of the grander homes, a staircase ending uncertainly in the air. Even the trees that had been planted along the sides of the main street had been cut down by explosives, leaving ragged, messy stumps. It was astonishing how rapidly nature had begun to cloak the mess; grasses and weeds and shrubs half covered the piles of broken concrete, and small trees grew in what had been living rooms. Birds nested in the shells of buildings. "This is a city for Casper the ghost," said Shaw, making a little joke.

The local leader's house was notable for its relatively untouched condition. Apart from having no doors or windows and missing a side wall, it was whole. Two kerosene lamps sat on the floor, which was mostly covered with a red carpet, and various rifles and pistols hung from nails in the walls. There were several people there, and when I asked if any of them had been present at the destruction of the city, one spoke up. He was a twenty-two-year-old man named Rizgar Rashid.

"The attack came on 17 March 1988, at four P.M. The fighters, more than twenty of them, come in from over the mountains and take one turn around the city. They drop paper to see which way the wind blows so they will know where to put the gas. Then they come back for a second pass, and come in very fast and low for the attack run. They attacked first with bombs that had gas in them. I was walking down the street when it began. The *pesh merga* had teached us if you smell bananas, it is gas, so run. I smelled this, so I put my hand over my nose and mouth and I run very quickly to the mountains. I saw many people fall down all around me. At first the body would become bloated and water would come from the eyes and blood from the nose; fifteen or twenty minutes it would take to die. The attacks lasted for two hours. The planes came back again and again. They used rockets on the people who were running in the road to Anab.

"I came back after one day in the mountains. I saw only bodies, too many bodies to count. I found my family in Anab, under a house. They were trying to get protection from the bombs: my mother Zorha, my sister Prishig, and my brother Nawzad. I cried and cried and cried. I could not watch. I sat down and cried."

A man sitting next to him picked up the story, speaking in English. "I am Dr. Fayak Muhammad, I have a practice here. I was here when the attack came and I treated many people. I can tell you that more than five thousand people died here and in the roads and villages around here. I can say from the evidence I saw myself that two types of gases were used. One was mustard gas, which affects the skin, eyes, and respiratory system and which was the lesser threat. The more severe damage was caused by nerve gas, which was the primary threat. I was able to treat those who had not received a lethal dose with atropine and IV drips, but many died upon exposure. The dead were buried in mass graves outside the city. I went to Iran afterward, and did not come back here until this March, when I heard the *pesh merga* had taken back the city."

The doctor offered to take us in for the night, so we got our bags from Shaw's car and walked with him to his clinic. It was the meanest of medical offices, a small, dark room in the shell of a government building that had not been destroyed. There were no windows in the room, and no light except the dim glow of a kerosene lamp. On a wooden table, painted white, were a small bucket of cotton swabs, a handful of surgeon's tools laid out on a towel, and a bottle of ether. A bookcase held a few more items, a box of vitamin B1 ampules, a couple dozen bottles of eyedrops, a scattering of antibiotics.

"I see two hundred patients a day, working from about eight in the morning to eight at night," the doctor said. "Most of them are diarrhea cases. Diarrhea is the number one problem, from too many people crowded together with no sanitation, no clean water. It is everywhere. You may say, at this point, that everyone has diarrhea. Unfortunately, I have no antidiarrhea drugs, none of the appropriate antibiotics for amebic dysentery, which is generally the cause. All I can do is treat the dehydration. In severe cases, I put the patient on saline and glucose IVs. In less severe cases, I tell them to go home and mix salt and sugar in water and drink it. I am almost out of IVs, though. I have no distilled water left, only a very little saline. I need saline IVs and tetracycline for cholera—those are the two most important

things. I need antimalarial drugs and antityphus drugs. I need
small cannulae so I can give IVs to children. I have lost one
hundred and three patients in the past fifteen days. If I do not
get supplies soon, I will lose many more."

I asked the doctor if he would take me to the mass graves, but
he said no. "My mother and brother and grandmother and
sister-in-law and nephew were martyred in the attack. I never
go to the graves. It makes me too anxious and I cannot work."
He assigned one of his *pesh merga* assistants to take me. We
drove in a jump-started Mitsubishi down a road through fields
overrun with thistles and with families squatting around fires
and lean-tos. The field with the graves in it had no squatters. It
was a lovely meadow, especially thick with thistles, the plants
growing two or three feet high, with big purple flowers. A light
misting rain had begun, and the setting sun had made the sky
a wash of pinks and purples and reds and lent a softness to the
air. The river snaked by in the middle distance, with the mountains beyond.

There were twelve graves in a rough row parallel to the road,
each about ten feet apart. The mounds were four feet high, five
or six feet wide, and perhaps fifteen feet long, in a crude oblong
shape. They blended into the landscape; it would have been
easy to walk by them without noticing. "Every one has more
than two hundred bodies," said the man who had brought me.
"There are more than two thousand four hundred bodies here."

Why here? I said. Why this spot? "Because this is where they
died, on the road along here. They run down this road to get
away from the planes, and the planes catch them here. I came
here three, four days later, with the *pesh merga* force, and this
road was everywhere covered with dead people. I called some
help and we brought up a bulldozer to dig the holes. The bodies
were smelling very, very bad. We had to wear cloths on our
faces. We pushed them off the road and over the field and into
the holes. It took seven days to bury all the people. My brother
was in the road and he was one of the people who was buried.

I saw his body but it did not mean anything to me because he was just one of so many people. We put him in hole number eight. For two months afterward, I didn't feel anything, then I started to feel very sad, and for a long time after that I thought I would go mad." This man's name was Ahmed Hama Razad, and he was twenty-three years old when he buried his brother, Hama Amim Razad, fifty.

We had a good dinner at the doctor's house, rice with raisins, potatoes boiled in broth, fresh bread, spring onions, and sliced tomatoes. The tomatoes delighted the doctor. "This is wonderful," he said. "We have not had fresh vegetables in a month." We ate on the concrete front porch, and afterward sat around smoking and talking. A group of young men came by for a visit. They were all university students or professionals of some sort, and the evening developed into an unlikely salon, there on the porch of a shattered house in a shattered city, with the sound of teenagers shooting off their rifles in the street making a backdrop to the talk of literature and politics. I spent a long time listening to a young writer. He had been studying English for fifteen years, but had never had a chance to really use it before, and was pleased to talk for hours. He spoke with offhand matter-of-factness of the difficulties of his writing life.

"Right now, writing is hard," he said. "I am not getting so much done because the war takes up much of the time, and the rest I spend trying to find food. It leaves very little time to write. I did write a newspaper when we held Sulaimaniya, and that was a good thing. It was the first uncensored newspaper to be published in Iraq since 1968, I think. I wrote the whole thing myself and we made copies of it on a mimeograph machine. I wrote about important things, about the function of censorship in a fascist structure and the nature of democracy versus the nature of the totalitarian state. We called the newspaper *Azadi*—'Freedom'—and it was very popular. We distributed four hundred copies, but it only lasted one issue because the army took back Sulaimaniya and we had to leave."

He had written two novels and two plays. "My novels have not been published, of course," he said. "Or my plays either. All publishing is controlled by the government censors, and I could not even bring my manuscripts to them. They would kill me if they knew about them. They are very dangerous, especially the second novel. It is four hundred and twenty-three pages and it is a very, very dangerous novel because it is about the president himself." He laughed nervously, understandably; writing a *samizdat* novel about Saddam Hussein was about as suicidal a thing as you could attempt in Iraq. "It pretends to be a dialogue between an unnamed field marshal and a general, but really it is a history of Iraq in the last twenty years, and it is very subversive."

He had educated himself by reading books in English and Farsi and Arabic smuggled in from Iran and Turkey and Lebanon. He had a library of one thousand illegal books, he said, hidden in his apartment in Sulaimaniya. "I like Alexander Dumas and Solzhenitsyn very much, but I am most impressed with Gabriel García Márquez. I read *One Hundred Years of Solitude* when I was younger, and it made a big impression on me. All my own writing is in the style of magic realism. Magic realism is very good for addressing the most important thing about Iraq, the losing of the sense of rationality. This is something I saw grow and grow over the years since I was a child. Life became every year more irrational, more crazy, more turned on its head. To express this in writing requires something much stranger than a realistic style."

We slept on the floor in a room that had been shaken by explosions but not knocked down. The walls had come several inches apart from each other at the corners, along fault lines that ran from floor to ceiling. In the morning we walked to the market for breakfast, and I saw how extraordinarily full of people and commerce the ghost city really was, how swiftly the rebuilding of Kurdish Iraq was proceeding.

There were hundreds and hundreds of people out in the streets, most of them young men, and a dozen new businesses perched on the wreckage of the old. Men with pushcarts and tables set up in the trash and junk, selling all sorts of things: toothpaste and cigarettes and sunflower seeds in cones made of paper recycled from a student's math notebook, rough brown bars of soap, razors and shaving brushes, playing cards, cookies and worry beads, aspirin, socks, eggs, batteries, dates, cartons of apple juice. On one corner, a butcher whacked great hunks from a freshly killed sheep hung from a tripod of poplar branches. He threw each piece down on the ground, and another man cut it into smaller pieces, which he threw in a basin by his side. Both men were dripping blood and gore, glistening red up to their elbows, with splotches on their faces, and with their feet in puddles of the stuff. Three as yet untouched sheep stood placidly watching them, in no way connecting what was going on before their eyes with what was shortly going to happen to them. Across the street, a barber had rigged up a rickety chair and a piece of mirror in the shell of a storefront and was giving a careful haircut to a boy. The owner of a battered minibus stood yelling, "Terwella, Terwella, Terwella," to indicate the destination of his run, and a boy trundled past him with a wheelbarrow piled high with figs. A restaurateur cooked fresh sheep's-liver *kebabs* on a brazier, and had a fire going under an urn of tea. Smelling the meat, I felt nausea overwhelm me, and I realized suddenly that I was sick.

I went to see Dr. Muhammad and he confirmed what I knew and said there was nothing he could do about it. It was best that I continue traveling, he said, and hope to find a doctor with supplies somewhere farther up the road. I knew by midmorning why Dr. Muhammad lost so many patients. It was a remarkably fast and nasty illness. From the first faint flutterings in the stomach it progressed, within a few hours, to violent diarrhea and a thriving fever. By chance, I was by then in a position to see what the sickness would progress to if left untreated. We had left Halabja in a minibus to Sayed Sadeq and from there hitched a ride to Penjwin, where, in the ruins of the city, ten thousand sick and starving people were living in tents and concrete caves.

Walking along the road, I came to a boy, ten or eleven years old I guessed, dying in the dirt. He was barely conscious. Thick ropes of mucus had run from his nostrils, and his skin was burning hot. He lay with his head turned to one side, and he could not move. Mozafar and I sat him up a little, so that his head was in my lap, and we tried to pour water into his mouth. He stared uncomprehendingly and let the liquid dribble from the corners of his cracked lips. A couple of other men came up, and one of them flagged down a *pesh merga* pickup truck, and we laid the boy in the back. "There is a clinic twenty miles from here," said the man. "They will take him there, but there is not much they can do for him. They have nothing to give him."

The man was, it turned out, the closest thing to a doctor in Penjwin, a Kurdish medical student from the University of Baghdad. "So far, more than a hundred children have died in this place," he said. "Every day, people die, mostly children and old people. And every day it is getting worse. Eighty percent of the children are sick, there is no medicine, no clean water, very little food. If this continues, fifty percent of the people will die."

There were levels of poverty in Penjwin. The best off had tents and vehicles and enough money to buy food. The worst off had nothing and lived in the concrete-rubble caves. I crawled into a couple of them. In one, about three and a half feet high by twelve feet wide by fifteen feet deep, I found ten people, seven of them children. A very old man lay in the opening. *"Salaam aleikum,"* he said when I walked up. "You are welcome in our home." A kerosene lamp hung from the ceiling, a tooth-brush and a bar of soap and a bowl of water stood in one corner. The dirt floor was covered in one patch by a piece of carpet. That was the extent of the furnishings. The children stared at me while I talked to their mother. She had the youngest child in her arms, a very small infant of fifteen days, swaddled in a green cloth and as unmoving as stone. Even when I touched her face, the baby gave no sign of consciousness. Only the shallow movement of her chest rising and falling showed that she was alive.

"We have nothing," the mother said. "No rice, no oil, no bread, no milk. We come here the 7th of April from Sulaima-niya. They destroyed our house. We have not had cheese or meat since then. I spend the last money to buy milk six days ago. Now we go around in the afternoon and ask for a little piece of bread from each family. We live on scraps of bread and water. We have no money. Everything costs too much."

Her husband said, "I will not go to Iran. If I die, I will die in my own land, in Kurdistan."

The wife said, "The baby is very sick. Very sick."

It had started to rain, and water was dripping through the cracks of the cave roof. I gave the mother five hundred dinars, and crawled out.

The horrible thing was that there was plenty of food in Penjwin. All up and down the road where this and many other families were wasting, there were piled up for sale things to eat—potatoes, eggs, apples, flour, rice, tall cones of sugar, pow-dered milk, even candy and cookies. The people who were dying of hunger and the vulnerability to disease that hunger brings simply didn't have enough money to buy anything. Post-war inflation had driven the price of everything in Kurdistan to levels that were, relatively speaking, astronomical. Isomil pow-dered milk cost three dinars a can, a kilo of rice or flour two. The average salary in these parts at that time was six to eight dinars per day, and there were no jobs anyway. Many of the people of Penjwin had fled Kirkuk or Sulaimaniya with no money at all. The nearest relief-agency food was fifty miles away and across a mountain range. And yet, I never saw anyone steal anything, nor heard of any such thing. Of all the things I saw in the war and its aftermath, I found this the most astonishing. A matter of culture shock, I suppose. I came from a country where even rich children shoplifted as a matter of course, and where people who would be considered fat and happy by the standards of Kurdistan looted the stores in their neighborhoods whenever the lights went off for a few hours.

The day wore on its wretched way, carrying me with it, sicker and sicker, weaker and weaker. Our way of travel was by its nature dependent on the kindness of strangers and the vicissitudes of chance, and on this day it broke down. Our first job was to get a ride out of Penjwin—there could not be a worse place to be sick in all of Iraq—to anywhere. We walked, spavined under the load of my big black bag, from one end of the terrible place to the other, two hours of walking, and at the end we hadn't found a soul willing to drive us anywhere. We stopped at a sheep-roasting stand so Mozafar might eat, and the sight— the haunches and shanks and livers of the butchered beasts hanging from the branches of a tree, and their bloody skins and glistening stomachs in the dirt, the fat bluebottle flies buzzing over all—drove me to such paroxysms of vomiting that I was soon on my knees, clutching myself and barking like a cat with hairballs. Mozafar was wonderfully solicitous. He held my head, and patted it, and murmured, "My dear, my poor dear," over and over. From this moment, I knew I hated him. I hated him for being able to eat, for not being down in the dirt with me, for patting my head and calling me Poor Dear, and for the fear that I might end up like the boy in the road.

In time, a truck stopped, and we got in it, and it took us, in a banging, bouncing drive, to the nearest place where the driver thought there might be a doctor, the camp of whatever faction this territory belonged to. There was no doctor there. The leader called me to his tent for an interview, and talked, and talked, and talked, while tea, and more tea, and more tea was served, and the sweat rolled off my face. I sat afterward on a rice sack in a scrap of shade from a shed, waiting, drenched. I thought I had never been anywhere as hot as the top of that hill, and I couldn't understand why the others walked around as if nothing was the matter at all.

For the next seven hours, I moved between the side of the shed and the outhouse some distance away, while we waited for a ride to wherever we were going next. Finally a truck full of rice pulled in to gas up, and the driver said there was room for us in the cab. In the dark, we couldn't see where he was heading, or where he eventually stopped to let us out, and it was an awful shock to realize as he drove away that we were back in Penjwin. We stayed there for three hours, Mozafar scouting for a connection, me lying in the dirt.

A pickup truck took us away, up into the hills again, nine or ten miles, to a farmhouse that was half knocked down, but still had a roof and three good rooms. I spent the night in teeth-chattering shivers and shits and delirium and in the morning the pickup truck came and took us again to Penjwin, where I lay in the dirt again and Mozafar looked for a ride. I was alarmed to find out that I could no longer drink anything to rehydrate myself; anything I swallowed, I vomited a few minutes later. In midafternoon, Mozafar found a car, and we set off.

We ended up that night in a house perched on the top of a steep and beautiful gorge, about which all I remember is that it was smoky and dark. I had lost sight of everything beyond each miserable moment as it occurred, and no longer gave much thought to where we were or whether we would find a doctor in time. Mozafar, who slept on the floor next to me and woke up every time I did to say "My poor dear" and try to pat me—I had taken to cursing him, but he didn't seem to take offense—

had a destination in mind, and the next day we arrived there, at the largest camp I had seen yet, centered around a former army barracks on a mountain plateau.

This was the headquarters of Jalal Talabani, leader of the Patriotic Union of Kurdistan, and Talabani had a doctor, and the doctor was the only one for a hundred miles around who still had the drugs and saline solution I needed. At the time we arrived, I was going through a phase of chills, so Mozafar led me to a second-story veranda that was in the sun and laid me down on the sleeping bag, where I fell into a light shaking sleep. The doctor arrived a few hours later and had two men carry me to the clinic, a small room with green walls marked by bullet holes and old stains. The men put me on a brown vinyl medical bed and the doctor took my temperature and poked around a bit and made a succinct, accurate diagnosis. "Bad fever, very bad dehydration. Amebic dysentery."

He popped a hollow needle into a vein on my right forearm and hooked it up to a plastic bag of saline solution hanging from a stand, and began the drip-by-drip process of returning fluid to my body. I didn't feel anything with the first IV bag, but halfway through the second one, I began to be aware of small bursts of liquid in the walls of my parched mouth. They were actual little explosions of water, delicious. A moment later, I felt my tongue growing wet again, swelling suddenly and magically, and rolling in the luxury of saliva.

Talabani had a satellite phone in his bedroom, and I got up sometime that afternoon to make a call to the *Globe*, and dictate a story. Talabani's wife helped me work the phone. She was a pleasant, efficient woman, as politician's wives generally are, and she made polite talk with me for a few minutes. She told me she had arranged for me to be taken north to the city of Rania, where her husband was. He would see to it that I made it to Turkey. Perhaps, she said, I would have company. I was only one or two days behind another group of journalists heading to the Turkish border, a BBC team made up of an English camera-

man and his wife and her brother. The cameraman was named
Nick something, she said. I guessed it was Nick della Casa, who
had stayed behind in Baghdad when I left after the bombing
started. I knew he sometimes worked with his wife and brother-
in-law.

When I returned to bed, the doctor gave me another saline
IV and a glucose one for dessert, an antidiarrhea drug and an
antibiotic. The sweat poured off me all night, soaking through
the sheets and the sleeping bag and three changes of shirts.
Mozafar helped me change shirts and wiped me down, mur-
muring "My dear" all the while. In the morning, the fever was
gone, and I had tea and a little bread.

Mozafar packed while I sat in the dirt and watched two men
conducting an inventory of arms. They were working through
a pile of rifles that filled a large room with a mound seven or
eight feet tall. One of them had waded into this, and he pitched
the guns back to the door, where his partner caught each one,
made note of it in a ledger, and tossed it to the side, where a new
rifle hill was forming. This was a store of second-string guns; a
few were relatively new Kalashnikovs, but most were old
Brownings and Gerands and bolt-action Springfields, and even
more ancient models. Some were very old—long, elegant guns,
made by Arab smiths, the barrels and trigger mechanisms hammered and filed and polished by hand. The counters hadn't
gone through a tenth of the pile when Mozafar came up to tell
me the bags were packed and the driver ready. Well, I said, we
had better get going.

"No, I cannot come with you. I will say good-bye here," he
said.

He saw I was surprised. "I think it is better," he said, giving
me a look that nicely blended reproach with hurt feelings. "I
don't think you wish to have my company anymore, and these
men will help you the rest of the way."

I felt, of course, ashamed, and pleaded with him to recon-
sider, but the truth was I didn't want his company, even if I did

know that I was being unfair. I couldn't take being called "my dear" anymore. I was careful not to plead too hard, and when it was settled I apologized for cursing him and gave him seven hundred dollars, adding two hundred to the five hundred we had agreed on at the start of the trip as a sop to my conscience. He kissed me on both cheeks, two times each, and patted me one last time on the head. "Good-bye, my dear," he said.

One of Talabani's lieutenants, a young man, took me to the next stop on the way, a former Iraqi army base outside the town of Schwarta, near Mount Azmer, which overlooked the Iraqi-held city of Sulaimaniya. We made it there in only two or three hours, and I hoped we would push on to Rania, but that was impossible. "You are an important guest," said Talabani's man. "And you must travel with the chief of this district himself, Shawat Haj Mujer, and he cannot go until tomorrow." It was just as well. I had lost all strength again. I spent the day dozing against a wall, and recovered enough by late afternoon to make an expedition to the top of the mountain. For days, I had been hearing about the famous battle that had taken place on Mount Azmer the month before. The Kurds had held it against a series of attacks by a larger army force, and this was considered a great victory. I was glad I went to see it, for it showed clearly the delicate nature of the balance of power in Kurdistan, a balance caused not by mutual strength, but by mutual weakness.

The *pesh merga* force holding the mountain was nothing but a few dozen men on a little scrabble patch of dirt on the edge of a small plateau. It was an unimpressive post. Those who manned it were armed with little more than rifles and RPGs. A 106-millimeter antitank gun stood next to two old mortars that looked like lengths of pipe some careless plumber had left in the rain too long. Near the mortars, in the mud, were a couple of hundred loose rounds of antiaircraft ammunition that had likewise been scabbed over with rust. A hut held a few jerry cans of water and enough bread and potatoes and rice for a few days at most. There were no fortifications or even trenches.

Six miles from this spot, the Iraqi army had thirty thousand troops holding Sulaimaniya. But when the army sent five hundred to six hundred men, three tanks, and a helicopter against Mount Azmer, 150 *pesh merga* drove them back, in battles over five days, between April 7 and 12. The rebels claimed to have killed 110 of the enemy while suffering only 15 deaths on their side. The physical evidence backed up their story. Three burned and bashed Iraqi tanks lay in the grass just off the road leading to the peak. "Two we hit with RPG and one got scared and drove off the side of the road," said the man showing me about.

I vomited on top of Mount Azmer, and all the way back down it, leaning out the window of the Land Cruiser. The men took me to the camp doctor, who put me to bed and gave me what he could spare, one bag of saline drip, a dozen tetracycline pills, and some Lomotil antidiarrhea pills. Added to what Talabani's doctor had given me, I had enough medicine, he said, not to get rid of the ameoba, but to cripple it until I could get to Turkey. I slept relatively well, being obliged to get up from bed only half a dozen times, and woke at dawn to dim shapes whirring in the air just below the ceiling. As the light turned from gray to pink, I saw that two hummingbirds had made a mud-daub nest in an old light fixture that hung from the center of the ceiling. They hovered and darted all about it, and it was a pleasure to lie there and watch them. I tried breakfast, tea and two pieces of bread, and was happy to see it stayed down.

We set off for Rania a few hours later, in an unusually large and serious convoy: six Land Cruisers, twenty-six men, and two .50-caliber machine guns mounted in pickups. "It is a difficult trip," said Shawat Haj Mujer. "The army holds some of the land we will go through, and we will take a cross-country route to stay away from them, but still, better to be protected if it should come to that."

It did not come to anything like that, though. We passed first through a long stretch of valleys and high pastureland, past tiny waterfalls that fell in silver pours as straight as plumb bobs, past entire hillsides blanketed in scarlet flowers, through valleys miles wide and ravines hardly wider than the car, going from paved roads, to dirt roads, and finally to no roads at all, the cars banging their way down paths made by sheep and streams. In a few narrow spots, we were blocked by boulders too large to drive over, but the men wrestled them out of the way, and we continued. The young men at the tripods of the machine guns had to stand at their posts the entire trip, and there were times the bounces lifted them right up in the air, and only by hanging on to their guns did they manage to stay aboard.

As we moved higher and farther north, the nature of the mountains gradually changed. In the south, they were made of volcanic rock and were heavily wooded and worn and gentled by age; here they were limestone and younger and sharper, with hard, craggy rock peaks that were tall enough to be half lost in mist. We arrived, at two in the afternoon, at Lake Dukan, a large high-mountain lake made by a dam across the Zab River, built by the British in 1956. The water level was only a few hundred feet below the tops of the mountains. At the narrow top end of the lake, a ferry of sorts sat in the muddy shallows, rusting and sagging and looking altogether sinkworthy. Its hull was made of two old giant pontoons, previously owned by an Iraqi army bridge-building unit. Across this had been built a deck of thick, rough planks. There was no engine; the boat was pushed across the strait by a skiff powered by a small Evinrude outboard motor.

After the first four cars made it on, barely—the tail of the last Land Cruiser stuck out three feet over the water—the ferry master began the delicate chore of coaxing the tub out of the muck of the shallows. First he tied a rope to what amounted to its bow, and attached the other end to the stern of his skiff. He gunned the outboard and set confidently off. The rope snapped. He tried it again. It snapped again. We dragged a fifteen-foot plank off the ferry and put one end of it up against the boat's fat rear end and the other wedged against the front bumper of one of the Land Cruisers still on shore. The idea was to use the car to push against the plank, which would push against the boat. The car moved forward, but the boat didn't. Slowly, the plank curved into a rainbow, and then a U, and then broke with a loud *crack!* that sent an eight-foot slab of wood whistling through the air. We tried the trick again, with the shorter of the two halves, and this time added manpower. Seven or eight of the men took off their clothes, waded into the muck, and heaved. At this, the ferry floated briefly free, but swung around and got stuck in a new position. We tried again, with the same results, and again, and again. On the fifth try, the barge floated full and truly free, and we all waded out and climbed aboard. The captain attached a towline again (this time he used a steel cable), and the little skiff chugged out to the end of it and pulled. For many seconds, nothing happened at all, but it was only a matter of overcoming inertia, and we moved, slowly at first, but then picking up surprising speed, across the water. We were all very pleased and proud of ourselves.

"This is something from medieval times, is it not?" Mujer said. "For other people, this operation would not be possible, but we in Kurdistan can do it because we must. This is the way everything is here, very hard. Only Kurdish people can live a life like this."

On the other side, we lolled about in the grass for a while, waiting for the second half of the convoy to make it across. I took the opportunity to clean up for the first time since I had gotten sick. Squatting by the lake's edge, I took off my shirt and shoes, and washed my feet and head and face and arms, and afterward shaved and combed my hair. When the rest of the men and cars arrived, we had a picnic. Several men gathered brushwood and made a fire. Two cut a goat carcass into pieces, two other men speared onto the metal cleaning rods from their rifles. Someone made tea, while someone else gathered spring onions. One of the men wandered over to the edge of the lake, took a pineapple hand grenade off his belt, pulled the pin, and tossed it in—a casual underhanded softball toss. The dull thud came a second or two later, and a second after that, half a dozen silver-bellied fish floated to the surface. The fisherman stripped to his boxers, dived in, and swam about the floaters, selecting two or three of the largest, which he pushed ahead of him as he swam to shore. Scaled and gutted and speared on gun rods, they were on the fire a few minutes later. When everything was done—charred, rare, steaming—we shucked the rods and ate.

Rania was the first undestroyed Kurdish city I had seen. It was a medium-sized place of about seventy thousand people, set high amid wheat fields surrounded by a range of snowy peaks the Kurds called the Black Mountains, difficult to approach, easy to defend. Talabani's people ran it, and compared to the rest of what I had seen of Kurdistan it was rich, with cows in the roads and rose bushes in the gardens. The market in the center of the city was spilling over with food: sacks of rice and flour, canned fish and cheese, apples, green beans, leeks, potatoes, bread and pastries, great tubs full of yogurt drink with hunks of ice floating in them to keep them cool, and a row of big lake fish gutted on the sidewalk. Prices for the essentials were regulated by the Patriotic Union of Kurdistan and written in chalk on a blackboard in the market: rice, 150 dinars for a forty-five-kilo sack; flour, 90 dinars for an eighty-kilo sack; sugar, 180 dinars for forty-five kilos; potatoes, one kilo for a dinar; a loaf of bread, a quarter of a dinar. PUK policemen in brown uniforms with Sam Browne belts patrolled the streets. One of them came up to me while I was inspecting a pile of eggplants.

"Excuse me," he said. "Are you from America?"

Yes.

"I must ask you a question. Do you know Arnold?"

Arnold?

With surprise: "Arnold Schwarzenegger. He is a very big man. You know him I am sure. He worked in Hollywood and he works in the White House now."

Talabani wasn't there when we arrived, and didn't come until the following afternoon. Half-sick still, fearful that my medicine would run out, counting my pills every time I took one, I was nearly crazy with impatience to get out of this country. But I couldn't do a thing to hurry the process along. In these parts Talabani was a great man, and I was only one of many people petitioning for favors. He showed up, at the head of a long, armed parade, my second day there. He turned out to be a short, mildly fat man with shrewd little eyes, faintly reminiscent of John Sununu. People shouted out his name when his blue Mercedes limousine passed, and followed him down the streets in throngs, and waited for hours for a chance to get a word with him. I waited too. The first day, he ignored me as I lounged about his house and dogged him on his ceremonial way around town, but in the afternoon of the second, he summoned me for an interview and a drive. We went in a convoy up a tiny, winding dirt road to a mountain about an hour from the city, a brooding, rocky peak named Kakok, arriving there at sunset. A mountain range and two valleys were spread out before us. I had no idea why we were there, but I followed Talabani anyway, both of us huffing against the wind as we walked up the last bit. He stopped at an especially dramatic place and turned to face me, the wind whipping at his suit. "This was the scene of one of my greatest victories. We came up this mountain on foot, fifteen hundred men, and we attacked five thousand Iraqi army and one thousand Kurdish mercenary troops and we defeated them. It was a famous victory."

Descending, like Moses and an acolyte, from the mountaintop, we went to dinner at the home of a rich man. There were twenty-eight guests, all men. For the first hour, we sat in an ornate reception hall, on black-and-gold sofa-seats lined up along the walls around a fine Kurdish carpet the size of a helicopter pad. We drank tea and smoked, and a boy with a video camera took pictures of us. After a long while, we moved into the dining room, where a huge feast had been spread out on plastic sheets on the floor. Two lambs had been killed, and their various boiled pieces were piled up with wagon-wheel platters of rice and currants. There was stewed goat too, and some sort of meat-and-potato soup, and platters of stuffed grape leaves and bunches of green onions and flat-leaf parsley, and bread, and bowls of yogurt and dill. The eating of all this lasted no more than ten minutes. The first person to finish actually did it in seven minutes. The men stuffed fistfuls of food in their mouths, shoveling with the monotonous dispatch of earth-moving machines. No one said a word during the meal, and when each diner was finished, he simply stood up and left the room. There was enough food for a group three times the size of ours—it is etiquette in such feasts to serve much too much—but the women and children would take care of the leftovers.

After washing at a sink in the hall, we returned to the reception area and sat for another three hours, drinking more tea, smoking more cigarettes, awash in boredom, under the slippery clatter of worry beads spilling through fingers. At eleven o'clock, the boy who had videotaped us wheeled in a television set and playback machine and showed us thirty minutes of gray-and-white pictures of ourselves three hours younger. At eleven-thirty, Talabani emerged from a long huddle and beckoned to me. I crossed the carpet and he stood up. "We have discussed it," he said. "It is impossible to get you to Zakho. There are too many army units between here and there. We will take you to Ruwandiz, and you will meet some people there who will make sure you get to the border at Amadiya, and you will cross there. You must leave now."

And so, like that, I did. Talabani wrote out a safe-conduct

pass on a scrap of paper, three men took me back to his house, where I picked up my bags, and we drove away at midnight. An hour or so later, I was asleep on the floor of an abandoned bakery just outside the village of Ruwandiz, in a place called Wadi Galli, perched on the top of a range of limestone cliffs that dropped two hundred yards to a fierce, fast rush of water, with an opposing wall of limestone rising on the other side. In the morning, after tea, we walked up the road to a building that had been a public library and was now, the spray paint on the wall told us, the local offices of the PUK. I gave to a fat man behind a desk my safe-conduct pass; he read it at length and I guess found it satisfactory. He wrote something of his own on another piece of paper and clipped it to Talabani's note. I had to transfer cars and drivers, though, and that kept me sitting around for the usual four or five hours; it was late in the afternoon before I made it to the town of Sari Peren, the next stop on the way. I slept there in a wood hut belonging to local nobility, Kharim Khan Bradusti, a chief of the Bradusti tribe, whose territory this was.

The next morning, Kharim and his son, Ghalim Kharim Khan, took me the final leg of the trip, in a train of four Land Cruisers. We drove six hours through wild country, past Mergason and Bazan to the town of Amadiya, maybe twenty miles from the border, and on past that on dirt roads that cut across the highlands. The son, Ghalim, was a cheerful and insistent show-off, in the way of rich kids, and he kept chattering at me all through the trip.

"I have many American and European friends, you know.... I have been to London many times. I am a student at the University of Baghdad.... I am a very important person, you know. I am a well-known guest at the Al Rashid Hotel and the Al Rashid is the best hotel in Baghdad...." He pulled a roll of American money from his pocket; it was as thick as a Coke can. "I have very much money. At home I have twenty thousand U.S. dollars. I have accounts in America and in Europe.... I have five hundred movies on videocassette, one hundred and five cowboy films. I like Charles Bronson the best." He wore Levi jeans and Ray-Ban sunglasses and lizard-skin boots.

The dirt road petered out in an area of gravelly, sandy flats and marshes that led down to a small river, about forty feet across and three feet deep. We left the cars and walked to the edge of that. On the way there, we crossed paths with a snake, a big bruiser of a dark blue-green. It had been dozing in the sun on the flat rocks near the water, and our arrival surprised it into an aggressive stance, coiled and reared-up. We could have easily avoided it—there was plenty of room to walk around it—but Ghalim became excited. It was a cobra, he said, a very poisonous snake, very bad. He ran back to the car and returned with his Kalashnikov loaded, and shot the snake three times from about fifteen feet away, blowing it to tatters.

At the water, Kharim said two of his men, Obeyed and Zahir, would take me the rest of the way to the border, about six or seven miles. The men and I took off our clothes, except for our underwear, and, with those and my bags on our heads, half swam, half waded across the little river.

We walked from noon to five in the evening, first across pastures and then up a series of long hills and finally down the other side through woods to the border itself. It was in some ways a glorious walk. The fields and hills were rich with bluebells and poppies and daisies, the sun was shining, and the temperature was in the high seventies, just right for a tramp. But, sweating and weak still with the sickness, I was in no condition for it, and I found it increasingly tough going. By the end of the first hour, we were almost always climbing uphill, and I already had fallen into the rhythm of the exhausted, concentrating on fulfilling one step at a time. I was carrying my shoulder bag, which didn't weigh more than thirty or forty pounds. Obeyed and Zahir were each carrying about thirty pounds of gear—rifles and ammunition, pistols, a few grenades, bedrolls, etc.—along with my other two bags. The big black bag weighed fifty to sixty pounds and the smaller duffel bag weighed at least thirty, but their loads seemed to have no effect on them. They didn't even sweat. Every so often they would turn and look worriedly at me—I was always in the rear—and motion that I should give them the shoulder bag, but I wouldn't. I had gotten it into my head as a point of pathetic pride that I had to carry out of the country a portion of my ludicrous luggage. We walked along lines of least resistance; the Kurds never tried to walk directly up a hill, but instead set a course across its face, making perhaps one step up for every four steps forward. They were adept at taking advantage of the little level spots and dips that came along, so that often just as it seemed to me I really couldn't go farther, we would have a patch of easy walking.

At the end of the third hour, as we were cresting the largest hill we had come to yet, we met two boys herding a couple of young cows along. Obeyed and Zahir struck a deal with them, and they gave us a teapot. We built a fire in the shade of a spreading tree that crowned the hill, and while that was heating up, walked down to a stream that ran through a narrow rift a hundred yards or so down from the top. I dunked my face in the stream, and although I knew I shouldn't, drank until my stomach hurt. We ate bread and cheese Obeyed produced from his sack. It was a hard, dry, white cheese, like a cross between Parmesan and assiago. With that we drank a pot of sugared tea, and before we left, Obeyed made another pot for the cowherds. He left it in the embers of the fire, and also left a bag of his bread hanging from a branch of the tree, thus satisfying his end of the deal.

When we picked up to leave, Zahir, without saying anything, took my shoulder bag and added it to what he already carried. I protested only a very little for form's sake. As it turned out, the worst of the climbing was over anyway. Two more hills later, we crossed the top and headed downward through suddenly different scenery, thick quiet woods of old trees, with a luxuriant bracken underfoot. We went along like this, closed in by green, for some time, to emerge suddenly into a clearing which led down to the river that was the border with Turkey. It was a beautiful, young river, about fifty or sixty feet wide, and very fast, falling all over itself in its rush, the water light turquoise and aqua and white, all bubbles and rapids and rocks. Looking upstream and down, I couldn't see a placid place anywhere, and I couldn't imagine how it could be crossed.

We worked our way upstream for an hour of mostly level walking until we came to a huge outcropping of rock that ran nearly to the water's edge. A path about eighteen inches wide ran up this, and it was just possible, bending double and half crawling, hauling ourselves up by tree roots and branches, to get to where, a few hundred feet above the river, the path cut across the bluff. We inched along that in a slow single file. On the other side, the terrain leveled out again, to fields and light woods, for another half hour's walk to the crossing point.

It was a smuggler's outpost, I saw. One of the items that had been most affected by the trade embargo against Iraq was untanned sheepskin, a perishable, bulky commodity. I had seen several piles of rotting sheepskins dumped by the side of the road by drivers turned back from Turkey. This place was a sheepskin crossing. Hundreds and hundreds of the oily, yellow pelts were piled up on the flat land by the river, and three packhorses were being loaded with bundles strapped to their sides for the trip across. When they were ready, they would be hooked up, one by one, to a system of ropes and pulleys that ran from two massive trees, one on each bank. The core of the system was a thick nylon rope that was stretched taut twenty feet above the water. Looped over this was an upside-down U made of rubber. From the ends of the U hung orange nylon ropes, which were somehow attached to the horses. Horizontally, the U was attached to a second rope line, which also ran from tree to tree, and was rigged on pulleys. The pulley system drew the U across, which guided the horse and kept him from

panicking and being swept downstream. The smugglers themselves were teenage boys, four of them, stripped naked except
for baggy white underwear. They were Turkish, from the nearest village on the other side, Obeyed said. They would take me
across and see to it that I got to someplace where I could hire
a car to take me further, eventually to Istanbul and a flight
home.

I watched the smugglers make a couple of crossings. They
didn't bother with the rope contraption, but made it over on
their own strength, by a combination of footwork and clever-
ness, as graceful a thing as I had ever seen, more like dancing
than wading or swimming. The trick was to half-surrender to
the water's force. They let the great rush of water sweep them
off their feet and downstream, but balanced themselves in it like
corks, so that their upper torsos were always above the water
and their feet always pointed to the bottom. The water was
shallow enough, and the bottom varied enough, that they often
touched up against a rock or bit of sandbar, and when they did,
they reacted instantly, pushing off against it to move laterally.
Thus, they made it across skipping from touchstone to touchstone, to alight in the end, panting but still upright, about a
hundred yards downstream from where they had started. They
were young and lean and brown and as hard-muscled as wolves.

In the past few hours, it had gotten much colder; the sun was
setting and a light rain had begun to fall.

"You had better get ready," Obeyed said. I shivered, undress-
ing. When I had dressed after my last crossing, I had left off my
wet underwear and packed it away. I wished now I hadn't, and
I thought of rooting through the bag for it, but I was too
embarrassed with everyone watching. Better, it seemed to me,
to just briskly and naturally go ahead and strip. I took everything off except for my glasses, and after a moment's thought I
took those off too and put them in the bag. I figured that
otherwise I would probably lose them as soon as I lost my
footing for the first time. Without my glasses, I couldn't see

much, but I could sense that the other men were looking at me strangely, with evident embarrassment. Finally, Obeyed spoke. "You should wear something." He made a vague gesture at my groin.

I cursed myself to myself. I was standing naked in the rain, by my own choice. I felt too old and weak for this, and my pinkness was suddenly overwhelming. I was the pinkest thing around for hundreds of miles.

It was mercifully and abruptly time to go. Two of the boys took my bags on their heads and ran off dancing in the water. Two more came up to me. Obeyed and Zahir kissed me good-bye, solemnly and formally, two kisses on each cheek, and then I returned the compliment, sixteen kisses in all. The brown boys led me to the water and I took a baby step in—my God, it was cold, and the rocks were sharp—and then we were off, them dancing and me slipping, stumbling, flailing with my pink arms and legs against the astonishing weight of the water. I thought twice I was being swept away, but the dancers held on to me, and never lost their footing, and never quit moving, and then we were in shallow waters, and then I was in no water at all, standing on the grass of Turkey, panting and laughing and pinker than ever, with the men on the far bank cheering.

I found out two things later. One, that I had lost fourteen pounds from the dysentery, which was welcome. Two, that Nick della Casa and his wife and brother-in-law had never made it out. Eventually the police found and identified two bodies as those of the men. They said a translator had shot them in an argument over money. They never found the woman's body.

THE COST OF
LIVING

I N A QUIET, MODESTLY RICH NEIGHBORHOOD in Baghdad, shortly
after Martyrs' Day, 1991, a woman was talking. She was
middle-aged, unmarried, and she had a strong, ugly-handsome
face, with a powerful nose and a large mouth full of big, slightly
yellow teeth. She was of an ancient, wealthy, learned family,
and she ran one of the family businesses, a small building
construction firm. Her hands were like a workingman's: stubby
fingers stained with chemicals and nicotine, palms hard and
horny with calluses. She used her hands with theatrical artistry
to emphasize her points as she spoke, making daggers and
pointers and cups as the need arose. She smoked one cigarette
after another, puffing furiously along.

"It breaks my heart, I tell you, it breaks my heart, what I see
in my country now. It is much worse than people going hungry,
or losing their money. What we are seeing here is the moral
disintegration of a society. Pimping, thieving, murder, prostitution—it is all going on all the time now. There is only two
percent of the country left that is honest, and half of that two
percent is sitting at home doing nothing. They are too afraid to
go out. Everyone is afraid. Even the government is afraid.

"Crime is everywhere. When you drive at night, you keep
the windows rolled up and the doors locked. Theft insurance
has doubled on homes, and insurance premiums on cars are up

three hundred percent. The shops on Kerada Street used to be
open until ten o'clock and now they shut down at eight o'clock.
People won't stay out late; it's too dangerous. The biggest
robbers are the police. There is a saying in Arabic: *Hami hara-
meim*, the protector is the robber. Well, that is the truth about
Iraq. Men in uniform come to your house and take you to the
interrogation center for questioning, and when you come back
six hours later, you find that they have stolen all the furniture.
Bastards.

"The only currency worth anything anymore is five- and
twenty-five dinar notes. The rest are forgeries. At first they said
it was Iranians and Saudis doing the counterfeiting, but the
truth is—I know from someone who knows—that the biggest
printing press in the country is right in the basement of the
Ministry of Defense, where Saddam's son-in-law is minister. It
is the counterfeiting that is making the big party officials and the
government men so rich. The way it works is they buy gold
with the counterfeit money. People don't want to sell gold for
dinars, of course, but when you are a man in power, you can
oblige them to sell to you. Also, there are merchants who will
give you sixty thousand in real notes for a hundred thousand in
counterfeit. You can make a lot of money very fast this way.

"A tube of toothpaste right now costs eighteen dinars. But
you cannot even find any toothpaste in the shops. Do you know
why? Because there is one merchant who has cornered the
toothpaste market. He bought all there was to buy in Amman.
And he has taken all that toothpaste and put it in warehouses,
and he is sitting and waiting for the price to go up to twenty-five
dinars and then he will bring it out to sell. It is this way all over.
Warehouses full of goods tucked away. Fat cats getting fatter.
But we, who are not those fat cats, we are white mice in a cage.
Marlboros cost ninety dinars a carton; last year it was eighteen
dinars. An ordinary pair of Lebanese shoes for a woman is now
nine hundred dinars, a woolen sweater is six hundred and fifty
dinars or more, an ordinary skirt and silk blouse cost two

thousand dinars. I wear only old clothes. I can afford better, but I will not enrich those bastards.

"I am rich, so since the war I have been able to eat, but there are so many people who are starving here. There are whole families that are slowly starving away. I don't know why people still want to bring babies into the world. The other day, a child fainted at a school near here. She said, 'My stomach is aching. I haven't eaten today.' The teacher said, 'Why have you not eaten today?' She said, 'It is not my turn.'

"Of course, the people in the government do not live the way we live. They have special food delivered to them. They can get whatever they want. They have not suffered. They are getting richer, in fact. These people are actually frightened that the sanctions will be lifted. They have made millions and they want to make millions more. The very concept of profit has changed for these men; they now only think in terms of one hundred and fifty percent profit or more."

All that this woman said was true. The war that had liberated Kuwait City had also liberated Baghdad, freeing it to reach, you might say, its fullest expression of self. It had become the ideal mob town, the perfect capital of a gangster nation. The new millionaires, Baathist bosses and government ministers and their merchant friends, tooled around the city in Mercedes-Benzes the color of *crème fraiche* and swaggered through the casinos tossing stacks of new money on the baccarat tables.

The biggest man about town was Udai, Saddam's oldest son, whose new newspaper, *Babel*, had attracted great numbers of readers with its gossipy tone and its daring columns poking fun at bureaucrats. Udai and his entourage were out most nights, dancing and drinking and whoring and gambling, and occasionally beating up passersby. People avoided them when they could.

Only the rich and the politically connected could afford to eat much. The government doled out some food, but never quite enough, and the Western relief workers in Baghdad had come to realize, after their offers had been stymied time after time, that the government wanted things the way they were. The deaths of the very poor served to turn the national anger outward, toward the United States, and the hunger of the middle classes kept them too preoccupied to plot rebellion.

If you had money, though, the city was a treasure pot. You could buy a two-hundred-year-old carpet for $150, a hundred-year-old gold pocket watch for $50, a twenty-year-old virgin for $20. The streets were crowded with trucks loaded down with liquor and cigarettes from Amman. The lobbies of the big hotels were busy with formerly respectable young women sipping tea and pretending they were waiting for someone they knew, with United Nations officials staggering under the trophies of their daily shopping sprees, with sleek, sly Jordanian hustlers whispering in the ears of large men in too-tight suits who looked like aging mob muscle, but were in fact ministers of state.

There are many private clubs in Baghdad for the use of high party and government officials: the Mansour Club, the Zowarak Club, the Hunting Club, the Alwiyah Club, the Al Khar Sporting Club (managed by Udai), the Saladin Club (for quisling Kurds), the Assyrian Club, the Armenian Club, etc. The evening of Martyrs' Day, a rich man (a well-connected lawyer I had met by chance on my first trip) took me to the Alwiyah, next door to the Sheraton Ishtar Hotel. The English built the Alwiyah in the 1920s, and although it has become somewhat run-down, it still looks very much like an English club, with three large drinking rooms on the ground floor and a huge dining room, eight tennis courts, and three swimming pools. "It is very nice in the afternoon to sit on the lawn and drink Pimm's Cup," said the lawyer. In the evening, coat and tie are required, and the crowd is mostly men; women are restricted to the dining room and the smallest of the bars.

We arrived about nine-thirty at night, late for the cocktail
hour, but the biggest of the drinking rooms was still packed, the
men in the blue cloth armchairs grouped in fours and fives and
sixes around low wood tables, each of which was crowded to the
edges with bowls and plates of food—*lebenah,* pickled beets and
carrots, bread and cheese—and many bottles, mostly of Scotch:
Johnny Walker, Haig & Haig, Pinch, Cutty Sark. The men
leaned forward over their paunches and ate with their fingers,
scooping up globs of *hummus* and *baba ganoush* and gulping down
tumblers of whiskey. They talked in loud, drunk voices.

"They will drink like this until midnight perhaps, and then
they will go out to nightclubs for more drinking or to stuff
themselves with more food," said the rich man, with contempt
in his voice. "Some will go to their prostitutes and mistresses."
He had been educated in England and wore fine tweed jackets
and fawn-colored trousers and silk ascots, and smoked a brier
pipe. He spent much of the year in London and New York, and
saw himself as a cosmopolite.

Across the hall was the main saloon, an old-fashioned English
men's bar, of the sort that was once strictly a stand-up place, a
long room with a high wooden counter running the length of
one side. Every stool at the bar was filled, and every man was
drinking. We drank with them for a short while, and afterward
we went to a fancy restaurant, a place with damask tablecloths,
a headwaiter in black tie, sub-waiters in white dinner jackets,
and everything soft and pretty in the candlelight. At the shining
black grand piano, a man played Cole Porter tunes. We ate
chateaubriand, with baby green beans in a butter sauce and
pommes soufflés. We drank a good Chianti Riserva, 1978, and
afterward snifters of Rémy Martin, which the headwaiter
warmed over a little brass candle contraption he brought to the
table.

*   *   *

Most of the drinking going on in Baghdad in those days, and there was a savage amount of it every night, was on a less exalted level. I went on a Thursday night to a little store a few blocks from the Sheraton to pick up a bottle of something to take to a friend's house for dinner. When I walked in, the proprietor was in the middle of counting the bottles in a shipment of several cases of Black Jack whiskey, a vile concoction made in Lebanon and trucked in from Amman. He was in his thirties, I guessed, but looked older; he was tall and very skinny, and the planes of his face had been thinned down to gray hollows. He wore an old gray suitcoat buttoned all the way up over a sweater, although it was a warm evening, and a red-and-blue muffler was wound around his throat. He sat on a three-legged stool behind the counter; I gathered from the awkward movements he made when he was obliged to stand and fetch something that there was something wrong with his legs or hips. Gap-toothed, he spoke with a faint lisp, very softly, all the time smoking a cigarette, and frequently coughing.

Behind him on the shelves were a few food items and some bottled water, but 90 percent of the space was devoted to liquor. There were seven brands of arrack and all sorts of whiskey, gin, vodka, Bulgarian red wine, and something called Kassatly Brut Pecher Mignon Vin, a Lebanese champagne made by mixing peach extract and alcohol.

"No one buys anything except booze anymore," the proprietor said. "If you ask a person 'Do you want bread or whiskey?' they will choose whiskey. They all want to drink as much as they can, all the time. Because they want to forget. Forget the war, the cause of the war, the war before this war, the man who makes us go to war, the people in the hospitals with no arms and no legs, the girls who cannot find husbands and the girls whose husbands are dead."

His own war had been a mixed thing. He had spent six months in the criminal carnival of Kuwait City without experiencing a bit of danger, and then, on the way home, had been bombed on the road to Basra.

"I see with my own eyes four trucks completely bombed and a lot of my colleagues killed, injured. And I tried to save some of these dead and injured people, but it was very hard. We were running and there was continuous firing on us, so it was impossible to help those who were hurt. After the attack was over, we put blankets on the dead and left them. It was all we could do. I was able to drive away. My truck still worked. But most of the vehicles were destroyed and most men had to walk. I don't know what happened to them. I see many bombs fall on my friends. Some of them are exploded by shrapnel, some of them there are no signs of shrapnel, they just burned. There was a lot of fire, very big flames. The flames would cover the men and they would run a few steps and then fall down and die. I still cannot believe I survived this."

Outside, in the street, a party was making its way to the Sheraton, a group of young men and cars parading with drums and kazoos and whistles and high-yelping brass horns. There was this sort of thing every night, mostly because of the weddings. The two wars back to back had postponed many unions for years, and now the pent-up demand was giving way to an orgy of marrying. This procession was seven or eight cars, mostly taxis, led by a rented (I guess) Mercedes done up with ribbons and streamers and blinking red and yellow and green Christmas lights. A taxi full of musicians followed the lead car, the three players leaning out of the open windows, one blowing a horn, one sawing on a fiddle, and one banging a snare drum.

Baghdad weddings traditionally end with the bride and groom going into one of the big hotels for a two- or three-day honeymoon, and at the front door to the Sheraton there were half a dozen couples—each with their own little clanging, tootling street band—waiting to check in, and to pose in front of the big statue of the goddess Ishtar in the center of the lobby. The brides were stacked up in a holding pattern, like jetliners over a busy airport, each young woman stiffly moving forward a cautious bit at a time so as not to walk on the train of the one before. In front of Ishtar, a very young couple were standing for their photograph, the girl all ruffles and flourishes of white, with fishnet gloves that went up to her elbows. I could see, high above, leaning over one of the interior balconies that ring the lobby, a couple who had already registered, still dressed in their finery, looking down on the scene.

Wandering later that night in the streets and in and out of bars, I fell in with two very drunk men. They were sitting at a table in the Palm Beach Disco Bar, a fat man in a suit and a skinny man in a gray *dishdasha*, with an empty bottle of Scotch, two small empty bottles of arrack, and another pint bottle of Johnny Walker, half empty. They were smoking from an *agila*, the ornate brass water pipe that Westerners call a hubble-bubble. The waiter brought a glass for me, and the fat man poured it half full of Scotch, and we drank and smoked the sweet tobacco, saturated with black honey and strawberry. The men were drinking to commemorate the loss of the skinny one's job; he had been a brigadier general in the army, and had been cashiered after the war. "Very sad, very sad," he said, shaking his head in loopy, drunk wobbles. "Saddam bad, very bad, very bad." He hauled his leg up onto the table and pretended to scrape filth off the sole of his shoe, wrinkling his nose in exaggerated disgust. "Saddam," he said, pointing to imaginary scrapings on the tablecloth. We drank a toast to that. The fat man blew his nose and held the handkerchief up. "Saddam." Another toast. The skinny man spit in the ashtray. "Saddam." Another toast, and so on until the whiskey was gone. Very late, driving wildly in the rain through back neighborhoods I knew nothing of, they took me to eat in a restaurant of the sort which, with its decor of tile and aluminum and plastic and its menu of two dishes, is the lowest common denominator of dining out in Arabia.

"This is very good," said the fat man as we sat down. "Very special Iraqi food."

The platters in front of us held three boiled sheeps' heads, steaming and covered with a grayish, whitish sort of skin or membrane. You had to peel this off with your fingers to get to the next layer, which was a slab of fat. The fat was yellow and half an inch thick. I learned how to eat it from the fat man, who was sitting directly across from me. With his fingers, he tore off a big hunk of the stuff, which slid greasy and wet in his hand. He opened his mouth wide and shoveled it in as if he were stoking coal.

I couldn't make myself eat the fat, but moving it around on my plate, I found there was another layer underneath, of a dark, oily meat. I pulled off a small piece and, with oversized gestures, to show that I was eating my share, held it up and put it in my mouth. It was spongy.

"Is good?" said the fat man. "Is tongue, next to lips the best part."

After the tongue was gone, I ate some cheek, but not much. The fat man was hugely enjoying the meal. He had finished the fat and most of the easily accessible cheek, and was working on the finer points of the skull. He held it up before him in both hands, propping his elbows on the table, and wrenched the lower jaw from the upper. He stuck the jawbone in his mouth and worked it like an ear of corn; he didn't miss a morsel, not even the little bits of gum between the shining teeth.

The party broke up around quarter to two, when the skinny man fell asleep with his head on the table. The fat man drove me back to the hotel. As I was saying good-bye, he reached over and put his big right arm around my shoulders and pulled me close, while with his other hand he reached down and, to my surprise, gave a sudden, sharp squeeze to my penis. Looking me deep in the eyes, he said, "Saddam bad. Bush good."

In the afternoons, in the same lobby where the brides paraded at night, the new prostitutes sat in armchairs on the mezzanine and nursed soft drinks or coffee. Many of them, I was told, were war widows, and I thought how odd and unhappy it must be for them to find themselves hooking where they had honeymooned a few years earlier. A Jordanian hustler I became friends with, a man named Samir, used to sit in the lobby in the afternoons and sip a beer and admire them. He was much-traveled and a connoisseur of international whoring, and he was impressed with the situation in postwar Baghdad.

"It is a very civilized system," he said. "The ladies come here every day. They dress nice so the security will look the other way. Some come alone and some with a man they made an arrangement with outside. If they come alone, they wait and drink their coffee, and if a man wants one, he sits down and talks and they come to an agreement. But they can't go upstairs to the rooms because the security will not let them. So they negotiate here and go elsewhere.

"Last night, I went to a club, a cabaret, and a man came over and asked me if I wanted girls, and I said sure, why not, and two girls came over, and I bought them a bottle of whiskey. They stayed until one A.M., and my God, they drank, you should have seen them drinking. You know, usually with these sorts of girls, they drink cider or tea and pretend it is whiskey or champagne, but I tasted what these girls were drinking and it was whiskey, all right, the most foul whiskey you ever drank—it tasted like raw alcohol. And one of the girls, she drank three quarters of a bottle; by one o'clock she was completely drunk. I thought, my God, she is twenty years old, and if she drinks like this every night, she will be dead by thirty.

"But the amazing thing is, the whole thing—the bottle of whiskey, talking with the girls all night, the cover price—it was all for only a thousand dinars. That's one hundred dollars. You can't find a price like that in any other city in the world! It's like Czechoslovakia was in '86, '87. That place was full of beautiful girls you could hire for next to nothing, and these weren't girls who were doing it because they were in love with prostitution, you know. They were young girls, nice, pretty; it was because the money was so good for them. Now this place is the same. The going price for a girl is a hundred dinars, a hundred and fifty dinars. If over thirty-five, fifty dinars or less. Well, you can give one of these girls a thousand dinars, she will do anything you can imagine. That's only one hundred dollars for you, but for her it's ten times the normal rate, enough to live on for a month in luxury. In one night, she can make this! So of course they are all doing it. Who could resist?"

A newspaper reporter friend of mine had given me the name and the telephone number of a man who was in the rackets. I arranged to meet him in the bar off the lobby in the Meridien Palestine Hotel. I expected him to be hushed and furtive, but he was as cheerfully loud as a man boasting about his golf game, chattering on over coffee and cigarettes.

"Well, of course, these are the days where everybody does what they must for the money. A lot of people are, what do you say, like in France, the *putains*? How do you say? Fucking for money! That is it. There is a lot of fucking for money. Oh my, yes. If a man likes a girl he will set her up in a little apartment, give her some money, and she will be a *putain*, but in a discreet way. No one will know about it except a few people, and me.

"Of course, there is a lot of stuff going on no one knows about. Everyone is very nervous these days. Especially they are nervous about Udai. He is all over town and when he comes into a place, everybody looks down. Nobody wants him to see them. Because if he sees you and he doesn't like you, he will kill you just like that. He is crazy. When he starts—what do you say—*en français, c'est frapper*—"

Beat.

"Yes, when he starts to beat someone he cannot stop with just an arm or a leg. He goes on and on until the person is crippled or dead. And Udai is getting richer and richer all the time. He has two newspapers now, *Babel* and *Rafidain*, and that is a lot of money.

"But getting back to the fucking thing. You know, we have in Muslim a concern about a girl if she is not *vierge*. For me that is not a problem, I don't like *vierge* anyway. Too stupid. But many men, if the girl has been fucking some other men before, they will not marry her. In ordinary times, this is not so big a problem, because the young men marry the young girls when they are still *vierge* and everyone is happy. But the wars have killed very many young men who were married. Now their wives are all without husbands, but they are no longer *vierge* anymore. So it is very hard for them to find new husbands. No one wants them because they have been fucked by other men. So what can they do? They work in a factory or in a shop, that is not very much money. But if they become a girlfriend to Udai or one of the other big shots, they can get a lot of money, enough in one month to live on for a year. There are a whole lot of apartments not too far from here, in a nice neighborhood near the ministries, that are just for Udai's girls. He keeps a girl in one of the apartments and he fucks her for ten days, twenty days, a month. Then he throws her out, but he gives her maybe one thousand, two thousand dinars, maybe ten thousand dinars. And so she is happy enough."

On Shatt Street, a small shaded avenue running along a branch of the Tigris, Udai was building a new home. The construction site was behind walls of corrugated sheet metal, and young men in black leather jackets and sunglasses waved on any car that attempted to stop. But it was possible to get a pretty

fair look at the place driving by slowly two or three times. The
principal buildings were four mammoth mansions of some
snow-white stone, of Federal design, and of grandiose proportions, with broad front porches framed by columns three stories
tall. Arched windows two stories tall flanked the front entrance.
Each building had a central hall and two wings, and each wing
was surmounted by a dome. The whole was set in the middle
of about a dozen acres of flat land, dotted with date palms and
orange trees.

Inflation, plaguelike, had swept through the land, destroying
and transforming. The official rate of exchange for the Iraqi
dinar was one dinar for three American dollars, or one third of
a dinar for one dollar. The black market rate, which was the one
everyone really used, was more than thirty times that; depending on the day and the dealer, one dollar would buy between
nine and twelve dinars.

Doug Broderick, the Catholic Relief Services field director in
Baghdad, had made up a chart and hung it on the wall of his
office in the Meridien Palestine Hotel. The chart showed the
increases, in real terms and by percentage, of basic food items
since the invasion: bread up 2,857 percent, infant formula 2,222
percent, flour 4,531 percent, eggs 350 percent.

"What you get with prices like this," Broderick said profes-
sorially, "is a Darwinian effect. The rich and the strong survive,
the poor and the weak starve. In any society, the very weakest
people are the children, so mostly it is children that die. The
number of child deaths during the fifteen months of sanctions
I would put at between sixty thousand and one hundred thousand. Now, the normal number of deaths would be about thirty
thousand in that time period, based on the normal rate here of
thirty-nine deaths per ten thousand and the seven hundred and
seventy thousand births recorded in this time. So, in essence,

the infant mortality rate has at least doubled and possibly tripled."

Al Quaddisya General Hospital, a featureless concrete square with 325 adult beds and 130 pediatric beds, serves the 750,000 people who live in the poorest part of Baghdad, the Shiite area called Saddam City. The front lobby of the hospital was bare except for a desk, vacant, and on the rear wall a photograph of a smiling Saddam holding one of his infant sons. The office of the hospital director was down a long, windowless hallway, and everything in the office—the carpet, the furniture, the paint on the walls—was worn and permanently dirty. As if he didn't want to clash with the decor, the director wore old polyester slacks and a laboratory coat that had been stained too many times, so that it was, while more or less white overall, subcutaneously mottled with patches of faded red and brown and gray.

"Really, nowadays most medicine is not available at all," he said. He was a small, round-shouldered man, and he sat humped over his little glass of steaming tea, as if he were trying to draw strength from its fumes. The lines of his face all drooped exaggeratedly downward, houndlike. "There are no antibiotics to speak of, no cough syrups, no bronchial dilators, no blood pressure medicine, no heart medicine, very few anesthetics. Really, it is very difficult for us." He was especially worried about a lack of cannulas, the plastic-and-steel disposable needle rigs that form the business end of the intravenous drips used to carry saline solution, drugs, and anesthesia into the bloodstream. "We have reached the point now where we are canceling operations because of the lack of cannulas," he said. "And because of this lack too, we are forced to treat all but the most serious cases of malnutrition and diarrhea as outpatient cases."

Most of those who were dying in Baghdad were very old or very young, and they were dying mostly of starvation and its complications. Like Broderick, the hospital director had made up a chart to quantify the phenomenon. Since January 1991, the neat red-and-blue bar graph on the wall opposite his desk showed, more than 50 percent of all the deaths had been caused by malnutrition, up from an average of 10 percent a year before. In February 1990, 15 percent of the deaths were due to malnutrition; in February 1991, the figure was 50 percent. In August 1991, the worst month, 63 percent of all the patients at Al Quaddisya who had died had died of starvation. In real numbers, this meant the hospital lost between 100 and 150 patients per month to starvation. Ninety-five percent of these patients were children. Very young children, especially infants, starve easily, although it is often the case that some opportunistic infection does the job quicker.

The director took me for a walk through the wards to see the malnutrition cases. We stopped first at the bed of a boy, Wa'ad Al, forty-four days old. He was a tiny thing, with calves no wider than the O made by my thumb and forefinger, and arms you could have snapped within that O. His belly was distended, the skin as taut as a drumhead, and the veins bulged like blue worms up against it. There was not a gram of fat left on him, so that his head had become almost a skull, and the flesh on his thighs hung in loose folds. "This boy is a typical case. His mother bought Pelargon for him, but she could not afford enough, so she heavily diluted the milk with water, and of course this is the result." A four-hundred-gram can of Pelargon brand powdered milk, which would have sold before the invasion for half a dinar, now cost twenty-two dinars, an increase of more than 4,000 percent.

At another bed lay Ala Husein, a girl of 105 days. Her mother sat with her (all the mothers stayed with their children at this hospital, sitting with them all day and sleeping on the floor, or in bed with them, at night), and she explained the situation. She fed her baby Isomil powdered milk, and since each tin of Isomil lasted three days, she required ten cans per month. Before the sanctions, Isomil cost six hundred fils per can, so that a month's supply cost six thousand fils, or six dinars. Now, Isomil cost 15 dinars per can, so that a month's supply cost 150 dinars. Her husband's pay was two hundred dinars per month. They had six children.

While her mother talked, Ala Husein lay completely still, and a fly crawled on her face. The doctor pulled apart the soft little blankets in which she had been swaddled (they were tied around her, with a ribbon of cloth, so that she looked like a papoose) and held up her wasted legs, pinching the flesh. "As you can see, there is not only no subcutaneous fat left, there is also no muscle left. Look at this chest." He thumped gently on the rib cage sticking out against the skin in sharp relief. "There is nothing left on these bones. What happens in malnutrition, you see, is that the child eats itself. First it eats the fat, then it eats the muscle. When there is nothing left for it to eat, it dies."

We walked through the crowded wards, stopping at this bed and that, examining this little shriveled-up husk and that little sack of bones and skin. One little boy he unwrapped had feces of an improbably vivid green, the shade of pesto sauce, smeared about his bottom and legs. "They call this 'hunger stool.' Very frequent in these cases. The bowel movement is watery and it is green."

The dead-baby situation made Doug Broderick so angry that his face twisted up when he talked about it.

"The terrible thing is that Iraq is, technically, overfed. The food stocks are at one hundred and twenty percent capacity, seventy percent of which is imported, thirty percent home-grown. But the government will not distribute the food, or allow anyone else to. They are only giving out twenty-five to thirty percent of what is necessary for the people to be decently fed. We—Catholic Relief Services—have fourteen hundred metric tons of food in this country right now, sitting in warehouses, waiting to be distributed. We cannot distribute that food because the government will not allow us to. They have blocked us from distributing it through the existing network of Women's and Children's Health Care Centers.

"It is simply a fact that the Iraqi government is free to buy food and medicine if it wants to. Nobody is preventing the government from going to Amman and buying truckloads of baby milk and bringing it back here. It costs thirty thousand dollars to buy a truckload of baby milk in Amman, and twenty-four metric tons of baby milk would be enough for the whole country, based on the number of births. So all it would take to stop all the infant deaths would be seven hundred and twenty thousand dollars. You telling me these guys don't have that amount of money?

"Of course they do. They could cope with this if they wanted to. But who wants to be seen coping with it? That would be a message they do not want to send. If they sent that message, it would take pressure off the United Nations to lift the sanctions. The fact is, the sanctions make Saddam strong. He can take the time to get rid of his enemies, take care of the Shiites and the Kurds, while his people are busy pointing their fingers at the U.S. and looking for food. Everybody in the country is too preoccupied with food to think about rebellion. The whole nation is dreaming about a nice dinner."

On Kerada Street, in a rich neighborhood, there was a fancy supermarket. The shelves were crowded with good food, much of it still bearing the stamp of the Sultan supermarkets, a Kuwaiti chain. There was Olio Sasso olive oil and good red wine vinegar, fresh-baked breads and fancy cakes, Swiss and Belgian chocolates in shiny foil wrappers, Edam and Gouda and Danish cheddar and Roquefort, cans of Dinty Moore beef stew, cans of kippered herring and cans of French potatoes and asparagus, packages of cookies and tea biscuits and crackers, tins of English toffee and Italian coffee and French pâté.

In one corner was a stack of U.S. Army field rations, still sealed in their big olive-green metal trays: omelet with ham, peas and carrots, turkey with gravy, blueberry cobbler, etc. "The Americans give it to the Kurdish people and the Kurdish people bring it here in trucks and sell it to us," the store manager said. "Myself, I would not eat it."

Samir, the Jordanian hustler, was the very picture of his type. He was lean, and fidgety always, even when sitting. He was not handsome—the skin on his face was too large-pored, and his mustache was scruffily trimmed, and he had only a middling chin—but he had large brown eyes that shone with an insistent and entirely misleading sincerity, and I thought he was one of those men that women wonder afterward how they ended up in bed with. He wore flashy clothes, wool and silk sport coats with overpadded shoulders and pleated pants and Italian loafers, that sort of thing. Yet he was unmistakably, irredeemably seedy.

My last night in the city, he and I sat up late in my room at the hotel finishing the last few inches of whiskey in a bottle, and he talked of the great days at hand.

"I remember what I told my father when I asked him for the money," he said. "Opportunity only knocks once, I said. It is true. This is my one opportunity knocking. After all, how many times in my life are you guys going to sanction this place?"

Samir's father, who owned a car dealership and a soft-drink franchise in Amman, had seen the truth in that, and had bank-rolled Samir at the end of the war with $300,000, to run goods from Amman to Baghdad and sell them for what the market would bear. Business had been good.

"I have made so far four hundred thousand dollars. Whiskey, cigarettes, beer, light bulbs, whatever. But do not sit there and think it has been easy. No, it is a very tricky business. Very tricky indeed. The big problem is that there are too many businessmen here at the same time—Iraqi, Jordanian, Lebanese, Egyptian, Saudi, they have come from all over to be in on the game—and everyone is looking for the same score at the same time. Now, the way you score is to see the need, the shortage, before everyone else does. Let us say you spot a shortage of razor blades. So you drive like hell to Amman and buy up razor blades and bring a truckload down here, and sell them for thirty times what you paid in Amman. Not so damned bad, eh?

"Now, how do you spot the shortage? By going around the city and looking in shops, talking to people, seeing what there is not much of, what items the prices are going up on. But here is the problem. This city is full of unscrupulous bastards who are hiding all sorts of items in warehouses, to make artificial shortages and drive up the price, and then they bring them out and sell. Maybe they open the warehouse just at the time you bring in your stuff, and—bang!—the market is glutted, you are screwed.

"This happened to me a number of times. For instance, two weeks ago, I saw Heineken beer was getting hard to find. So I go to Amman and bring back three container loads of Heineken. I get here, what do I find? This bastard has socked away two hundred container loads of Heineken in warehouses, and suddenly let them out in the four days I am gone. The shortage is over, the market is glutted, the price is steady again, and I cannot find anyone who wants my beer. So now I have three container loads of beer sitting in a warehouse that I have to pay rent on and I cannot sell it and maybe some government bastards will come steal it in the night.

"Even the matter of being paid is a problem. Let us say you conclude a deal for two million Iraqi dinars. Well, you cannot take payment in anything other than twenty-five-dinar and five-dinar notes. Everything else is phony. Once I was offered payment in American dollars. The best, I thought. I was told they were fresh from the central bank in Kuwait City. Very good. The deal is almost done, I have examined the money; it looks good. I am just counting one last time and I notice—just by the merest chance—one last thing. On every note, all the serial numbers are exactly the same. That is the kind of thing I have to worry about.

"So, you make a deal for two million dinars, and let me tell you, two million dinars in twenty-five-dinars and five-dinar notes is a big amount of money. It is paid to you in a rice sack, or a flour sack, and there are many problems with doing business this way. You walk out of a business establishment with a sack on your shoulder, and everyone knows you are carrying a sack of money. Now, a sack of Iraqi dinars is not such a valuable item in Amman, or New York, but in Baghdad, where the average person is making a salary of one hundred and fifty dinars a month, it is a lot of money. So you are a very tempting target. And there is not a goddam person in this town who does not have a gun. So, you can see, it is the kind of thing that is a problem.

"Then, let us assume you get safely to your office. You now have to count the money. You know how long it takes to count two million dinars in twenty-five-dinar and five-dinar notes? I have ten employees here in Baghdad who do nothing but count money. They do it all night long. Every night, and we still can't keep up. We have to take a certain amount of it on trust. A man gives me a sack, says there are one point six million dinars in it, I sometimes just have to take him at his word and ship it to the bank.

"Thirdly, of course, the counterfeiting problem means that not only should you count your money, you really should check each bill under the ultraviolet light to make sure it is not a phony, because even some of the small bills are fake now. This takes forever. But you have to do it, because half the money in circulation is no damned good.

"But," he said, and he lifted his glass, "to hell with all that. By God, I love America, and thank you! By God! Do you know I always said—my whole life—I had one goal, to be a millionaire by the age of forty. And do you know—thank God for

America!—if these sanctions last three more months, I will make it."

The woman with the workingman's hands was on her fourth cup of coffee and fourteenth cigarette.

"Sometimes I wonder why I stay. I am rich. I could go. My last letter from my sister in Paris, she said, 'Why do you not come?' But I wrote her and said I could not go. I cannot leave my country now. I cannot. I believe that if I stop going on, if I leave my country, my country is defeated.

"Saddam and George Bush, they have together tried to defeat us, each in his own way. George Bush could have sent his army to Baghdad and killed this bastard Saddam, and he did not. We really thought democracy would save us. Now, I do not believe in democracy. I don't believe in anything. Except God. He will save us because there is no way he will allow good people to be destroyed by evil.

"And of course Saddam and his criminals, those bastards, are stronger than ever. The only people left in the army are people who are loyal to Saddam. He has given them all new cars and more land and new medals. They know that if anyone else took power, they would disappear from the face of the earth. You must realize this is a class of people who were scum, who came from families that were scum. Their fathers were scum and their fathers' fathers were scum."

She lit another cigarette, inhaled, grimaced.

"It is as if both sides—the Americans and the criminals of Saddam—are using us to work out their experiments. And they are interesting experiments. It is fascinating to see what it takes to bring about the total degradation of a people."

ABOUT THE AUTHOR

MICHAEL KELLY was born in Washington, D.C., in 1957. He majored in history at the University of New Hampshire. After working for the ABC television program *Good Morning America* for three years he became a reporter on the metropolitan desk of *The Cincinnati Post.* He was also the Washington correspondent for *The Baltimore Sun.* In 1989, he became a free-lance writer and moved to Chicago. He wrote for *The Boston Globe, Gentlemens' Quarterly, Esquire,* and *Playboy.* During the Gulf War he was a special correspondent for *The New Republic,* earning both an Overseas Press Club Award and a National Magazine Award. Following the war, he went to work for *The New York Times* as a Washington correspondent, covering the 1992 presidential campaign. He is married to Madelyn Kelly, a producer for *CBS Evening News.* They live in Washington, D.C.

ABOUT THE TYPE

The text of this book was set in Janson, a typeface designed by Anton Janson who was a punch cutter in seventeenth-century Germany. Janson is an excellent old-style book face with pleasing clarity and sharpness in its design.